Who are you really?

Moon in Aries—chatty, charming, enthusiastic.

Moon in Taurus—wildly romantic.

Moon in Gemini—creative and eternally youthful.

Moon in Cancer—sensitive and caring.

Moon in Leo—loving and lovable.

Moon in Virgo—dauntless and determined.

Moon in Libra—considerate, winning, good-willed.

Moon in Scorpio—persistent, achieving, ever victorious.

Moon in Sagittarius—confident and independent.

Moon in Capricorn—unsentimental and successful.

Moon in Aquarius—imaginative and unusual.

Moon in Pisces—artful and *avant garde*.

Also by Sybil Leek

ASTROLOGY AND LOVE

MOON SIGNS

Sybil Leek

A BERKLEY MEDALLION BOOK
published by
BERKLEY PUBLISHING CORPORATION

Library of Congress Catalog Card Number: 76-28502

SBN 425-03586-7

*BERKLEY MEDALLION BOOKS are published by
Berkley Publishing Corporation
200 Madison Avenue
New York, N. Y. 10016*

BERKLEY MEDALLION BOOK ® TM 757,375

Printed in the United States of America

Berkley Medallion Edition, DECEMBER, 1977

*For my mother, who with her moon in Cancer,
has been the caring, protective bulwark
of our family life.
With love and gratitude.*

CONTENTS

MOON
SIGNS

CHAPTER I

Celestial Equal Rights

The queen of night, whose large command
Rules all the sea, and half the land.

—Samuel Butler, *Hudibras*

Sun-sign astrology is moonshine.

It has been rammed down your throats during the latest escalation of interest in astrology. Most professional astrologers are sick of this diet, mostly because sun-sign astrology has provided a legitimate weapon for enemies to use such as those slick scientists tired of arguing among themselves, turn bleary eyes on the materfamilias of their own sciences, and cast her out with the same equanimity with which they raped Mother Nature. Flaunt two words to scientists today—astrology and ecology—and most of them go into a tirade against the first and a pious eulogy for the second about how they invented the atom bomb to save mankind and that atomic waste does not really disturb the balance of nature. Astrology to scientists is like the proverbial red rag to a bull. It inflames them to stampede

1

and the newspapers love the controversy. Sadly I have to admit that we have allowed the scientists to get away with too much bad-mouthing of both the subject and those who practice it. For in the allegations that astrology is not a science and all astrologers are charlatans, we have allowed popular sun-sign astrology to inflate itself so that it overshadows everything else astrology can offer.

It is the ultimate male chauvinistic insult to the feminine principle of life because (wouldn't you know it?) the sun is given all the attributes of the male. It is the first beat toward life, the remnants of a religion based on the male as the supreme sex. It lost its religious connotations to become the patriarchal symbol of the celestial heavens. It is even immune from the attentions of modern-day scientists in the space program; they know better than to try to get too close to the sun. It is still the all-powerful luminary, to be examined from a distance. On the other hand, the moon has had most of her dignity stripped away from her since man made those footsteps on her aged, dusty surface on July 20, 1969.

Since science has ripped the veil of mystique from the moon, it is time astrologers revealed her rightful place in astrology. Like the sun, the moon was once worshiped as deity; then patriarchal religion swamped the old matriarchal religion of Diana and Astarte, and the female had to start on her long fight back to equality. Somewhere along the line, King Sol, alias Ra the Sun God, pulled a fast trick on many of the people who knew him as the male principle of life and spoke of his influences on all living things in a science called astrology. Sun-sign astrology became the roaring chariot, with spokes of golden fire; the influence of the sun was woven into the horoscopes of a new generation of people who had only a vague idea that Ra was another name for the sun god.

As interest in astrology escalated, so the sun-sign theme rose in popularity and became a conversation piece at parties

2

where one person told another that he was a Virgo because he was born within the sun sign of Virgo. Such a statement became blanket coverage for all involved in being a Virgo and the ascendant; the planets and the moon were forgotten. So we got the retaliation by smart alecks who said, "But I am a Virgo, too, and look how different we are. That proves astrology is nothing but bunk." What it proved was that the person saying this knew enough about astrology to write on a pin head. What makes two Virgos different is the ascendant and/or the placement of the moon within the chart so we may find someone born in the sun sign of Virgo, who has Taurus ascendant or a moon in Taurus. The influence on the basic sun-sign personality changes very radically.

Why are so many people sun-sign conscious? I believe it is the result of the constant flow of astrological journalism both in magazines and newspapers carrying astrological columns. This type of writing became popular in 1930, but it did not make too much impact until after World War II when the world really hit its astrological stride. If you think the purists created the popular trends in astrology, forget it because it was businessmen, Madison Avenue, and newspaper owners who saw that astrology represented the green commodity they love so much—money. The purists, of which I was one at that time, continued with astrological research and marveled at former students of ours who suddenly blossomed as commercial astrologers. We sat in our ivory towers and watched astrology become a pop science manipulated by puppeteers who pulled strings to get the names of famous people at the head of their newspaper astrological columns. When the purist woke up to the knowledge that 32,000,000 Americans were interested in astrology, King Sun had been elevated to his former godlike status as if no other celestial body ever influenced a sign.

I suppose it was the blast-off from Cape Canaveral of Apollo II to the moon which really shook my own ivory tower to the foundations and sent me scurrying down to earth. There I took a long, hard look at modern astrology and I did not like

3

what I saw: an old science debased to the art of reading sun signs as if they were sacred words, and an entire continent content to believe it. Having survived decades of ferocious attacks by religion, astrology at the height of its newfound popularity was ripe to have verbal tomatoes thrown at it by its new enemies, the scientists. The experience was like seeing an old lover belonging to my youth suddenly stepping out like a middle-aged swinger trying to be young. It hurt.

Running around with the advocates of sun-sign astrology were flower-power people, instant astrology programs on talk shows, long-haired, bearded youths with old eyes looking like gurus in search of an ashram and bright young ladies who, having discovered that Leos are passionate lovers, all managed to get a giggle when being interviewed by a Leo talk-show host.

The moon, with all her feminine qualities, shivered as more space vehicles landed on her surface and men left their footprints on her aged face. I marveled that the Women's Liberation movement never saw the value of the moon as an influence on their own activities or thought of the ancient moon goddess, Diana. Anyway, she has been relegated to third place as more and more witches bounced through the pages of magazines, all vowing adherence to Hecate and Astarte, two faces of the triple-faced Moon Goddess. If the Women's Liberation movement had adopted Diana as their own celestial symbol, they could have combated male chauvinism with a few silver shafts of pure astrological wisdom. Sol and his sun signs would never have made the best-seller list of books, and astrology would have been again in its rightful position as an acknowledged science. Truly to those who go beyond sun signs and acknowledge the expression of the feminine quality of life, astrology reveals itself as a fabulous science equally as exciting as that of mathematics. It has helped to alert man to the pitfalls in his life, enabled him to appreciate that cycles recur again and again, and that if he catches the high cycles he can achieve success with less energy expended than when he relies on change. It has shown him ways to relieve tension, taught him that relaxation is as important as hard work and, most of all, brought man to a point in his life when he has the means to apply a system of checks and balances so that he can be in harmony with himself and his environment.

Astrology is as important to man as is psychology. This branch of knowledge deals with the human soul deriving awareness of the mind from the careful examination of the facts of consciousness. Astrology complements everything in psychology because it examines the facts of the planetary influences on the conscious and the subconscious, providing a guideline towards harmony of mind, body, and spirit. Those who deride astrology show their own ignorance about a subject that has been around for many thousands of years. I think this is where the hope for a sound astrology emerges because it has survived just about everything from religious intolerance, scientific disregard, and the public menace of sun signs extolled as the be-all and end-all of modern-day astrology. Those uninitiated to the science of astrology can be forgiven for their ignorance, but there is no excuse for astrologers themselves fostering the mistaken and outrageous idea that sun signs are the only reference points.

Sun-sign astrology is just about one grade above the astrology doled out at fair grounds from a machine giving a ticket stating your weight. The Ascendant, the moon, the life ruler and the planets are not acknowledged by sun-sign buffs, and the sun sign is so rooted in the public mind today that real astrology is practiced only by a few elderly practitioners. We are an endangered species and must now rally under the banner of the crescent moon.

Sun-sign astrology goes well with instant coffee, predigested foodstuffs, plastic flowers, pablum, the instant divorce syndrome, and TV dinners. Like all these items, the so-called solar horoscope is indeed convenient. Solar horoscopes are set up when the birth time is unknown, and it saves the immense labor of rectification by events. But

5

convenience does not make for validity. The solar horoscope, while having some slight value from the position of the sun and planets in the signs, is missing the important factors. These are the Ascendant, the Mid-heaven, the correct house cusps, and the moon. To construct a solar horoscope, all that is needed is the birthdate. The degree in which the sun was moving on that date is taken as an artificial Ascendant, and the horoscope is set up as if it is fact instead of fiction. Those who employ this method argue that everything is built around the sun and so the method is justified. I disagree in toto. How can the establishment of a false Ascendant, Mid-heaven, house cusps, and possibly the sign positions of the faster-moving planets—Mercury, Venus, and Mars—lead to anything but misinterpreation? Also, in this type of chart the moon is either omitted or placed in the wrong sign.

Another method, neither better nor worse, is to place 0 degrees Aries on the Ascendant and go on from there. Both methods are taboo to any astrologer interested in a correctly set up chart from which he can make factual interpretations. If a person does not know his exact time of birth—and very few people do,—a good astrologer can and will work this out through taking into account major events which have occurred in the subject's life, and his appearance and mannerisms.

Assuming that all difficulties have been resolved and an accurate horoscope has emerged, we can begin to examine and understand the importance of the moon in the horoscope.

CHAPTER II

The Moon

The moon is nothing
But a circumambulatory aphrodiziac
Divinely subsidized to provoke the world
Into a rising birth rate.

—Christopher Fry, *A Sleep of Prisoners*

Throughout history, the moon has inspired man's wonder and challenged his profound curiosity. To primitives and ancients and to the poets of all ages, the satellite of our earth-planet was a wandering goddess of the night, the celestial embodiment of remoteness and chastity. Even today, we perpetuate this moon-worship in our "Monday" or "Moon-day," designated by the Romans as the sacred feast day of the moon.

Man's modern concept of the universe began to emerge in 1543 when Nicolaus Copernicus astounded the Renaissance world with his theory that the sun—not the earth—was the center of the solar systm. "In the midst of all," he wrote, "dwells the sun, as if seated on a royal throne. The sun rules the family of planets as they circle around him."

Eventful years followed as refined instruments and improved observational methods led first to the Danish astronomer Tycho Brahe (1546-1601) and then his talented assistant Johannes Kepler (1571-1630) discovering more and more data about the moon's orbit and motion. Finally they were able to establish its path as an ellipse. Another gigantic step forward in understanding the moon came in 1687, when Sir Isaac Newton published his three-volume masterpiece, *Principles*. This work laid down the universal law of gravitation and the classic laws of motion that, until Albert Einstein, stood as the final statement of the principles of the celestial mechanics.

The first to bring man materially closer to the moon was Galileo Galilei of Pisa, Italy who, in 1610, fashioned a primitive telescope and trained it on the moon's mountains and valleys. He was even able to estimate the heights of the peaks and the lengths of the shadows. "I am quite beside myself with wonder," he wrote, "and I am infinitely grateful to God that it has pleased Him to permit me to discover such marvels as were unknown to preceding centuries."

A full century before Galileo's discoveries, the fantastic mind and genius of Leonardo da Vinci was also turning to contemplate the nature of the moon. He began to design a bat-winged machine for manned flight and, in the light of the limited technical knowledge of his day, the Florentine genius arrived at an amazing conclusion. "The moon has every month, a winter and a summer, and it has greater colds and greater heats than our earth. . . . The moon is an opaque and solid body and has no light of itself but so much of it as the sun sees, it illuminates. Of this illuminated part, we see as much as faces us. . . ."

Leonardo's predictions about flight and his mechanical "bird" strangely foreshadowed across four and a half

8

centuries what was to become a fact when the astronauts of the space program landed Apollo II on the surface of the moon. "The great bird," wrote Leonardo, "will fill the whole world with amazement and all records with its fame. And it will bring eternal glory to the nest where it was born."

The world certainly was amazed, and with it came some fear that the celestial embodiment of romance had had its day. But the space program alerted many astrologers to begin to study more seriously the effect of the moon on all living things and to check its placement in horoscopes much more thoroughly. Throughout the centuries man has deviated from the notion that celestial bodies influence events on earth. All too often astrology fell from grace not only through conflict with religion but because of the very men who practiced it. We almost fell into the trap in this century by publicizing sun-sign astrology at the expense of the moon. Fortunately, I believe we are over the danger period. While a group of scientists can get their opinions into press by making wild invalid statements about astrology, more and more news creeps into columns about "amazing scientific discoveries." All these discoveries boil down to facts which astrologers throughout the ages have accepted, although some generations have forgotten them.

Let's look at the grunion fish. In my native land, it is not unusual to use the phrase "The fish will be running well after the next full moon." Behind such a conversation there is a host of fishermen anxious to prove the veracity of such a statement. Some years ago I went to a meeting of the government fish and game commission and asked about the idea of fishes running better at the time of the full moon. He stated with some ferocity that fish are not affected by the moon. This official should read a pamphlet issued by his own government department published in the state of California.

"During the high tides of March, April, May, and June, a small smelt comes along the sandy beaches of California. It comes with the sweep of the water upon the beaches as the waves break and lie for a moment, then squirms and flops back into the wash of the next wave. Probably the only exact statement which can be made is that the spawning runs come shortly after the full of the moon, or in other words, after the highest tide of the series."

After this bit of information, I became quite interested in the spawning habits of the California grunion after the full moon. Those nonscientifically minded smelts make a special point of depositing their eggs—generally three clutches—at the fullest point of the tide at the time of the full moon—that is, within perhaps half an hour after the culmination of the full moon but never before. It is absolutely essential for the development of the fish that they be deposited out of reach of the disturbance of the tide for a given period. This period is contained within one full lunar cycle, approximately twenty-eight days.

Imagine, those strange little grunion can even count. Not only this, but they are aware that their eggs must remain undisturbed for twenty-eight days, so they drop them where the seawater will carry the young fish on the wash of the receding waves into the ocean where they belong. It is obvious that to obtain these conditions it would be useless to spawn any time before high tide because the newly laid eggs would be completely washed away. Since there is no reason to suppose that there is any qualitative difference between the three high tides preceding the full moon and the three succeeding tides, nor any physical influence that would vary at the time of the full moon, it is logical to assume that direct influence of the moon on the fish is the main factor in producing this phenomenon. Grunion are simple fish, but they know their moon cycles even without the help of an ephemeris. So, next time you have a moment to spare after listening to scientists telling you the moon does not influence your moods, consider the case of the moonstruck grunion. The basic laws of the universe—those of action, reaction, and polarity—are exactly the same as the laws of the moon in astrological research.

You may even have cause to blame the moon if you are cold or thinking that the summers get shorter and the winters longer. Greater influence on the earth's weather may be exercised by the moon than by the sunspot cycle, says Leningrad geophysicist Sergei Timofeyev. This, he believes, is due to tidal effects in the atmosphere influencing the circulation of air masses of differing temperatures. Timofeyev has compared the mean air temperatures for many years in Leningrad and other areas of the Soviet Union with the various positions of the moon relative to the earth. He found the dependence on temperatures on the nine-and nineteen-year cycles of lunar motion to be shown even more sharply than dependence on the eleven-year solar cycle.

Temperature fluctuations within the lunar cycle reach almost two degrees. With a higher position of the moon over the horizon, the scientist found that cold winters and summers predominate. In the past, such catastrophic phenomena as the freezing of the Amu Darya River in 1405 and the freezing of the Black Sea at the Crimean coast in 1500 took place in the years of the very high position of the moon. In those years, both maximums of the moon's tidal force coincided with minimum solar activity.

Registration of the lunar effects on the movement of air masses in the earth's atmosphere is important in making weather forecasts. It is particularly important not to forget them in long-term forecasts of climatic changes. Having studied the course of weather from 1959 onward, Timofeyev has drawn the conclusion that Europe has now entered a period of cooling like the one that occurred at the beginning of the second half of the eighteenth century. While science has rejected so much of moon-lore—particularly the astrological forecasts—it has always accepted the moon's responsibility for the tides of the oceans of the world. What they have never been able to accept until recently is that man himself is mainly composed of water, and that barometric pressure and the influence of the moon has had an effect on the watery content of man himself.

The monthly menstrual cycle of a woman is also affected by the moon. She conceives because she is injected with the liquid male sperm, and the baby swims in a pool within her womb. One of the major breakthroughs in updating astrology came when Eugene Jonas, a Czech doctor, discovered that by considering the position of the moon at the birth of a woman, he could also deduce her fertile periods and her chances of knowing the sex of the child. The knowledge was important to many women who wanted to have children and could not understand why they had not been able to conceive. After studying the moon's position, Dr. Jonas prepared lunar charts, and his test cases produced excellent positive results. Many marriages rest or fall in the birth of children; when a woman does not conceive, with ultimate chauvinism the male generally blames the woman and she carries a load of guilt. If this is not enough, there are some marriages when one sex is desired more than the other, and a woman producing a daughter when a son is ardently desired is also expected to carry the blame. Astrology shows a way to circumvent these difficulties. There are clinics in the United States that follow Dr. Jonas's idea of watching lunar cycles so that the periods of fertility can be gauged. You can also check your own moon-sign position to see whether you might be happier with a boy or a girl, as the moon indicates many of your basic reactions to both sexes.

CHAPTER III

The Feminine Principle

As unto the bow the cord is,
So unto the man is woman,
Though she bends him, she obeys him,
Though she draws him, yet she follows,
Useless each without the other

—Longfellow, *The Song of Hiawatha*

The moon rules the fourth sign of the zodiac whose symbolic creature is Cancer, the crab; it is associated with the home and domestic life. It relates very much to the second chapter of Genesis in the Bible, which tells how woman was formed and how dual souls sprang from one single ego; it also gives details of life in the home of these dual souls in the Garden of Eden, which corresponds to the spiritual plane of the involving soul. It is interesting to note that the first serpent of the sky starts in the middle decan of the constellation of Cancer. This constellation's water snake, Hydra, extends the full length of the four constellations—Cancer, Leo, Virgo and Libra—its head in Cancer and its tail in Libra,

13

connecting the two domestic constellations of Cancer and Scorpio. The creative serpents of the sky start in the constellations that correspond to the "companionship houses" in astrology. This is appropriate because the serpentine spiral which we call life is the result of the interaction of positive and negative forces. Hydra, the water snake, is the feminine creative energy of Cancer, while Serpens is the masculine energy in the first decan of Libra.

As with all the symbolic creatures of the zodiac, the crab is very appropriate for those born in the sun sign of Cancer. When the sun reaches Cancer, it is in its farthest northern declination and consequently starts its backward movement toward the south. This backward movement is common to the crab, which does not move directly forward but with a sideward or slightly backward movement. According to a Greek legend, Cancer was a gigantic sea crab which came to the assistance of the water snake, Hydra, when it was attacked by Hercules. To kill Hydra was one of the twelve labors of Hercules. While Hercules was battling with Hydra in the Lernean marshes, the crab attacked him by seizing his foot. In mythology, the foot is the universal symbol of understanding because it supports the body, even as understanding supports the individual.

The constellation Hercules belongs to the spiritual decanate of Virgo, and it is in the center decan of Virgo representing the more spiritual side of work. The labors of Hercules relate to each of the influences of the twelve signs of the zodiac. Even the great Hercules could not complete his task alone. He secured help from Iolaus. The water snake, Hydra, had one hundred heads; when one was cut off, another grew immediately. Iolaus was very cunning; when Hercules cut off a head, it was Iolaus who seared the stump with a hot iron, thus preventing growth. In astrological lore, the two acts of cutting and searing are symbolic of the inharmonies of domestic life, bringing with them impure desires and licentious thoughts which must be seared over by the image of a true soul companion. The last head of Hydra was

14

reputed to be immortal. The immortal head of the domestic hydra is the undying desire for a soul mate. When Hercules hewed this apart from the body, he carefully buried it under the rock of ages to preserve it forever. As the moon reflects life from the sun and represents the feminine principle of life in polarity to the father principle of the sun, so Cancerians, the moon children of the zodiac, thrive better with a mate and must always seek their twin soul.

The greatest change of polarity—the greatest magnet stress possible in the zodiac—occurs when there is a transition from a fixed fire sign to a movable water sign, or vice versa. This occurs when a heavenly body passes from the dividing line between Cancer and Leo and, to a lesser extent, when a heavenly body passes from the fixed air sign Aquarius to the movable earth sign Capricorn. Annually the sun passes these points about June 23 and January 20, times we are likely to experience extremes in hot and cold weather. When the sun enters Cancer for the first time, its strength is attacked as the days begin to shorten. In Cancerians, the constitution can be delicate because of the debilitation of the life force rays of the sun. The Chaldean astrologers called Cancer "the gate of men" and had a tradition that this was the region of the stars through which, when humans were born, the spirit about to be incarnated must descend from heaven to earth to animate the new bodies. There are other traditions in which the summer solstice, or the beginning of Cancer, is referred to as the gate to hell. It is also the gate to which Cephas, or Peter, holds the keys; the dividing line between the superior and inferior regions, the point where the sun reverses its north and south motion.

Cancer is the home sign of the moon, in ancient astrology referred to as the mother sign. The Chaldeans and other ancient people knew astrology as the religion of the stars and did not believe that the spirit or soul had its beginnings at the moment of birth. This premise was totally incorporated into their astrological lore. The Chaldeans believed that the spirit, having evolved through lower forms of life, existed in the astral realm and was attracted to the parents at the moment of copulation. They stressed the part played by the mental aspiration originating from Gemini (the first double sign of the zodiac) and the emotions represented by Cancer. The mental aspirations and the emotions determined the quality of the spirit. As all human beings enter life through the mother, and astrologically the mother is signified by the sign of Cancer, it is easy to see why the ancient astrologers called this sign "the gate of men." As Cancer represents the gateway to life, so its opposing sign, Capricorn, represents the gate to death, through which the spirit passes to the astral realm to await another moment to be born.

The influence of astrology as the religion of the stars did not pass away quickly and we find threads of it still appearing in the Old Testament. You may remember that Jacob had a vision: "And he dreaded, and behold, a ladder set upon the earth, and the top of it reached to heaven, and behold, the angels of God ASCENDED and DESCENDED on it." Then follows a description of the increase and spread of his family, a typical Cancerian activity. Finally: "This is none other but the house of God and this is the gate of heaven." Then Jacob set up a pillar of stone, just as Hercules set up stone pillars—this pillar being the solstitial column. Note that the angels ascended and descended rather than first descending, as one would expect. This is a relic of astrology as the religion of the stars and so described because the sun ascends higher and higher until the solstitial pillar is reached and then descending. It is also significant as depicting evolution and involution.

The first decan of Cancer is Canis Minor, the Lesser Dog. It is not nearly so important in mythology as the Greater Dog. It is identified with the favorite dog of Helen that was lost in the Eripus. Helen represented the moon in its alliance with Cancer, the home to which she was restored. The loss of her dog signified the loss of faithfulness and the commencement of the loss of the sun, or its waning power in Cancer. According to another legend, the Lesser Dog was one of the fifty dogs of Actaeon that devoured their master. Diana, representing the moon, was discovered bathing with her nymphs in the vale of Gargaphia, when Actaeon discovered her. To prevent his betraying her, Diana transformed him into a stag, and his own dogs tore him to pieces. We have a reenactment of this legend again in the Old Testament in the biblical account of King Ahab and his wife Jezebel. Elijah—or Auriga, the Master of Wisdom—is present throughout this account as prophet of their end; horses and chariots are prominent in the deaths that take place. When the king died, "And on washed the chariot in the pool of Samaria; and the dogs licked up his blood." When his immoral wife, Jezebel, was slain "and some of her blood sprinkled on the wall, and the horses, and he trod her underfoot." The wall is the solstitial pillar between Gemini and Cancer, and the horses those which the faithful heavenly twins were reputed to ride; horses, on account of their speed, being universal symbols of the mind. The biblical reference goes on to say, "This is the word of the Lord, which he spake by his servant Elijah the Tishbite, saying, in the portion of Israel shall the dogs eat the flesh of Jezebel."

The Lesser Dog of Cancer is the dog that devours and symbolizes the unfaithfulness to domestic ties which Cancerians detest. In the major arcanum of Tarot cards, the eighteenth one corresponds to Cancer. It depicts two dogs and the card is read as "deception," for one dog represents the lying spirit. Jezebel was killed because of her unfaithfulness and was a deceiver and Ahab was sent a lying spirit: "And the Lord said upon him, wherewith? And he said, I will go forth and I will be a lying spirit in the mouth of all his prophets. And he said, thou shalt persuade him and prevail also, go forth and do so." It seems strange that a deity should encourage a lying spirit, but if we use the word "law" for "Lord," the matter becomes much more clear. King Ahab was the husband and companion of Jezebel who would attract lying spirits, and those would lead Ahab astray as he placed his trust in irresponsible mediumship.

*   *   *

17

As the rays of the sun are cut off in the Cancer solstice, in human life this symbolizes the soul's turning from fidelity to domestic infidelity and promiscuity, the two insecurities most feared by Cancerians. Cancer corresponds to the house in any chart ruling the home, and the various decans of Cancer and the legends concerning them are all primarily concerned with some phase of domestic life. The third decan of Cancer is Argo, the Argonautic ship and the Ark of Noah, which are associated with The Flood. The records of the Egyptians as reported by Solon, the Greek lawgiver, point to the period of the last great deluge as the time when the equinox passed from the first decanate of Leo back into the last decanate of Cancer, about 8919 B.C. Both astrology and geology testify, as well as Egyptian and Chaldean traditions, that there has been not one but many deluges and that these appear within periodic cycles. In the history of Masonry, there is a story that two pillars were made, one of marble to withstand fire and the other of brass to withstand the flood. No matter which holocaust took place, the wisdom of Masonry would be preserved forever on these pillars. The Egyptian priest and the Greeks believed that the world had been devastated not once but many times by fire and flood. The Bible records the Deluge as well as the destruction of Sodom and Gomorrah by fire and brimstone pouring out of the heavens. The Sybils of Rome predicted the world would perish by fire and the Stoics, according to Seneca, held the same belief. Every civilization has had its own tradition of devastation by deluge or fire, and it is interesting that these legends are not exclusive to the sophisticated intellectual Greeks but also belong to the Arawaks of Guyana and the Tupi-Guarani of Brazil.

In the destruction of Atlantis, a Mayan codex indicates that 64,000,000 people perished. The Mayan Codex Cortesiane says, "Twice Mu jumped from its foundations. It was then sacrificed with fire. It burst while it was being shaken up and down by the earthquake." Plato reports that Solon the Greek stated the Egyptian priests told him that Poseidonis—that is, Atlantis—sank about 9,000 years before his time.

18

This was approximately the date when the equinox passed from Leo into Cancer, from the fire decanate pictured by Crater, the Cup, into the watery decanate pictured by Argo, the Ship or Ark. If a cataclysm occurs at this point in the zodiac and causes a watery deluge, then a cataclysm of an opposite nature will occur at the opposite violent point; hence the legends of great clouds and devastation by fire.

Many people are confused about the Age of Aquarius and do not know that each constellation and sign of the zodiac has its own "age." The calendar year is divided into twelve months; the Great Year is divided into twelve periods of approximately 2,150 years. The Great Months are named after the constellations but are eras of time, not areas of space. The Age of Pisces, from which we are just passing, commenced 2,150 years ago, and we are at the beginning of the period which is called the Age of Aquarius. The Age of Cancer, under the rulership of the moon, occurred from 8850 to 6700 B.C., the time when Atlantis disappeared in the deluge. Since Cancer is a lunar sign, the uprise of the sea may have been caused by a shift in the relationship of the moon to the earth.

The transition from the Age of Leo to the Age of Cancer was as drastic as our present transition from the Age of Pisces to the Age of Aquarius is likely to be. The devotion to sun worship gave way to a pantheistic religion teeming with nature spirits. The goat-footed Pan, associated with Capricorn, the opposite sign to Cancer, was succeeded by the matriarchal religion in which Diana, the Moon Goddess, was also the Great Mother. At this time, Wicca as a nature religion flourished (although some cults remained faithful to Pan and the Horned God). It was virtually the transition from a magical religion with male domination to an equally magical religion in which the moon and the feminine qualities achieved domination. Works of art from this time show a preponderance of Mother-Goddess figures, often crude female torsos with huge breasts and distended stomachs, marking them as part of a fertility religion. At the

19

same time, the family became the basic unit in the matriarchal society, with this came the learning of new skills including those of making homes, bringing family life from caves and primitive huts. An entirely different type of civilization was in the making in this Age of Cancer, an age of emotion and mysticism. In ancient religions, mythology, and folklore, the moon plays just as important a role as the sun. This is not surprising because night is the time when spirits walk; the night has its own sounds which strike the ear more mysteriously than those of daytime. The day and sunlight were associated with the sights and sounds of working life, but nighttime and moonlight were associated with lovemaking, the act of procreation, in itself a mystical union. Moonlight softens the harshness of the day; nocturnal birds and beasts prowl in its rays. Most of all, it was the feminine qualities of the moon which presented a much more subtle, emotional religion than that of sun worship, with its constant demands for human sacrifice.

In the Age of Cancer the previously veiled spiritual world was related to everyday life. Later, when the Age of Cancer gave way to the Age of Gemini, remnants of moon worship lingered in some parts of the world, but the sex of the moon was seen as masculine.

The Dieyeris of Australia believed that man and all beings were created by the moon. In many American Indian languages, the moon was regarded as male and the sun referred to as "his companion." The Ipurinas, a Brazillian tribe, addressed the silver orb of the moon as "Our Father" and spoke of him as a little old man, their mutual ancestor who still watched over his numerous descendants. The eastern Eskimos say that their ancestors came from the moon to the earth and, if we accept the idea that ancient astronauts once came to the earth and left it, then it may well be that the Eskimos are descended from the original space travelers. Several tribes in Borneo use the moon as the chief basis for their religion and, as such, it is venerated.

* * *

Even the familiar nursery rhyme of Jack and Jill is not immune from the influence of the moon. The source of this legend goes back to Scandanavia. A boy and girl named Hjuki and Bila were drawing water from the well when the moon decided they must serve her. She carried them off to the heavens in a bucket; the story of Jack and Jill fetching a pail of water is acted out in the heavens and is related to the waxing and waning of the moon. As the children ascend the hill, the moon waxes; on their descent, it wanes. In the Scandanavian language, Hjuki means "increasing" and Bila means "decreasing." There is a universal belief that the physiological life of women is linked with the moon; most of these beliefs relate to that astrological understanding of the characteristics and influences of the moon. In England, there is a belief that from time to time women are impregnated by the moon and carry a child which is fed by the emanations of its radiance. The child never develops perfectly and is aborted as a "moon calf." There is some scientific acceptance that the physiological life of the female is linked to the moon. The cycle of human ovulation conforms to the twenty-eight days of the lunar month . . . in fact, the word menstruation signifies "monthly."

With the influence of the moon on religious rituals also came the added veneration of water entering into numerous rites of purification, penitence, and sanctification. Baptism by sprinkling or immersion belongs to the most ancient sacred rites, long before Christianity. The use of water in divination, lustration, and libation was worldwide and always linked to the moon. In emerging from the sun worship of primitive religion, the magical power of the moon was quickly appreciated; it was supposed to draw into itself the hidden potencies of the stars and constellations. The Babylonians, the great astrologer/astronomers of the past, worshiped the moon as queen of the night, hailing her as the ancestor of the sun, then linking this into their astrological calculations. The earth was thought of as the child of the moon. Madame Blavatsky, founder of the Theosophical movement, stated, "The moon is far older than the earth, which owes its being to the moon." This brings us back full circle, for this is exactly what is being proved scientifically since the United States started on its space program. What astrologers and occultists have always accepted by faith will soon be proved to be a fact by the very people who have tried to discredit astrology and occultism.

In astrology we find clues to the true personality through studying the aspects of the moon in the natal chart. We may see ourselves as one type of person and be surprised that the world sees another type. If the sun and moon are in conjunction at the time of birth, then we find a rare type of human being, someone who is really what he appears to be. When the moon has numerous aspects to it, we find a person capable of varying his behavior to suit his companions and circumstances. In rare cases of one aspect alone to the moon, we find a person whose behavior is consistently uniform; he is often a very dull, predictable person. If the moon is strongly placed on the meridian, then the subject is an archetypal female. Even though he may be male, he will have many feminine attributes dominating his character. A woman with this placement will flaunt her femininity and be influenced by the latest fashions; she will keep to the strictly acceptable feminine form. She is more likely to read *The Total Woman* than be interested in books about women's liberation.

When the moon is well placed in a natal chart, the subject usually chooses a profession which takes him into public life, although this public life may not make him famous, such as an actor. He could also be in public life through being a chauffeur to a famous man or even the commissionaire at a hotel where celebrities gather, or a beautician who deals with famous faces.

CHAPTER IV

Your Moon Profile

Having established the enormous importance of the moon, we can now carefully examine the role that the moon plays in everyone's life. To find out what your own moon sign is, turn to the Ephemeris (Chapter XI). Do bear in mind that this Ephemeris is simplified; if your moon seems to fall close to the beginning of a sign or the end of a sign, you may want to read the sign that falls before or after it.

Ideally, of course, you should have your chart done by a professional astrologer who will carefully chart the moon's position and give you its exact placement.

The moon profile for each sign gives you the following information: basic personality characteristics, physical characteristics and weaknesses, and a guide to relationships with natives of each sun sign.

As you know, the moon rules the emotions. As its impact on your love life is obviously considerable, romantic considerations are examined in great detail in the next chapter.

CHARACTERISTICS OF MOON
IN ARIES PEOPLE

Aries is the first sign of the zodiac, literally the beginning of springtime, the ideal time to take a new look at life, relating past experiences to the present and looking hopefully toward the future. It is a fire sign, and its astrological symbol looks like the horns of a ram, the symbolic animal of the sign. Metaphysically the horns of the ram also represent a fork in the road of life, giving a person the opportunity to go one way or another, relating freedom to decision-making, thus implying that free will is dominant in the Aries subject.

When we consider the moon in Aries in contrast to the sun in Aries, we get a slightly different picture because the moon is a water influence and in a fire sign, water and fire can turn to steam. Thus Moon in Aries people often talk a lot and give the impression of being more knowledgeable than they are. For instance, a Moon in Aries type can talk about big plans and invoke a lot of enthusiasm for these plans, but when called on to deliver more details, he falls apart. Still, he always has a newer, brighter and better idea and goes on with equal enthusiasm to the next subject. Tremendous energy is wasted on ideas that fall apart and cannot be followed up by action. Because of this, the Moon in Aries person must always be seeking new friends; in fact, he always needs an audience who for a brief moment in time will allow him his place in the forum. There is a lot of charm in this placement of the Moon in Aries, plenty of vivacity and verve; there are moments when the person shines like a bright star, expressing himself like a firebrand, only to be dashed apart when it comes to details. He is a Chinese firecracker, but never a damp squib.

*   *   *

A person with the Moon in Aries can rise to positions of authority very quickly, but then he reaches a point where he stays—there is no other place to go. No matter how much he concentrates on his rapid rise to authority and the pleasure he has had in achievement, there comes a time when he becomes frustrated simply by the difficulties in holding on to what he has got.

His quick temper rises, but it fizzles out to become steam dispersed into the air. Gradually the person with Moon in Aries, having achieved success in business, becomes militant at home and very self-centered and conceited. For the Moon in Aries person who does not achieve a modicum of personal success at work, the attention will turn to a series of personal conquests with the opposite sex, but his love life is never very stable. The Moon in Aries person thrives on novelty and he can manufacture excitement through his own enthusiasm, often through aggravating a situation or embroidering facts. If other planets give him an outlet for his imagination through some source of creativity, then he can be a much happier person. His keywords are enthusiasm at its best and impulsiveness at its worst. Between the two he manages to have a very sparkling life, always keeping up appearances among friends. He can be the life and soul of a party, but when the party ends there can be lengthy periods of depression until his quick mind decides on the next thing to do. Neither anger nor depression last for any length of time; ugly moments can be forgotten with ease, and there is rarely any resentfulness against others. His pride and independence bolster up his self-esteem.

PHYSICAL CHARACTERISTICS

Variable height, rather fleshy body and plump, round "moon" face, a good complexion. Light brown or flaxen hair; strong, noticeable nose with small nostrils; full, round eyes with well-shaped full brows.

WEAKNESSES

Eyestrain, headaches, often of a migraine intensity, catarrh, alopecia, weak sight.

HOW MOON IN ARIES PEOPLE
RELATE TO THE SUN SIGNS

TO SUN IN ARIES

This combination produces great activity in thought and more than a few verbal fireworks. They are friendly—in a volatile manner. The Sun in Aries dominates the relationship, and the Moon in Aries person is quite happy about this because it takes away a lot of responsibilities. The strength of the lunar Aries is that there is a great deal of understanding in the need for the solar Aries to be always active. The weakness of the Moon in Aries in this relationship is that both sexes are incapable of standing up for themselves in arguments even when they are right and the Sun in Aries types are quick to take advantage of this weakness.

TO SUN IN TAURUS

The lunar Aries respects the stability of the Taurean; they can tread the same path in business or romance amicably, though not without a few setbacks due to the quick Aries temper. There is a mutual respect here which is recognized by both parties. The Moon in Aries supplies an inspiration to the Sun in Taurus person and is able to bring out the best qualities of that sun sign. Once each party has established its own definitive qualities, there is no domination by the strong sun in Taurus.

TO SUN IN GEMINI

The lunar Aries can dominate the Geminian, but once Gemini feels he is being exploited, he is quick to move away. This relationship is always on a seesaw. Its primary weakness is that the fickleness of the Gemini seems to mar the relationship, making it ultra-painful on the romantic level. The relationship thrives when it is kept on a very intellectual level—which is good for business and bad for romance.

TO SUN IN CANCER

The sun in Cancer struggles to dominate this relationship but never really manages to do so. It is a relationship that has to be worked on and often has an off-on period when both retire hurt, then try again because of their mutual interests. The strength of the Moon in Aries is that it has a deep understanding of the erratic sensitivity of the Cancerian; but trouble comes when the Aries cannot hold his tongue about Cancer's faults. Both can go overboard in excesses when there is a romantic involvement.

TO SUN IN LEO

The moon in the first fire sign of Aries relates very well to the higher echelon of fire in the Leo. There are many common interests both in romance and business. There is a natural attraction here; this can be a very equal relationship with each party dominating for a short period. Both parties are stubborn and neither likes to be proved wrong. The Moon in Aries has a great ability to enjoy the flamboyancy of the solar Leo.

TO SUN IN VIRGO

Aries dominates this relationship because the Sun in Virgo person will withdraw from any trouble and allow the lunar Aries to hold the reins. The Moon in Aries can easily relate to the Virgo Sun on the intellectual level; in a business relationship the capricious Aries can spark off ideas and rely on the Virgo to put them into effect. To make such a business partnership work, both parties should clearly define areas of work before getting into financial considerations. In romantic matters, the relations begin on an exciting level, but the lunar Aries can seldom live up to the Virgoan's discriminating ideals.

TO SUN IN LIBRA

Aries dominates the relationship, but its strength lies in the fact that it is motivated to help the sun in Libra, and so there is mutual appreciation. The weakness of the Moon in Aries person is that he cannot understand the vaccilation of Libra, and the constant struggle to keep Libra on an even keel can result in temper tantrums in which the Moon in Aries generally comes off the worst.

The lunar Aries enjoys the perception of the Sun in Libra person but can get very irritated when the Libran becomes indecisive or makes too many demands on him to accept responsibilities. When the Libra recognizes that his needs can be fulfilled by the more dynamic Aries, then he is content to leave more and more responsibilities in the hands of the lunar Aries, who is not quite able to fulfill them. The same flaw exists in business matters.

TO SUN IN SCORPIO

When the rapidly moving lunar Aries meets the immovable force of the Sun in Scorpio, there is bound to be chaos, if not a head-on collision. There is an abrasive quality in this relationship as both parties try to dominate, but at times this is not a bad thing and both the Scorpion and lunar Aries love a challenge. The Arian rarely instigates any trouble, but has enough pride to fight for its rights, unfortunately the Moon in Aries is overly sensitive to Scorpio's verbal onslaughts. The greatest difficulties come in the modus operandi because these two will seldom see eye-to-eye in achieving an end result. In business these two are good with a third partner— as long as it's not the spouse of the other party. Romantically, it can be a passionate pursuit of sensual and sexual pleasures.

TO SUN IN SAGITTARIUS

Both love the activity of the other, and this becomes a basis for mutual needs to be achieved, especially in business. But both personalities are strong, and clashes of will and personality are very likely, the more philosophical Sun in Sagittarius can take this more easily in his stride than the quick-tempered lunar Aries. When both join together in a pioneering effort, they can attain spectacular results since the combination of energy and ideas merges very well. They make good traveling companions, but both are erratic enough to change the point of destination at will. Romantically, this can be an exciting relationship mutually rewarding to both, but the female with the Moon in Aries cannot always take the rough edges of the male with his Sun in Sagittarius.

TO MOON IN CAPRICORN

This relationship thrives in business because both are ambitious but there are times when the lunar Aries becomes totally irritated with the slower-moving Capricorn. Each likes to get into a position where he can be in the driver's seat, and often has to make compromises so that they take turns. In terms of romance, there is little attraction unless one or the other has attained a degree of financial security. Marriages occur more to expedite a better position in life, to reach a higher social position. But both will sacrifice emotional security for the security related to material needs.

The great strength of the lunar Aries in this relationship is that the Arian can understand the glum moods of the Capricorn. When the Arian is female, she may be ultrasensitive to periods of neglect; the Arian male may not ever understand the parsimonious nature of the Sun in Capricorn female.

TO SUN IN AQUARIUS

The Sun in Aquarius recognizes the main attributes of Aries—the quick, sparkling ideas—and can generally be helpful in putting them into a practical form. The attraction is mutual, a sort of psychic awareness that one can contribute to the other. This works well both in business and romance, although the lunar Aries may make too many sexual demands on the Aquarius for a truly harmonious personal relationship, and may have difficulty in keeping pace with the spiritual and mental growth so necessary to the Aquarian.

TO SUN IN PISCES

The attraction generally comes from the lunar Aries, who may recognize that the Sun in Pisces type need his help and know-how. At its worst, the attraction may be one in which the lunar Aries, seeing the weaknesses of the Piscean character, may seize on it to assert power over another human being. There can be a very strong romantic attraction, the ardor of the lunar Aries contributing the Piscean's need to be loved on any terms. In business it is an unstable relationship—prospering for a little while, then falling apart almost without each party's being aware of it. While Aries can relate sympathetically to the needs of the Piscean, he cannot cope with too much vacillation.

CHARACTERISTICS OF MOON
IN TAURUS PEOPLE

The person with this placement of the moon has plenty of resources available all through life, many of which relate to material needs. The moon is exalted in Venus-ruled Taurus, enabling it to gather in and conserve resources for the proverbial rainy day. Much of the inconstancy of the moon becomes stabilized in the practical sign of Taurus, consequently a Moon in Taurus person is not likely to be so impulsive as a Moon in Aries person. This is a position where the moon strongly influences romantic attitudes, and most subjects enjoy such things as candlelight, soft music, and gracious companionship in their love life. Indeed, both sexes demand that love must come with all the frills attached, and both sexes pay great attention to good grooming and pleasing manners. They will often marry for status; this status is as likely to be familial as financial.

There is a great attachment to family life, to lineage and traditions and to memorabilia relating to heritage. Moon in Taurus people are always able to get support from relations and friends, and in business are able to use contacts to further their ambitions. The Moon in Taurus brings with it an appreciation of music, and in many cases, the chosen profession may be linked to music. It brings devotion and perseverence and, most of all, good old-fashioned common sense. In love the head will rule the heart, but never to such an extent that a love affair becomes a painful experience. In business matters, while the subject can be hardheaded in his dealings, he is also able to be philanthropic and very much interested in community work or simply doing good for a friend who has hit hard times.

Moon in Taurus people are able to consolidate ideas and ideals, applying common sense to all situations and problems. They can rise to most emergencies without falling apart.

PHYSICAL CHARACTERISTICS

A strong body, but inclined to corpulence at an early age. Rather short in stature. Good complexion; full, fleshy nose

31

with wide nostrils. Dark brown or black hair. Small eyes with full arched brows.

WEAKNESSES

Swelling of the throat, such as quinsies; in cases of influenza, the throat will be the most vulnerable area; ulcers.

HOW MOON IN TAURUS PEOPLE RELATE TO THE SUN SIGNS

TO SUN IN ARIES

The first attraction is through mutual respect, but the persistence and exactitude demanded by the solar Taurean can make heavy demands on the short-fuse temper of the lunar Aries. The Taurean appreciates the good things in life which the Aries also enjoys, but the Moon in Taurus does not have the vitality for the physical activity so necessary to Aries.

TO SUN IN TAURUS

There is little conflict in this relationship based on mutual likes and dislikes. One looks at the other and recognizes much of himself. While they both have mutual likes, they also share their dislikes—heaven help the person who finds himself on the wrong side of this pair! The lunar Taurean has a very charming personality that complements that of the solar Taurean. The only weakness in this relationship is the lunar Taurean's inability to be as practical in everyday affairs as the solar Taurean.

TO SUN IN GEMINI

This is generally a short-term attraction rarely leading into any deep relationship, since the earthy Taurean is often outraged by the more extroverted character of the Sun in Gemini type. Not good in business relationships unless there is a third party available to arbitrate, the lunar Taurean is not often agreeable to this while the Geminian could not care less. Romantically there is a physical attraction but not an enduring romantic one, since the lunar Taurean demands what the Geminian is incapable of giving: total, unabated loyalty.

The Moon in Taurus likes orderliness, but in relationships with Gemini, this passion for order is carried so far that it becomes mere nitpicking.

TO SUN IN CANCER

The lunar Taurean is conscious of the softness of the Cancerian, and when this attraction is based on love, it will never seek to exploit it. But beware the lunar Taurean who uses the weaknesses of Cancer in any business pursuit—for then the Cancerian will suffer emotionally and physically, and in all probability come out the loser.

TO SUN IN LEO

It is easy for the lunar Taurean to build up the confidence of Leo through flattery. The Moon in Taurus person has a knack for gaining the confidence of Leo and will provide him with loyal support. This can be a mutually rewarding relationship in both business and romance. When it doesn't work, it's usually because flamboyant Leo may be irritated by the retiring Taurean nature.

TO SUN IN VIRGO

Taurus usually dominates this relationship, especially if the Sun in Virgo person is young. The Moon in Taurus person can be a guardian angel to Virgo, always understanding

Virgo's unspoken needs. Money considerations will dominate this relationship. As both persons have hearts ruled by their heads, this relationship is likely to be unsatisfactory at the romantic level.

TO SUN IN LIBRA

The lunar Taurean seems able to attract respect from the Libran, but many relationships are based on the May-December motive... The December lunar Taurean is likely to be the dominant party attracted to the charm of a more youthful Libran. The romance can be good, although gradually the sexual and sensual aspects decrease, often in relationship to the increasing desires for material rewards that the Libran cannot give. In business the partnership can again be related to an older lunar Taurean seeking the help of a younger associate, and he will then take on the role of guiding. This aspect is common to both sexes.

TO SUN IN SCORPIO

This is a love-hate relationship all the way. It can be very hard on the lunar Taurean if the relationship is a romantic one. If the female has her moon in Taurus, she can relate well to a male Sun in Scorpio, and may not mind being dominated. When the sexes are reversed, the Sun in Scorpio female will want to dominate, and there is an inevitable clash of wills. While the Moon in Taurus person's greatest strength is his practicality, his weakness is physical overindulgence. The Moon in Taurus will pick up the Sun in Scorpio's weaknesses and add them to his own. In a business relationship, they may be able to cope with their difficulties if they have mutual goals. They are both quite capable of compromise when the end result is to their joint benefit.

TO SUN IN SAGITTARIUS

Both are capable of recognizing that each is a workhorse,

and both can accept responsibility without moaning about it. The Moon in Taurus is aware that the Sagittarian is overly optimistic, but he allows Sagittarius to think he is carrying the burdens while Taurus works in subtle ways to make things easier. Both the lunar Taurus and the solar Sagittarian work hard for success and pull their hardest when the going is rough. After success has been achieved, they are likely to go their separate ways.

This same thing applies to romance. Once the sense of challenge and achievement is gone, romance fades, and they will go their separate ways—unless there is a family involved. In many cases, taking an interest in grandchildren will bring the responsibilities necessary to rekindle the attraction.

TO SUN IN CAPRICORN

The mutual attraction here is hard work. In business this can be a spectacular combination, especially on long-term projects. The danger here is that Capricorn may work so hard that Taurus allows himself to get lazy. In romance, a youthful Taurean may be attracted to an older, achievement-oriented Capricorn. In this case, the lunar Taurean will forego sexual pleasure for what he considers the greater benefits of material security and loyalty.

TO SUN IN AQUARIUS

The moon in Taurus can dominate with gentle guidance. The attraction is one tinged with wariness by the lunar Taurean for the virtuosi qualities often apparent in many Aquarians. He demands that Aquarius prove himself by setting a few Herculean feats as a challenge. If Taurus is satisfied with the performance of the eccentric Aquarian, they can make a powerful combination in business. In romance the relationship seems to remain tinged with wariness. Neither quite trusts the other and it is better when the Aquarian is many years older than the lunar Taurean and especially beneficial if the lunar Taurean is female so that she can develop a father-figure image which quite suits the solar Aquarian.

TO SUN IN PISCES

There is a mutual attraction—especially in romance—since Pisces seeks love and Taurus is prepared to give it especially at the beginning of such a relationship. But the lunar Piscean needs to allow some of the practicality of the Taurean to brush off and become more in tune with reality if the relationship is to mature. Alternately the lunar Pisces can be helpless enough to keep the loyalty of the Taurean, who is quick to recognize that weakness is not a fault but a chance to give him power over another human being. The lunar Piscean will try hard to be a good business partner but will always allow the Taurean to dominate the relationship and in most cases this turns out to be to their mutual benefit. This relationship can thrive when there is no conscious desire on the part of either party to be dominant.

CHARACTERISTICS OF MOON IN GEMINI PEOPLE

This position stimulates the imagination, sometimes manifesting itself as a means for highly creative work, but at its worst producing the type of person who enjoys telling lies and forgets everything about truth. The Moon in Gemini has many good things about it when the mind is kept active and directed into areas such as education; the subject can be a fine teacher or a quick-witted student. He can rarely keep to one thing at a time and loses some impact in carrying projects through to a level where he gets the best results, so he is constantly searching for new experiences.

In business, the Moon in Gemini person can sparkle, but he

does best with a strong, practical partner who does not mind calling the shots. If the Moon in Gemini person respects his partner, he does not mind this supervision, providing he has been allowed plenty of freedom during his youth. If this is missing, he can become resentful at first, have a quick spurt of temper, and then cheerfully walk away. Quick to rise to any physical or mental emergency, the Moon in Gemini often does not know the meaning of fear and consequently will take chances that would devastate anyone else.

In romance, this type of person is not averse to indulging in several affairs at once and manages to survive without anyone hating him, due to his charm and the ease with which he can make explanations. Marriages do not start with any stability, but can be maintained if the partner is easygoing and understands the duality which is exaggerated in the Moon in Gemini. He covers a lot of faults with total optimism even when everything seems to be going wrong; he can bounce back into activity after a major setback.

With this position of the moon, both sexes seem to retain a special kind of youthfulness and in old age always relate well to younger people. They are vain about their personal appearance.

PHYSICAL CHARACTERISTICS

Tall, well-formed lithe figure. Coloring varies between pale and sanguine, with a good complexion and brown hair. Oval eyes wide apart with finely arched brows.

WEAKNESSES

Pneumonia, varicose aneurysm, a variety of lung problems.

HOW MOON IN GEMINI PEOPLE
RELATE TO THE SUN SIGNS

TO SUN IN ARIES

The lunar Gemini is attracted to the volatile nature of the Arian, but relationships dissolve into thin air as both tire of playing games designed to outdo the other. The Sun in Aries dominates for limited amounts of time. The strength of the Moon in Gemini is its ability to withdraw from situations before they become too difficult. Gemini's fickle nature is not something that Aries can understand or tolerate. In business and romance the relationship will be short-lived; but partings are made without malice, and a degree of friendship will remain.

TO SUN IN TAURUS

The lunar Gemini can never understand the stability or down-to-earth qualities of Taurus and has little respect for them, and therefore little time to spend on trying to understand. It is a one-sided attraction with the Taurean being intrigued by the versatility of Gemini but being quite incapable of catching up with the speed at which the Gemini mind moves. Business relationships are passing phases— lunar Geminis may be employed for short-term projects by Taureans. On a romantic basis, the charm of the lunar Gemini appeals to the beauty-loving Taurean but rarely burgeons into marriage. If marriage is the outcome, it is always for different reasons than love. The main attraction here is generally through the arts or sciences.

TO SUN IN GEMINI

There is a mutual attraction in which neither dominates, but it is often a "hail and farewell" short-term relationship that can be picked up again from time to time. There's definitely no dullness in this relationship, but it's unlikely to be enduring. The attraction of like minds can produce results in educational and research ventures. On an everyday level, this relationship is quite pleasant—while it lasts. In romance, each gets a childlike enjoyment out of the affair; no one gets hurt. Sexual instincts here are not too strong; gradually the affair will break down with little regret by either party. Gemini's quick intuition always tells him when to move on.

TO SUN IN CANCER

Cancer will probably be dominant, but this is almost never a satisfactory relationship. Gemini is quick to understand the moods of Cancer, but he is usually bored and quickly loses interest. The Cancerian is likely to become possessive of the lunar Gemini, and the last thing a Gemini wants is a trap closing around him. The lunar Gemini does not like to be around when anyone is upset, and both sexes of Cancerians can become very emotional. In business the good mental abilities of the lunar Gemini can be useful to the Cancerian. The acquisitive Cancerian is willing to share things with the lunar Gemini, but the relationship will come to grief when it's time for Gemini to repay Cancer.

TO SUN IN LEO

It is amazing how the lunar Gemini can grate on the nerves of the solar Leo. Sometimes this seems deliberate, but it usually comes about without the lunar Geminian's even trying. When the solar Leo retaliates in no uncertain manner, Gemini knows there is advantage in making a strategic retreat. In romance this is not always possible, and then the lunar Gemini sulks and becomes despondent and the battle is won for Leo. There is a physical attraction, and it thrives until the abrasive quality of the lunar Gemini exerts itself, spoiling the romantic image. In business matters, Leos often grit their teeth and put up with the Gemini when he has something spectacular to bring into the relationship, but it is very much a hit-and-miss state of affairs, and in time both parties give up. While Gemini recognizes the strong vital force in Leo and is able to absorb it almost by osmosis, he may underestimate Leo's smartness and take him for granted.

TO SUN IN VIRGO

Both share the ruling planet of Mercury, and Moon in Gemini types seem to have the advantages which go with Mercury, the planet of communication and education, both areas in which Virgoans take an interest. The attraction is at first intellectual, even when there are romantic overtones, but the relationship is far better when it is kept on the level of business; although it is not unusual for business and pleasure to mix well, if for a limited time. The Moon in Gemini appreciates the intellect of the Sun in Virgo, but lacks Virgo's perseverence and will tire more quickly, losing interest in joint projects.

TO SUN IN LIBRA

There is a tremendous attraction here. The quick-witted, pleasure-loving lunar Gemini appeals very much to the beauty-loving Libra. As they move in the same social circles, this is generally where they are likely to meet and start a friendship. When Libra becomes possessive, Gemini leaves. When Libra becomes excessively indecisive, Gemini will stay around to give advice. This relationship can succeed well in business or on a romantic basis. In the latter case, there are a few sobering moments in store for the Libran, but Gemini's charm can generally placate Libra (unless Gemini gives in to his most basic weakness and tells one white lie too many). Neither is forgiving if the other party strays in marriage.

TO SUN IN SCORPIO

The lunar Scorpio can exert charm at will, and since there is a physical attraction to Gemini, there is generally enough will to find a way to start and maintain a relationship. Both are inquisitive and enjoy gossip while maintaining great control on any secret areas of their own lives, and both have sense enough not to probe too deeply into taboo areas. In business the combination can be good and long-lasting, and sexual attraction lasts a long time in a romantic situation with both parties eager to maintain this mutual need. Gemini can challenge the Sun in Scorpio and get away with it purely on the basis of charm. But if Gemini goes too far and the Scorpion gains ground, the slash of the Scorpio tongue and barbed stings will be more than the lunar Gemini can cope with.

TO SUN IN SAGITTARIUS

The attraction is linked to financial needs and both recognize they can make a contribution to mutually benefit each party. The versatile mind of the lunar Geminian works well with the driving power of Sagittarius; when the business side is at its best, both can make money and enjoy success. Romantically, the lunar Gemini can enjoy the passions of the solar Sagittarius, but compensations have to be made when the lunar Gemini decides to make too many friendships away from the domestic scene. There is an alternating current of domination here, and the parties may seem to be on a seesaw.

TO SUN IN CAPRICORN

The lunar Geminian finds it hard to cope with the moodiness of Capricorn. There is mental stimulus to both parties, but once the Capricorn lapses into depression, the Geminian will rarely stay around to cheer him up. It is this aspect which also ruins many a lunar Gemini romance with Capricorn, although it can be good if the lunar Geminian is female and younger than the Capricorn. She can generally coax him out of his saturnine depression, especially if there is a stable financial situation. The lunar Gemini knows how to use the Sun in Capricorn, and when the relationship wanes, he is able to walk away without being hurt. The lunar Gemini has no time to spend in trying to understand the Saturn-inspired moods of the Capricorn and rarely learns anything from sharing sorrow.

TO SUN IN AQUARIUS

If a lunar Geminian wants to find someone to take on the bulk of responsibility and iron out many of the hard ruts in life, then there is no better companion than the solar Aquarian. The attraction is at first intellectual, then resolves into a caring companionship. It is often one-sided, with the lunar Geminian having most of the advantages, but this does not seem to upset the solar Aquarian. This is especially true in a romantic relationship, but is harder to establish in a business one unless the lunar Geminian is exceptionally brilliant and the solar Aquarian exceptionally tolerant.

TO SUN IN PISCES

To a certain extent, each is aware of the fact that he can exploit the other, but it is never done maliciously; often both parties get a lot of pleasure out of fun-inspired exploitation. The attraction is based on contrasts—Pisces marvels at the daring of the lunar Geminian, and in turn the lunar Geminian enjoys the placid nature of the solar Pisces who is rarely dull and has a good sense of humor.

In both business and romance, this relationship is often subjected to friends who advise that it can never amount to anything. The surprising thing is that these two unstable types often get a great deal out of life and enjoy each other's companionship for long periods.

42

CHARACTERISTICS OF MOON
IN CANCER PEOPLE

Here the moon is in its own bailiwick, comfortably emotional when necessary, always enjoying domestic life but given to moments in life where they are on a high plateau of excitement or down in the depths of depression. Neither mood lasts long; this is often called the "sunlight makes shadows" position.

The subjects can be very possessive about material things especially when they are in love. The females make good (but overly possessive and sometimes obsessive) mothers, and the fathers are conscious that they must provide for their children in the best possible way. Both sexes demand excessive returns for any favors bestowed on friends, relations, and offspring. When this is not forthcoming they are hurt, and lapse easily into sulks, forcing people around them into trying to appease them. In extreme cases, moon in Cancer people can produce excessive guilt in the very people they love most; but they never know how much damage they have done because they really believe they are doing their best for others. When there are scenes on the domestic front, the Moon in Cancer person does not use temper as a weapon, but may resort easily to tears followed by an attitude of martyrdom. This can cause a great deal of strain on friendships and business relationships.

Moon in Cancer people always make preparations for their old age and are capable of very strategic planning to meet this part of their life. Paradoxically, when they are over forty, they want to slip back into youthfulness. After fifty they become self-indulgent, and at sixty are still making those important preparations for the old age which seems as if it will never catch up with them. Becoming grandparents is important to them, as another generation in the family allows them another degree of control and further planning for the future. In business deals the moon in Cancer person can be very shrewd and is capable of making money quite easily, especially if they can work in real estate or do work from their own homes.

PHYSICAL CHARACTERISTICS

Short stature, well-proportioned, inclined to a pleasing type of fleshiness. Round, full face with pale complexion and light brown hair. Round eyes, limpid and rather protruding.

WEAKNESSES

Inclination to put on weight; dieting will reduce this, though flesh is quickly regained. Diuretic pills may be helpful, as there is a tendency to retain water—even to the point of dropsy. Carcinomas.

HOW MOON IN CANCER PEOPLE
RELATE TO THE SUN SIGNS

TO SUN IN ARIES

This is doomed to be an on-off relationship. While the Moon in Cancer person has an appealing charm, eventually Cancer's inconsistency becomes too much for the solar Aries. Although the lunar Cancer knows all about vacillation and erratic behavior, he doesn't find it interesting in others. Aries can behave erratically, and this distresses Cancer, who reserves the right to change his mind and views at any time, but hates this quality in another. In business relations, the lunar Cancerian can dominate the seemingly stronger Aries in the early days of the relationship. This will all change when Aries refuses to tolerate changes of schedules and business tactics. This partnership can survive if there is a third party involved.

On the romantic level, Aries can be passionately attracted to the lunar Cancerian, quick to appreciate the loving and lovable qualities, but this relationship relies a great deal on sexual attraction. Once it begins to falter, it can rarely be revived.

TO SUN IN TAURUS

This can be a good personal and romantic relationship with Cancer dominating. The lunar Cancer understands the home-loving part of the solar Taurean's personality. Problems occur if Cancer tries to become too dominant; Cancer may be overpowered by the force of the Taurean's stubbornness. There is often an attraction between Cancerians and youthful Taureans. It is an especially good combination if the solar male Taurean is many years older than the lunar Cancerian. Many older lunar Cancerians are attracted to youthful Taurean males and help them in their careers.

TO SUN IN GEMINI

This can be a very short-term relationship because Cancer cannot understand the versatility of Gemini, and Gemini cannot relate to the conservative, overly protective character of Cancer.

TO SUN IN CANCER

A favorable relationship in which the strength of the Moon in Cancer supplements the weaknesses of the Sun in Cancer and vice versa.

TO SUN IN LEO

The lunar Cancerian can be very adroit in fostering a relationship with the solar Leo because there is a mutual attraction to begin with and plenty of room for the relationship to develop. The lunar Cancerian is very adept at drawing out Leo, although the Leo may think he is having his own way. Trouble can begin when Leo wakes up to the fact that he has been outsmarted, but so great is the charm of the lunar Cancerian that even this can be overcome although the same activities will occur again and again. It can be a great romantic association with Leo giving the passionate love that the lunar Cancerian craves. As Cancer is not physically one of the strongest of signs, there may be a lot of debilitation in trying to keep up with the robust, outgoing solar Leo. This can also be a successful business relationship if the business is one that is linked with the pleasures of personal companionship.

TO SUN IN VIRGO

The lunar Cancerian is very good with youthful Virgoans, but relationships are apt to go astray as the Virgoan grows older especially in the parent-child association. In adult life there is an attraction because the solar Virgoan seems to understand the frailities of the lunar Cancerian and is prepared to tolerate them, always with the hope of improving the harmony within the life of the lunar Cancerian. The wayward moon in its own bailiwick does not always want to respond to the teacher-student association and sometimes rejects the very thing which is good, retreating into emotional upset.

TO SUN IN LIBRA

This relationship can be like a game of Monopoly in that domination fluctuates according to the material possessions of either party. Whenever the lunar Cancerian comes in contact with the solar Libran, there is a conflict of personalities as they enter into competition with each other. It is usually only a good relationship in that sometimes the parties can profit from the challenges of the other. Libra does not respond to Cancer's charm, but ultimately cannot resist the temptation to manipulate and exploit the Cancerian, resulting in wounded feelings. This is a wearing association at best.

TO SUN IN SCORPIO

The lunar Cancer and the solar Scorpio have a mutual attraction, the sympathies of the Cancerian being easily engaged by the emotional Scorpio. They respond intuitively to each other. The lunar Cancerian senses when Scorpio does not need company and withdraws, but is always responsive to any call for help. The secretive Scorpio enjoys the lunar Cancerian's sensitivity and sense of privacy. The biggest danger spot in this relationship comes when sensitive Cancer is confronted by the Scorpion's sarcasm. This is not likely to be a successful business relationship because the constant gauging of emotions adds a strain to normal business procedures.

TO SUN IN SAGITTARIUS

Cancer is quite able to enjoy the extroverted solar Sagittarius and show great appreciation, though the lunar Cancerian may be unable to sustain the quick pace always adopted by the Sagittarian. Lunar Cancerians can be very calculating in this association and dominate the relationship through a clearly expressed need for a shoulder to lean on. There is, though, always a danger that the Sagittarius will revolt against the constant demand for sympathy and will make a few demands of his own.

This can be a good romantic association if the Sagittarian is an older male; it rarely works if they are the same age. If the lunar Cancerian is young, the female Sagittarian can be helpful in furthering a career or even be a good business partner.

TO SUN IN CAPRICORN

The lunar Cancerian generally handles the solar Capricorn very well. The relationship has the greatest chance of success if the male is Capricorn and is old enough to have achieved some financial success. It does not work out so well in reverse, though there is a basis for superficial companionship. The lunar Cancerian can be just as moody as the solar Capricorn, but the moods never last as long. Cancer thrives on drama and Capricorn on tragedy.

TO SUN IN AQUARIUS

If the lunar Cancerian is female and relies on physical charm rather than intellect, this association is short-lived, but Cancerians can be very determined in their pursuits. The Moon in Cancer tries to dominate, but a solar Aquarian is not likely to be intrigued, and the Cancerian will probably not know when to stop pushing.

This can be a good business relationship as the lunar Cancer has a hidden toughness when material things are at stake, and a quick-witted Aquarian may sense this.

TO SUN IN PISCES

A pleasing relationship with little domination. It can be a very lasting relationship. The strength of the Moon in Cancer lies in the strong psychic awareness of the needs of both. The weakness is that the psychic awareness is not combined with the tiniest bit of logic, but the Sun in Pisces can often provide this. These two will have many common pursuits in the creative arts which they will enjoy exploring together; they will also have an enthusiastic and pleasurable sexual relationship. This can be a good business partnership as well, provided that both parties define goals before setting off on the venture.

CHARACTERISTICS OF MOON
IN LEO PEOPLE

These people are very lovable and loving; they enjoy entering into any relationship where there is potential for growth either by understanding, appreciation, business deals, or affection. They will go more than halfway to make these things happen and will generally succeed. There is a great deal of idealism in this position of the moon, and it is important that people having this in their charts choose their friends and lovers with discrimination because any deviation from their high ideals can produce sadness and ultimately bitterness.

When a man with the Moon in Leo falls in love, he puts the object of his love on a pedestal, forgetting that this may be the most uncomfortable position for the loved one to retain. He is apt to endow her with virtues far beyond those she may have, and nothing is likely to change his mind about this unless she herself lets him down. A woman with the Moon in Leo is not quite so idealistic, but she knows what she wants from a romantic relationship and if it is not there already, she will persevere to achieve it. Since this is not always possible, such females go through a form of humiliation and self-abnegation, blaming themselves for the love affair's going wrong. Both sexes enjoy children but see them as reflections of themselves and can rarely cut them free. Generally the Moon in Leo parents find their great love for children is returned with respect.

In business relationships, the Moon in Leo person is capable of asserting authority and shouldering a massive amount of responsibility which he is reluctant to share with anyone else.

Their life-styles are a source of great pride which helps to boost up their morale when things go wrong.

PHYSICAL CHARACTERISTICS

Generally above average height for both sexes, well proportioned body, strong and large-boned, sanguine complexion. The eyes are large and prominently set in a full, round face; eyebrows without too much arch, rather low set. The hair ranges from light brown to tawny brown.

WEAKNESSES

Heart afflictions, muscular pains in back.

HOW MOON IN LEO PEOPLE RELATE TO THE SUN SIGNS

TO SUN IN ARIES

The natural attraction comes through the two personalities sparking off against each other. The solar Aries recognizes a good opponent in the lunar Leo, and so they are worthy adversaries. But they both have the good sense to use a neutral ground for any verbal battles, and generally there is a Mexican standoff which leaves neither party unduly worried. They both want to make their point but are willing to leave a question mark in the air as to which one is right. This does not seem to affect the friendship, which may last for many years. It is interesting that either one will insult the other, but woe betide anyone else who does it; each will spring to the other's defense. This makes for some interesting situations on the romantic level, where sexual instincts are mutually shared and appreciated. The business relationship can thrive under strange conditions and become mutually profitable. Both will take turns in wanting the greater share of the limelight while calculating who put in the biggest amount of energy and initiative to achieve success. In their hearts they know they have both done their best. Any departure from true friendship can be very verbal and both can make dramatic exits—until the next time around.

The lunar Leo and solar Aries can take turns dominating the relationship in all its phases. Unfortunately, the Moon in Leo sometimes produces physical disabilities which can slow down the Leo and produce impatience in his Arian companion.

TO SUN IN TAURUS

The lunar Leo recognizes the best characteristics of the solar Taurean such as devotion, loyalty, and the ability to do well in material things; he is not averse to using the Taurean. In business relationships the solar Taurean will dominate the lunar Leo, but this is no hardship because Leo enjoys spending the money made and adds a dash of verve to the ponderous Taurean business methods. This can be a very satisfying romantic relationship since the moon is exalted in Taurus and there are many complementary interests, such as the desire to have a pleasing environment and both will try hard to attain and sustain it. The lunar Leo understands the basic honesty and childlike quality of the solar Taurean, but problems may occur when the commonsensical Taurus is confounded by Leonine extravagance.

TO SUN IN GEMINI

The astute lunar Leo is not averse to using the solar Gemini. He comes out very well in the relationship, which is generally satisfying to the solar Gemini until it becomes dull and prosaic and that is no part of the solar Gemini's life-style. Their relationship will generally be short-term. In a romantic relationship, the lunar Leo can always keep the solar Gemini interested; the Leo has more control of the situation than he has in business when Gemini is likely to walk away from any difficulties which arise. In romance, the lunar Leo is very capable of sizing up the need for Gemini to have an exciting love life and will be there as a steadying influence when Gemini is in a mood to walk away. It is a romantic relationship which can have many ups and downs, but generally it is an interesting one with periods of mutual satisfaction.

TO SUN IN CANCER

The lunar Leo is very attracted to the solar Cancerian and both seek to charm each other without the competition that both abhor. The attraction is very positive and mutually responsive. A solar Cancerian female can be a very good romantic match for a lunar male Leo; the relationship is only slightly less harmonious with a solar Cancerian male and a lunar female Leo. In both cases the relationship has to be worked on with constant attention and endless expressions of affection and demonstrations of love. Such a relationship, depending as it must on the personal charm and graciousness of both parties, is not likely to succeed when business relationships are mingled with personal pleasures. This inability to merge business with pleasure may make this remarkably good association fall apart; it is impossible to sustain the relationship by business alone. Love and caring is what attracts them in the first place and becomes the cohesive force holding them together.

This relationship may be weakened by Leo's long memory, which is always dredging up old incidents to remind Cancer of his past mistakes.

TO SUN IN LEO

There is a swift attraction between the lunar Leo and the solar Leos; they magnetize each other and enjoy comparing notes about past adventures as well as planning great ones for the future. They are well matched in verbosity, charm, and good looks, all attributes they know how to use. They can present glamour to the world and in business can be a force to be reckoned with in terms of success. They make money easily enough, but both can spend it as rapidly as it comes in. For this reason, romantic partnerships can come unstuck for financial reasons, but if there are children in this union, they are concerned enough to try to curtail their spendthrift ways. Most of all, they have the ability to attract and enjoy very good friends.

TO SUN IN VIRGO

The attraction is generally intellectual; the lunar Leo provides a nice foil for the Virgo alertness. In this mutually profitable relationship, the lunar Leo is able to draw out the best qualities of the more reticent solar Virgoan, making him feel at ease and more inclined to expand his mental horizons and express his well-thought-out views on any of his favorite topics. The Virgoan gives the lunar Leo the admiration he needs to give his best performance. In business, the relationship can be very good if areas of work are clearly defined so that the lunar Leo is primarily involved with the public and the solar Virgoan is working behind the scenes. Romantically this is not a very exciting union except when the lunar Leo is male and is prepared to look after the female Virgoan, who in turn will be devoted and attentive providing she can have a secure environment.

The relationship is endangered, however, if the lunar Leo ever suspects he's not on an intellectual par with Virgo.

TO SUN IN LIBRA

The lunar Leo is very attracted to the solar Libran, and the relationship soon gets into a romantic groove. Conflict comes as both begin to recognize selfish traits in the other but refuse to acknowledge their own faults. In this way a powerful romance can deteriorate into a bickering match, with the solar Libran getting the worst of the verbal battle. Marriages can last when there is plenty of money and both parties agree to ignore the other's faults, while remaining good friends. This sort of détente is necessary in business relationships, and if the lunar Leo is allowed his own way, the business will prosper.

Leo can appreciate all Libra's good points, but may become a little bored with Libra's need for peace and harmony.

TO SUN IN SCORPIO

The mystery which generally surrounds the solar Scorpio is enough to intrigue the lunar Leo, who wants to know everything. Both are inquisitive about the affairs of the other, but both are determined to maintain a wall of privacy. This wall can be broken down when romance creeps into the relationship. It can be a long and meaningful relationship as the lunar Leo understands the passionate Scorpio nature. There will inevitably be a number of quarrels which are likely to wound Leo's pride, especially if Scorpio has been telling lies. They will always unite quickly to present a good front to friends.

This can be a good relationship, but will be probably short-lived as both parties are inclined to check up on the other's activities. If a flaw is discovered, the business relationship will come to a stormy end.

TO SUN IN SAGITTARIUS

In this relationship, Leo is able to give just enough flattery and appreciation to please the solar Sagittarian. There can be a problem in the priority that Leo assigns to personal loyalty; the lunar Leo is not likely to be tolerant of the solar Sagittarian's other friends and is not above stirring up a little mischief in that area.

In a romance, this can be a case of fire meeting fire. This is an affair based on strong sexual desires and not too much everyday understanding. In time it smoulders and dies away. It won't be revived again unless there are children. Although the passion is there, and the sexual attraction, this union is not without a large number of sexual aberrations and problems which often find their place in a psychiatrist's casebook.

In business the lunar Leo is very attracted to the strength and directness of the solar Sagittarian and takes pride in gaining his confidence. Apart from the first sexual attraction, the relationship is on a much safer base when activities are directed to business rather than intimate personal association. However, both are inclined to want to mix business with pleasure, although both areas of life then suffer.

TO SUN IN CAPRICORN

There is not much emotional attraction of the lunar Leo for the more somber solar Capricorn, but marriages are often made for reasons other than love and romance. If both parties understand their commitments from the beginning, a short and not very exciting courtship can result in marriage. Then it rests on how well each party is determined to fulfill the original commitments, and the solar Capricorn is not averse to reminding the lunar Leo that he is expected to fulfill them. It can deteriorate into a sulky relationship in which the lunar Leo behaves like a spoiled child and the solar Capricorn becomes morose and exacting. The lunar Leo male can dominate the solar Capricorn female (often to a degree of subtle cruelty), but she will bear it with fortitude if material needs are met.

In business the relationship is not so tense, as the shrewdness of the lunar Leo appeals to the hard-working Capricorn, and the two can produce good results in business achievements even when they are barely on terms of moderate friendship. Gradually, through achievements and mutual needs being met, the two earn the respect of each other; this is probably the best part of this unusual relationship. If there is a recurring problem in the relationship, it is that Leo always underestimates the practicality of the solar Capricorn.

TO SUN IN AQUARIUS

There is a strong surge of natural attraction between the lunar Leo and the solar Aquarian. Both are capable of ignoring the advice of friends who cannot know how this relationship will succeed. It is generally sustained in a most meaningful manner in which mutual respect and admiration enhance the friendship. The lunar Leo has the ability to understand the subtle workings of the Aquarian mind; the solar Aquarian will treat the sometimes outrageous ideas of the lunar Leo with respect. This unlikely pair can produce some unexpected coups, especially in business. If there's a weak link in the relationship, it comes from the lunar Leo's need to look for and find fault. The solar Aquarian cannot abide this.

On a personal basis, this union can produce delightful children. Both parents enjoy fostering unusual talents.

TO SUN IN PISCES

The lunar Leo has no difficulty in twisting the solar Piscean around his fingers. There is great physical attraction, and some of the more robust elements of the lunar Leo are made more tender by the contact with a solar Piscean. Amazingly enough, there is a great deal of understanding for each other's needs, and the relationship can be very loyal if it can survive the efforts of well-meaning friends and relations who somehow seem to try to disrupt this particular alliance. The lunar Leo meets such interference head-on to protect the solar Piscean.

In business, money worries can defeat many bright ideas, but somehow the two types manage to get a great deal of fun out of this association. Any problems will come from Leo's inability to relate to the intuitive instincts of the solar Pisces, and he will be very vocal in expressing his distrust.

CHARACTERISTICS OF MOON
IN VIRGO PEOPLE

With the moon in this position, Virgo people are very conscious of keeping fit and enjoy admiration expressed for body fitness. Providing they do not become obsessed with specific routines such as yoga, exercising machines, and way-out diets, they manage to maintain a good degree of health. When they become obsessed, they can be very irritating, especially when they insist that everyone else should follow the same exercises and diets which they have taken up.

Keeping the mind healthy by intellectual pursuits is also important to Moon in Virgo people: They love to criticize or analyze everything they read and are not averse to expressing their opinions on the views of other people. Provided that Moon in Virgo people do not become bigoted or deliberately provocative with their own relations and friends, they can be one of the finest groups in the zodiac. They enjoy taking an interest in their local community and then broadening their interests to include the wider issues of national government and political issues.

Sheer dedication to hard work is rarely enjoyed by Moon in Virgo people, but they will work hard to attain a chosen goal. They are good providers and investors. Many doctors who excel in diagnosis have the Moon in Virgo, and it's remarkable how this position of the moon helps so many professional people achieve that extra touch of greatness in practically any profession.

In business, Virgos make good, stable, partners, but the Moon in Virgo is not conducive to any great exciting romances. True, the moon softens a lot of brittleness of the Virgo nature, but the result is that Moon in Virgo people suffer in silence during courtship and marriage. In housewives, the females are very conscientious in struggling against any bitterness which may occur in the marriage; and they must be really stricken and unhappy before seeking solace through the divorce courts. The male Moon in Virgo person is not quite so self-sacrificing, but will always struggle to make provision for his family even when love has flown away. There is always the ability to retreat from material concern to intellectual studies. Both sexes, when emotion is negated in their personal lives, are capable of using their talents to shape the destinies of others in the realms of industry.

PHYSICAL CHARACTERISTICS

Rather tall stature for both sexes. Oval face with keen deep-set eyes and a piercing glance. Well-shaped eyebrows, fully arched well above the eyes. Tolerably clear complexion inclined to ruddiness. Dark brown hair which at first sight may appear to be black, or highlighted with dark reddish tones.

WEAKNESSES

Looseness of bowels, pneumonia, skin irritations.

HOW MOON IN VIRGO PEOPLE
RELATE TO THE SUN SIGNS

TO SUN IN ARIES

The lunar Virgoan is apt to ignore the solar Aries, or at least would like to, but it is not always possible since the solar Aries has a gift for drawing attention to himself. These two have little in common at first; it is a relationship which has to be nurtured very carefully through chance meetings until both learn to respect each other; then there is a glimmer of grudgingly given attention. Such conditions are not conducive to the ripening of a romance, but if it does happen, it will be a low-key affair initiated by the solar Aries and received with more politeness than passion by the lunar Virgoan. In business it is often the fate of the lunar Virgoan to be in the same office as the solar Aries—or even, in extreme cases, the relationship is inherited and forced to exist because of financial matters. The lunar Virgo can seldom come to terms with the erratic behavior of the solar Aries.

TO SUN IN TAURUS

Youthful lunar Virgoans have a natural attraction to youthful solar Taureans and these romances may lead to early marriages which start with a degree of passion and then emerge as fairly stable ones due to the practicality of both parties. A lunar Virgoan going into business early in life with a Taurean may end up as a millionaire; the two merge well in business, and both accept equal responsibilities. Both have passive natures, but the lunar Virgoan will use sarcasm as a weapon against the pragmatic Taurean, who at times can be goaded into quick spurts of temper only to find that he has lost the battle against the more astute lunar Virgoan. In this relationship, the lunar Virgo will work very hard. The Virgo may however, be undone by his desire to attend only to material things. Neither the lunar Virgo nor the solar Taurean is good at sharing, and they may become competitive as more possessions are acquired.

TO SUN IN GEMINI

The lunar Virgoan tolerates the whims of the solar Gemini, but never in a patronizing manner. They can become very good friends, although most of the understanding has to come from the lunar Virgoan. Gemini can bring a sparkling spirit of adventure and hint of potential freedom of spirit to the more down-to-earth lunar Virgoan. Both are inclined to have a mutual admiration of the arts, which may cement their friendship. In business, the lunar Virgoan will dominate and take most of the responsibility, but he will make good use of the talents of the quick-witted Gemini.

In romance, the Geminian generally initiates the affair, and it can be very meaningful, although not very exciting sexually. Satisfaction comes from the mental stimulation they give each other. Gemini's flirtatiousness may spoil this relationship, as the lunar Virgoan can tolerate anything except infidelity.

TO SUN IN CANCER

Many solar Cancerians come on too strong for the more plodding lunar Virgoan. The Virgoan hates to be hunted. He is not always smart enough to know when to accelerate the pace in romance. The male lunar Virgoan does not enjoy a good romantic marriage with the female solar Cancerian because there are too many feminine wiles for him to cope with patiently. It is not much better in the female lunar Virgoan relationship with the male Cancer because she makes too many demands; her own sense of timing is erratic enough to make her want to go out for the evening when he has an important business deal to put together or merely wants to do some repairs in the house. In business relationships, the lunar Virgoan acts as a brake on Cancerian moods and will stand no nonsense when financial matters need attention. Both thrive best in a good environment where there is no shortage of money.

TO SUN IN LEO

There is considerable attraction here, and a lot of compatible factors come into play if both are more intellectually inclined than materialistic or physical. There can be a great sexual attraction, but it is less likely to survive than good old-fashioned noncompetitive friendship. Should marriage take place, the lunar Virgoan is the first to put the marriage on a harmonious companionship level in which the solar Leo is expected to share everything; but Virgo does not mind if the solar Leo does not wish to share his more adventurous life. Both are prepared to make allowances for the failings of the other and are quick to boost each other's good attributes. Lunar Virgo must guard against becoming withdrawn and noncommunicative. They can be a very well matched pair in business matters.

TO SUN IN VIRGO

The lunar Virgoan reacts very well with its solar counterpart. This is an exceedingly good business combination which can lead to the accumulation of a great deal of wealth, indeed to the status of millionaire. They understand each other; their attraction is one of mutual respect, and neither will take advantage of the other. They can be lifelong friends. If they are born into the same family, they will demonstrate little evidence of sibling rivalry.

Romantically, many of the usual attributes are missing. Instead of gushing with sentiment, they relate to each other with loyalty and patience. The only danger in this relationship is the possibility that on some occasion lunar Virgo and solar Virgo will direct their considerable powers of criticism toward each other. Each of them is capable of totally fraying the other's nerves.

TO SUN IN LIBRA

The lunar Virgo male is attracted to the female solar Libra; but the attraction does not seem to be so vital when the sexes are reversed, as the lunar Virgo female is inclined to try to dominate the solar Libra male. The female Libran could dominate the lunar Virgo male easily, but the relationship changes as they get to know each other and live with each other's faults. The lunar Virgoan may overindulge the solar Libran; this often backfires to the detriment of the well-meaning lunar Virgo. The lunar Virgo is just too down-to-earth to play the games that the Libran enjoys so much.

This is a workable business relationship. The lunar Virgo is content to be in the background, providing he has control of the financial side of the business. He is perfectly happy to be behind the scenes, making use of the social contacts of the solar Libran.

TO SUN IN SCORPIO

If this relationship is to succeed, the lunar Virgoan must first express his interest in the solar Scorpion. The patient lunar Virgo is likely to be lost in admiration for the Scorpio, content with a small role in the background. This relationship will probably not work well in business because the inquisitiveness of the lunar Virgoan is in conflict with the business intrigues and game plans of the solar Scorpio.

It is a strange fact that the inquisitiveness of the lunar Virgo does not extend to being curious about the personal life of a chosen solar Scorpio mate, but rather he is intrigued by the aura of mystery and perhaps fears to pull away the veil and face any unpleasant truths. While this can be a good relationship, the lunar Virgoan cannot always satisfy the sexual demands of the passionate solar Scorpio.

SUN IN SAGITTARIUS

The first attraction and reaction of the lunar Virgoan to the solar Sagittarius generally comes through business and is retained on a high level with integrity and dedication on the part of both. The solar Sagittarian supplies the necessary drive to keep things moving, and the Virgoan applies intelligence and service in maintaining a good employer-employee relationship, an area which the more reckless Sagittarian is not so diplomatic in negotiations. The lunar Virgoan can also act as a brake on the speedy Sagittarian.

The lunar Virgo is attracted during youth to the solar Sagittarian; the romance is hectic enough while it lasts, but is rarely sustained, and while the Sagittarian can exit from romance and marriage without showing too many emotional scars, the lunar Virgo is always hurt, and has difficulty adapting to changes. Later in life, suspicions of the opposite sex make for difficulties in romances.

TO SUN IN CAPRICORN

These two earth signs find a lot in common although the lunar Virgo is much more sensitive than the solar Capricorn. Both are tolerant of each other's faults, and this can be as good a basis for a relationship as one which relies on sentimentality. Both are capable of hard work and envisioning long-term projects. They both enjoy ascending the ladder of social success, although they have totally different motivations. The lunar Virgoan is a great student of people, which encourages him to seek a viewpoint other than his own. The solar Capricorn sees social life as a means to furthering business interests.

Romantically, there is a nonsexual attraction, but the possibility of a long-term marriage. A lot of the warmth of genuine affection on a one-to-one basis is missing here. Nevertheless, this can be a successful marriage because the lunar Virgo can be impervious to the dark moods of the Capricorn and can completely ignore them. The danger here lies in the fact that both are secretive, and the Moon in Virgo person can be very uncommunicative.

TO SUN IN AQUARIUS

The lunar Virgoan views the solar Aquarius warily and moves carefully into any relationship. It may take many years for full confidence to enter into the friendship because the lunar Virgoan is politely respectful but never very complimentary. After a slow start, such a relationship logically ought to have all the rough edges eliminated, but unfortunately this is not the case. The lunar Virgoan can generally find faults with the solar Aquarian and never hesitates to expound on them until mutual ill feeling disrupts the friendship. Still, they are content to repeat the experiences from time to time. The same distrust mars the rare romantic interludes between lunar Virgoans and solar Aquarians; marriages are generally more a convenience than a truly exciting romantic adventure.

TO SUN IN PISCES

This is a natural attraction from which the lunar Virgoan benefits as much as the solar Piscean. Each recognizes the best in the other, and when faults are observed, the lunar Virgoan is tolerant enough to overlook them unless a third party intervenes and deliberately seeks to disrupt the relationship. The solar Piscean likes the practicality and loyalty of the lunar Virgoan and can rarely see any faults even when they are pointed out.

The romantic prospects are good and, the same rules apply in business relationships; however, there are frequent periods of trouble, as it seems all too easy for a third party to engineer them. Fortunately the lunar Virgoan and the solar Pisces have strong survival instincts and quite a lot of basic intuition which they manage to line up with logic. They survive, not because of the advice of friends and interlopers, but in spite of them. The only problem that pops up here comes from the lunar Virgoan's occasional insensitivity to the psychic and intuitive powers of the solar Pisces.

CHARACTERISTICS OF MOON
IN LIBRA PEOPLE

Notable for their charm, people born with the Moon in Libra know innately how to use this attribute. They get the goodwill of others simply by turning on the charm, having good manners, and being considerate, all attributes which can be mistaken for weaknesses. Yet within the charming exterior there is a tough core of steel which can produce some surprising results if anyone takes a Moon in Libra person for granted. These people always try to understand the other person's point of view, but the instincts for self-preservation saves many Moon in Libra people from making mistakes in judgment. What they seem to be and what they are varies a great deal, and no one should underestimate these types.

The Moon in Libra enables many of them to attain success in numerous diverse professions such as law, architecture, politics, the arts; this position also produces unusual homemakers. On the surface, the homemakers do not appear to be concerned with the humdrum things of housekeeping, yet they can create a pleasing environment which others enjoy. Indeed, sharing in the good things is very much part of the lifestyle of Moon in Libra people (even though they are often more willing to share other people's things than to bring in a fifty-fifty proposition). Men with this position of the moon are attracted to very feminine women, and romance blooms as much through gracious companionship as through pure sexuality. The female born with the moon in this position generally has the chance to make a good marriage, and if it fails she seems able to repeat the best parts of the first marriage and even improve on it. Both sexes understand that knowing the right people in the right places can enhance their own chances of success and happiness. In business, the male will flourish on his own while the female does best with a partner who supplements her natural propensity to charm and her desire for the beautiful things of life.

PHYSICAL CHARACTERISTICS

Tall in stature, but an awkward-looking body. Though body is fleshy and well developed, the bones are small. Pink and white complexion. Forehead broad and rather full oval face. Smooth light brown hair with good highlights. Clear, round eyes with well-arched brows, rarely bushy.

WEAKNESSES

Various kidney disorders, allergies.

HOW MOON IN LIBRA PEOPLE
RELATE TO THE SUN SIGNS

TO SUN IN ARIES

The natural attraction of the lunar Libran for the solar Aries is often the basis of many true-life love stories which go through the boy-meets-girl cycle, high school courtship, and marriage at an early age. Though it seems too good to be true, many case histories demonstrate that this is one of the most romantic of all love stories within the range of the zodiac. The lunar Libran needs the fire, drive, and protective force of the solar Aries and thrives on it, while the solar Aries is happy with the charm and intelligence of the lunar Libran. Aries must be aware that lovely, charming Libra may suffer inwardly and the lunar Libran must try to curb a natural bent for extravagance.

*   *   *

This is essentially a love match and the same principles do not apply to a business relationship unless the romantic interest is there as well. In that case, business and pleasure mix well enough to bring success as well as a harmonious personal life. Of course, some of these idyllic love stories have unhappy endings, but generally it is not through lack of affection so much as undue stress placed on them by friends and relations. All too often, well-meaning people cannot bear to see two people so happy, and some mischievous quirk demands that they interfere.

TO SUN IN TAURUS

This is a magnetic attraction that can ultimately engender a very stable friendship. The solar Taurean offers a great deal of guidance and always looks after the lunar Libran. While the solar Taurean is charmed by the lunar Libra's personality, he may be a little put off by the Libran's vanity. This can be a romantic affair, but it is more likely to produce a good friendship than a lengthy marriage.

In business matters, the prospects are not good in terms of longevity, but short-term projects are successful. It is generally the lunar Libran who moves on to another area of business while maintaining friendship with the solar Taurean. Though both are under the influence of Venus, the usual sexual stimulus necessary to many marriages gives way to a mutual enjoyment of the beautiful things of life. If sexual activity is part of their concept of the good life, then it will be there, but the happiest of these marriages generally is characterized by a lesser sex drive and plenty of consideration.

TO SUN IN GEMINI

This is the attraction of the honeybee for the nectar-giving flower—the solar Geminian is the honeybee and the lunar

Libran the flower. The attraction lasts just as long as the lunar Libra has something to give either sexually, through mental stimulation or by verve and vivacity. The impact of meeting is felt by both, and youthful lunar Librans and solar Geminians can have a lot of enjoyment together. The relationship survives by fits and starts but rarely ends in any animosity when it is kept on a personal level. In business the relationship can be at its best only when there is mutual respect for each other's talents and ignorance of faults. It is preferable to be ignorant of each other's faults because once they are revealed, both the lunar Libran and the solar Geminian can literally pick each other to pieces. The patient lunar Libra can withstand Gemini's moods, but is not able to enjoy fantasy the way the solar Gemini can.

TO SUN IN CANCER

What a battle of wills the lunar Libran and the solar Cancerian can get in although they both maintain a great degree of charm in public. Left to themselves, they make no pretense in throwing down the gauntlet and charging in to verbal battle. Yet they are unbeatable when they gang up on a joint adversary since both have strong elements of destruction within their makeup (even though both cover it with a veneer of youthful guile and excessive charm). In business neither completely trusts the other, and this can work well enough since they are dedicated to catching out the other in some fault. The amazing thing is that in business they can make money especially in Venus-dominated professions such as beauty culture and hairdressing. It is always a battle of wills without any victory for either party. The lunar Libra must give up any hope of wanting to improve the solar Cancerian, as nothing could be more boring.

TO SUN IN LEO

The lunar Libran often feels threatened by the solar Leo and relationships develop best when the lunar Libran can respect and admire the solar Leo, from a safe distance. The lunar Libran needs encouragement from the Leo before stepping out to get to know him better. If the lunar Libran is female she can appreciate the macho maleness of the solar Leo as a protective force. If the lunar Libran is male the chances of a deep relationship developing are very slight because the lunar Libran develops an inferiority complex and the solar Leo does not hesitate to hurt the vulnerable, sensitive areas. This can be quite a sadistic relationship at its worst, while at its best it can be ultra protective and caring.

TO SUN IN VIRGO

There is a natural attraction between the lunar Libran and the solar Virgo. Unless the lunar Libran deliberately tries to provoke Virgo's jealousy, this is one of the few relationships which can make the intellectual Virgo soar to dizzy heights which seem like a fantasy. Romantically, the relationship can be sustained because the lunar Libran has a great gift for appealing to the solar Virgoan's protective nature. In business, the careful solar Virgoan is much wary of involvement and proceeds only if the business is a highly specialized one connected with creativity.

TO SUN IN LIBRA

While polarity often produces the most magnetic attraction, this is the rare occasion when like meets like and is happy with what it sees. This combination produces a good friendship. There is an inherent wisdom in the fact that few lunar Librans are romantically involved with solar Librans as there will be too much competition between the two. The lunar Libra maintains this same attitude about business ventures with the solar Libran, unless there are other people involved.

TO SUN IN SCORPIO

The attraction here is always tempered with mental reservations on both parts. Each party appraises the relationship callously, wondering, "What can I get out of this?" If they enter into a relationship, it is generally because both parties see something they want, and the romance will not be long-lived. There can be romantic involvement here (especially if the lunar Libra is female and the solar Scorpio is male), but the attraction is brief. Although Scorpio dominates this relationship, this particular combination releases the lunar Libra's latent aggressiveness; the abrasive qualities of the sun in Scorpio cause this, but the solar Scorpio is not prepared to deal with it and is thrown off balance.

In business it can be totally different if the lunar Libran is content to be exploited by the solar Scorpio, knowing that the end product of this exploitation will be considered financial reward.

TO SUN IN SAGITTARIUS

As with all lunar Librans, there is always a strong physical attraction which the sun in a fire sign produces, and the accent is nearly always on sex no matter what sex the lunar Libran is. But the lunar Libran may have many changes of mind and seems to sense what is necessary in life; if it is sex, then it is always obtainable, and there is little thought to the ephemeral quality of this overpowering part of human relationships. Luckily, the lunar Libran knows when to move away from a bad situation—and this instinct can save the Libran from becoming overtrustful of the solar Sagittarian.

Solar Sagittarians are very good in business relations with lunar Librans, especially in specialized lines relating to any of the Venus-inspired businesses connected to beautification or the arts.

TO SUN IN CAPRICORN

The usual physical attraction is there, but in most cases this happens when the solar Capricorn is male; the elderly solar Capricorn can become absolutely besotted by the lunar Libran (though the Libran may be unhappily surprised by the Capricorn's ability to see through that charming insincerity). In business matters, the female solar Capricorn can be just as valuable to the Libran male or female as the solar Capricorn male. It is an arrogant, authoritative relationship which many lunar Librans enjoy because it frees them from responsibility and lets them get on with less mundane things than being involved in making money.

TO SUN IN AQUARIUS

This is a very positive physical attraction in which the lunar Libran and solar Aquarian relate to each other very well in terms of long-lasting friendship or romance. In the latter case, should the lunar Libran cease to want romantic overtures, the solar Aquarian will not relinquish interest, although the relationship will change from one of high physical attraction to one of parent-child indulgence. In business, lunar Librans are not inclined to trust solar Aquarians as much as they do in affairs of the heart; these relationships are always fraught with problems even when they actually get established.

TO SUN IN PISCES

The lunar Libran and the solar Piscean are closely attuned—intellectually and physically. Both have a high degree of psychic awareness which stimulates the relationship on several levels—business, romance, or friendship. This pair can effectively combine business and romance. Libra has a great ability to appear vulnerable, which appeals to the sympathetic Piscean; but the lunar Libran must be careful not to hurt the sensitive Piscean inadvertently.

CHARACTERISTICS OF MOON
IN SCORPIO PEOPLE

The moon in this position gives a phenomenal memory; nothing from childhood days is ever forgotten. At first this seems like an asset, but if the childhood days were bad, Moon in Scorpio people carry many scars on their psyche. They are very clever at hiding their true feelings, but it is necessary for them to develop optimistic points of view and seek friends who are tuned in to positive thinking. The lunar Scorpion's delicately balanced sensitivity is often forgotten because the moon also imparts strong sexual urges. The moon is in its detriment in Scorpio, and in this case limits the potential of the moon to encourage growth; this may manifest itself in secrecy. It can be hard to get a relationship started because of this need for secrecy.

Life is rarely easy for Moon in Scorpio people although they are persistent and will overcome seemingly impossible challenges. Even when success comes it brings more problems, especially overindulgence in drugs or alcohol or intense family worries. (The late Aristotle Onassis had his moon in Scorpio; while he was a much publicized figure, there were many secrets in his life and many personal tragedies.) Though many good things come into the life of those born with the Moon in Scorpio, it is a strange quirk of fate that so much is also taken away from them.

In business, these lunar Scorpions work well in quiet offices; if they go into partnership, they generally end up with buying out the partner or somehow gaining control of the entire business. In romance, it is not easy to relate happiness to lunar Scorpions—their sexual drive is often a substitute for long-standing companionship. They take what they want but are rarely satisfied when they have attained it. The constant search for new challenges goes on endlessly.

PHYSICAL CHARACTERISTICS

Thick, short body with large head and fleshy face; a poor complexion. Dark hair, generally black. The eyes are full and round; it is not unusual for the pupils to be flecked. The eyebrows are full, and in the male will often meet over the bridge of the nose, adding to the heaviness of the face.

WEAKNESSES

Hernia, urinary complaints, aneurysms.

HOW MOON IN SCORPIO PEOPLE RELATE TO THE SUN SIGNS

TO SUN IN ARIES

This relationship is always a dramatic one; whether it is through friendship, romance, or business, it will be dominated by many highly explosive moments. Each party has a finely honed cutting edge and a gift for spotting vulnerable areas in the other. This can be a volatile love-hate relationship, characterized by anything from pure hostility to a highly charged (if short-lived) sexual attraction.

Yet, to everyone's surprise, this can be a long-lasting relationship. Friction makes the relationship interesting (if difficult); both parties have plenty of energy, and the abrasiveness seems to produce something which is necessary to them. This lively relationship is an enduring one; it never seems to come to a truly final end after the initial physical attraction wanes, despite the many disruptions. The one thing that is likely to bring it to an end, however, is the lunar Scorpion's inability to let go of a quarrel; this trait is a source of major irritation to the solar Aries.

73

TO SUN IN TAURUS

Scorpio will completely dominate this pairing unless the solar Taurean gains control through finances or an exceptional professional talent; the lunar Scorpion has great respect for both these things. This is a high-powered relationship with strong romantic overtones. The lunar Scorpio, with his turbulent subconscious, has a basic respect for the solar Taurean, admiring the ability to be direct and down-to-earth. In a way, both can live vicariously with a great empathy for the other's feelings; these friendships can last a lifetime. The solar Taurean is a very good business partner for the lunar Scorpio. Romantic involvements seem capable of retaining the original power which first precipitated the relationship. Regardless of money, the relationship in romance, friendship, or business will be just as good after many years as it was in the beginning.

Mutual respect and affection are the two qualities both need and find here. The lunar Scorpio instinctively responds to the romantic Taurean nature. Scorpio must be extremely careful not to sting the solar Taurus with wounding sarcasm.

TO SUN IN GEMINI

The attraction here has to start on an intellectual level if it is going to be meaningful to both parties. Both the lunar Scorpion and solar Gemini love to impress, so there is some jockeying for position in terms of limelight and appreciation. The romantic overtones are strong but generally result in some heartbreak for the lunar Scorpion who never wants to let go of the relationship once it has gone beyond friendship. In business relationships, the lunar Scorpion holds all the cards and is very much in control of the solar Gemini; this can work to their mutual advantage despite the fact that it is not an easy association.

TO SUN IN CANCER

There is a strong natural affinity between the watery elements of the lunar Scorpion and the solar Cancerian; a lot of intuition comes into play in all relationships. It is as if they sense the times when they need each other and then are content to drift apart until the intuition alerts them to mutual needs. In almost all relationships, Cancer seems to have the power to dominate the lunar Scorpio, probably because the lunar Scorpio feels an unusual sense of trust in the solar Cancerian. This can be a good romantic relationship or a longstanding friendship and an exceptionally good one for business, as the solar Cancer can always retreat into his shell when things get too difficult.

TO SUN IN LEO

This is a twofold attraction—the solar Leo responds to the lunar Scorpio's sexy vibrations and is intellectually intrigued by the mystique that surrounds the lunar Scorpion. It is not easy to assess which is the stronger attraction, but it works well in all relationships. Friendships can be undyingly loyal, and business associations will be highly profitable. In romance there is a strong chemistry which does deteriorate with time. Like most lunar Scorpion relationships, this one is not exactly free from trauma, but there is enough depth to the relationship to rally and renew interest. The solar Leo is intrigued by the ability of the Scorpio to stay one step ahead of him (as long as Scorpio is clever enough to allow the solar Leo to feel he dominates the relationship).

TO SUN IN VIRGO

The lunar Scorpio does not have much tact; the blunt solar Virgoan finds this impressive. Both parties could use lessons in diplomacy. Although the lunar Scorpion is quick to take offense or become hurt, something in this relationship allows both to indulge in their own particular bluntness without any hard feelings or noticeable deterioration in the relationship.

This is a good business association, as both are able to clearly define areas of work before becoming committed. Friendships can be long-lasting. Romance is not as high-powered as many lunar Scorpions may like, but it can succeed, probably because of the solar Virgo's capacity for understanding the more delicate and sensitive areas within the lunar Scorpion. The Scorpio must be careful not to take the solar Virgo for granted.

TO SUN IN LIBRA

The lunar Scorpion will always try to dominate this relationship—and will be surprised when the solar Libran simply moves out of the sphere of influence. In romance or friendship, this relationship will have an on-again off-again quality, although the lunar Scorpio is capable of an intuitive alertness to the needs of the solar Libran even when they have been apart for some time. The solar Libran is charmed by the Scorpio, who knows just how to manufacture the right type of charm, but the solar Libran will simply move away from the lunar Scorpion rather than face a difficult and quarrelsome relationship. This combination can be durable in business when there is a common need.

TO SUN IN SCORPIO

This can be a most formidable team as each understands the attributes and faults of the other. Although there is some danger of loss of identity on the part of the lunar Scorpio, these two can merge interests very well—especially their sexual interests. Although they may have occasional spats, they will unite to fight against any outside force. This is the one lunar relationshp which lacks malice—even the sting of the Scorpion's tail is not so deadly here. This is a dynamic business combination.

TO SUN IN SAGITTARIUS

The physical attraction is very strong and can last for lengthy periods. However, the solar Sagittarian may become bored with pandering to the Scorpion's highly sensitive nature, and break off the relationsihp for awhile; after parting, the intensity of the physical attraction is renewed. The lunar Scorpion's friendship also has its off-on cycles. As the lunar Scorpion never admits to any mistakes, the forgiving solar Sagittarian is the one to kiss and make up. In business the solar Sagittarian is in the driver's seat; it is best not to mix business with sexual pleasures. Since the chemistry of both parties is geared to sexual adventure, a good business association suffers through the impact of physical needs.

SUN IN CAPRICORN

The lunar Scorpio seems to have remarkable capabilities for getting involved in a clandestine association with the solar Capricorn. Curiously, the relationship does not offer much in terms of mutual attractions of a truly sexual nature. However, the lunar Scorpio and the solar Capricorn are both secretive, and sometimes there is a spirit of adventure in clandestine relationships that is sufficient motivation for both parties. The kick is obtained through knowing something no one else knows, and such associations remain well-guarded secrets for a long time. In business the solar Capricorn can bring good benefits to the lunar Scorpio as long as the Scorpio is able to fulfill the high moral and ethical standards of the solar Capricorn. This is often tiresome to the lunar Scorpio, who relies on his ability to fake this for quite some time.

TO SUN IN AQUARIUS

The lunar Scorpion is too dramatic, intense, and emotional to make any instant appeal to the solar Aquarian.

Relationships generally develop through the Aquarian's being nearby in some emergency; once he responds, he is committed to extending the relationship and trying to become friends. Once the break in the ice is achieved, the lunar Scorpion can become a very good companion. The relationship prospers through the concern of the solar Aquarian, who is able to recognize the frailness of the lunar Scorpion. Because of this, the solar Aquarian can be fairly useful to the lunar Scorpion in business, although there are likely to be many unsettling emotional times. The Scorpion's possessiveness may destroy this relationship.

TO SUN IN PISCES

The lunar Scorpion has very friendly feelings to the water sign of Pisces. He will try to offer friendship and protection; he will be ready to fight some of the battles in which the Piscean hates to get involved. But the solar Piscean must never take anything for granted. What the lunar Scorpion offers willingly is one thing, but if too much help is demanded, the friendship becomes shaky.

Romantically it is far more likely to be a good strong sexual association if the lunar Scorpion is male; this is a remarkably friendly and harmonious pair. It does not work similarly if the lunar Scorpio is female because the male solar Piscean cannot cope with so much strength in his opposite number, and feelings of inadequacy lead to breakups of the romance. In business, the lunar Scorpion and the solar Piscean need a third party from one of the earth signs to bring stability and success to their projects.

CHARACTERISTICS OF MOON
IN SAGITTARIUS PEOPLE

Lunar Sagittarians rarely feel the urge to go into group movements in order to discover who they are; they KNOW who they are and where they are going. When they have to make mental adjustments en route to their chosen goal, they are quite happy to do so; they may adopt the attitude that the "end does justify the means." If the original motivation is on a high level, this is a good enough attitude, but it can cause trouble if the motivation is only for personal gain. In this case the directness of the Moon in Sagittarius becomes ruthlessness and will achieve results even if a few old friends are left behind.

Lunar Sagittarians can envision seemingly impossible projects and then, despite advice by well-meaning and less courageous friends, will go on to achieve the project. They maintain a great deal of control over their own lives and will combine business with pleasure until a time comes when they have to make a decision about priorities. Business wins in the long run. Personal freedom and causes connected with freedom are very close to the heart of the lunar Sagittarian, but their interest in causes is more philosophical than emotional. They can be very practical revolutionaries, championing minor revolutions in the home or business; political concerns need not be at issue.

The biggest danger that Moon in Sagittarians face is optimism to the point of carelessness. Always eager to progress, they can overestimate their own talents and those of others. Gambling can be a problem not because of greed but because they are convinced they are lucky people and always see success as the end product of any endeavor. Many lunar Sagittarians are attracted to evangelistic religions and this becomes another type of gamble—they bet their time, fervor, and energy that they will be able to save a great number of souls.

In romance, lunar Sagittarians are great companions; sex is assigned its proper place in life according to their needs rather than basic desires. As the higher echelon of the fire signs, romantic passion exists but is tempered by spirituality. After the first flush of courtship, most lunar Sagittarians settle down to a life of companionship in which the companion follows the lead of the Sagittarian. Only when there is a direct conflict of interests does the lunar Sagittarian resort to divorce; it will be handled very shrewdly and to the Sagittarian's advantage. Failure of a marriage or any other partnership is not something the lunar Sagittarian likes to face so the relationship will be terminated completely and quickly. There is never any looking back at the wreckage. With his usual optimism, the Sagittarian is convinced that something better is waiting just around the corner.

PHYSICAL CHARACTERISTICS

A well-proportioned body, tall and thick-set. Oval face with ruddy complexion, inclined to bronziness. The hair is bright brown and shining. Full, oval eyes with a kindly expression and fully arched eyebrows.

WEAKNESSES

Gout.

HOW THE MOON IN SAGITTARIUS
RELATES TO THE SUN SIGNS

TO SUN IN ARIES

The lunar Sagittarian is attracted to the solar Aries like a moth to a flame. He recognizes so many of the forceful qualities that are not so strongly expressed in his own personality; the lunar Sagittarian can easily anticipate and fulfill the solar Arian's driving needs. Friendship can be long-lasting; each enjoys the other's companionship and the exchange of bright (though impractical) ideas. They are both great conversationalists (even though much of it is good-natured hot air), and they both appreciate this quality in others.

Romantically, this association starts off with strong sexual interest, but this interest eventually becomes a firm friendship. In business, the relationship is adventurous and potentially dangerous as both parties are inclined to overestimate their potential. It is always better if there is a third party involved who can act as a brake on abundant enthusiasm, excessive optimism, and the inability to be practical about finances.

TO SUN IN TAURUS

Although the solar Taurean is impressed by the energy of the lunar Sagittarius, he soon recognizes that without guidance the wheel-spinning lunar Sagittarius gets nowhere. So the role in friendship, romance, and business—as far as the solar Taurean is concerned—is to offer the necessary guidance which is generally accepted in good faith. Keeping the lunar Sagittarian going along at an even pace is difficult to achieve, but somehow the steady solar Taurean can manage this.

Romance is better if the lunar Sagittarian is male, so that the feminine qualities of the solar Taurean are fully appreciated and the lunar Sagittarian can offer his protective cloak. Generally the solar Taurean is quite capable of looking after himself but has sense enough to realize that the lunar Sagittarian sees himself as gallant knight whose duty is to protect his fair lady. Friendships can be long and satisfying to both parties, as the lunar Sagittarian is able to accept the large responsibilities that the solar Taurean conveys.

TO SUN IN GEMINI

This is a good relationship, though not a consistent one. Its strongest point is that even when it is at a low ebb, there is a mutual understanding which helps make most setbacks temporary. The lunar Sagittarian and the solar Geminian are very compatible in just about everything, since each makes allowances for the other. Keeping active in joint projects is the secret of the success in this relationship, whether it is through friendship, romance, or business. Both can be examples of perpetual motion; it is rare that the solar Geminian can find anyone else in the zodiac who moves with the same alacrity as he does. In business, the solar-Sagittarius can cope with any dull moments, shielding the solar Geminian from them; the same thing applies in romance. While neither is very tactful, when working in tandem they manage to keep in step.

TO SUN IN CANCER

The excessive good nature of the lunar Sagittarian appeals to the Cancerian. This appeal is a better basis for friendship than romance, although there may be a few romantic interludes. In marriage the good humor of the lunar Sagittarius can become too much for the Cancerian to cope with, in turn, the lunar Sagittarian cannot take the ever-changing moods of the Cancerian when they are in close quarters. Without the tie of marriage, they can do very well, for both have escape routes into which they can retreat from time to time. The lunar Sagittarian is always a good friend in an emergency and the intuitive instincts of the solar Cancerian are immediately alerted to this appealing quality. The business relationship is not very positive unless it is clearly understood from the beginning that the lunar Sagittarian is in command, as the solar Cancerian is likely to dance away into whatever activities appeal at the moment.

TO SUN IN LEO

These two fire signs feel a mutual bond of attraction. The solar Leo will dominate this match—look out for trouble here! When the lunar Sagittarian feels he is being taken for granted or exploited by the aggressive Leo, there can be a real explosion of temper. Luckily for this relationship, the lunar Sagittarian does have the ability to apologize and make amends when necessary.

In friendship, the solar Leo and lunar Sagittarian can share a great deal. The solar Leo is not very fond of sharing, but the lunar Sagittarian is able to bring out the giving nature of Leo. This combination makes for a torrid sexual relationship, but once that physical pull deteriorates, they cannot return to simply being good friends. In business, they are both capable of extraordinary vision and energy; however, it is usually best for them to have a third party around to keep the business in good financial shape since both are very extravagant.

TO SUN IN VIRGO

The lunar Sagittarian is always impressed by the intellectual qualities of the solar Virgo; Virgo likes the drive and enthusiasm of the Sagittarian and gets a big boost in energy from the Sagittarian. The only serious problem that is likely to crop here is the solar Virgo's total inability to relate to the lunar Sagittarian's inherent sentimentality. This combination can produce a formidable partnership, but it is one better suited to business than romance. It also makes for a very solid, old-fashioned friendship in which each makes a distinct contribution and is around when the other is in need.

TO SUN IN LIBRA

The lunar Sagittarian relates very well to the solar Libran on a personal basis. There is a strong physical attraction and plenty of the protective force for which the lunar Sagittarian is famous and which the Libran needs all through life. The lunar Sagittarian is able to estimate the moods of the sun in Libra and recognizes that Libra's selfishness is really a form of self-preservation. There can be a problem if the lunar Sagittarian is overly sentimental and allows the solar Libran to exploit him in a romantic relationship.

In a business association there can be friendship based on mutual needs; the enthusiasm and objectivity of the lunar Sagittarian rubs off on the solar Libran and gives him more confidence. In business, the lunar Sagittarian must be careful not to expect too much cooperation from the solar Libran.

TO SUN IN SCORPIO

In the beginning there is strong physical attraction. Unfortunately, in time both begin to make impossible demands on the other, a series of herculean tasks designed to prove love or friendship. If the relationship is not an intimate and personal one, the lunar Sagittarian and the solar Scorpio can direct all their energies and emotions toward a common financial goal. The lunar Sagittarian is able to take any amount of responsibility and is good at covering up the solar Scorpio's mistakes. A business association is likely to be much more satisfying and long-lived than a personal one.

TO SUN IN SAGITTARIUS

This is one of the like-attracts-like relationships in which birds of feather do indeed flock together, enjoying every moment of the association. The intuition of the lunar Sagittarian is appreciated by the fiery solar Sagittarian; both have plenty of enthusiasm to meet common goals. The relationship is not so happy on a marriage basis since the novelty of liking so many of the same things begins to wear off, and then they begin to find a common denominator in the negatives in life. This saps their inner resources and makes it difficult to meet emergencies. In business the relationship can prosper providing both are allowed equal responsibility and neither lets the other down.

TO SUN IN CAPRICORN

The lunar Sagittarian seems to be quite fearful of the solar Capricorn, probably because the optimism of the lunar Sagittarian has little to offer to alleviate the saturnine qualities of the Capricorn and has very little patience with moods of depression. In friendship, the lunar Sagittarian will try to be helpful, but inevitably the time comes when he gives up. There is not much joy in any business relationship unless there are other people involved. If the enthusiasm of the lunar Sagittarian and the wariness of the Capricorn can be guided by a carefully chosen third party, the association will result in some financial success, but it will never be a totally enjoyable business relationship.

TO SUN IN AQUARIUS

The attraction here is never instantaneous. It will most likely develop over a period of time, especially if the lunar Sagittarian has come to the aid of the Aquarian. The appreciative solar Aquarian will struggle to pay back one good with another, thus providing the basis for their friendship. The lunar Sagittarian is quite good at bolstering up the confidence of the Aquarian, although the Sagittarian will feel the Aquarian's intellectual domination. This combination is not likely to produce any passionate romances or even remarkable business alliances; it is most successful on the friendship level. Both parties here are likely to be a bit critical of the other; the friendship is generally saved by the lunar Sagittarian's "forgive and forget" attitude, which the Aquarian accepts easily.

TO SUN IN PISCES

The lunar Sagittarian is always attracted to the solar Piscean. This is a ready-made opportunity for the service-loving Sagittarian to be helpful, and it generally results in long-term friendship. The romantic yearnings of the lunar Sagittarian literally sweep the solar Piscean off her feet and can be very good for both, especially if there are children from the marriage.

The same characteristics prevail in business. There is no doubt that the lunar Sagittarian must take the lead in guiding the solar Piscean, who is generally willing to be led and can produce many bright ideas for the lunar Sagittarian to work on. The lunar Sagittarian has the ability to convert Piscean dreams into realities as he brings practical experience to the Piscean's fantasy world.

CHARACTERISTICS OF MOON
IN CAPRICORN PEOPLE

The moon's sensitivity is hindered in the weighty sign of Capricorn. Lunar Capricorns seem to be driven into complex areas of life; in time there is little or no attention paid to sentiment. The lunar Capricorn can be quite a workhorse, seeing work, the making of money, and the resultant power become an acceptable compensation for the absence of personal relationships. Unfortunately, not every lunar Capricorn has the talent or ability to rise to a position of power, and it is these types who suffer most; their frustrations inevitably bring about conditions of failing health. It is a specially tough position for the moon to be in the female horoscope, men seem to cope with it much more effectively. In the female there is often a point in life when they become martyrs to the family or to a bad business partner; the amazing thing is this acceptance of life dominated by sorrow dominates. The list of lunar Capricorns who achieved world fame (or infamy) is very interesting since it includes Disraeli, Lord Nelson, Napoleon, George Washington, Abraham Lincoln, Adolph Hitler, and Goebbels. Female lunar Capricorns who decide to go into business often do so when they deliberately relinquish the traditional feminine roles and then they take on positions of authority normally associated with the male.

Deep psychological problems in adult life generally relate to a bad relationship with the mother. In both sexes this can cause complications in establishing a strong romantic relationship, but the lunar Capricorns are capable of compensating. Men often marry women who can help their career, and the females frequently put material security before the emotions and marry older men. Both sexes have a stoic acceptance that whatever they do, there is a price to be paid; they seem willing to pay it.

PHYSICAL CHARACTERISTICS

The moon in this position gives a thin body, but with an inclination of fleshiness. Short stature. The hair is black and the male has a tendency to baldness; the female has thin wispy hair. The complexion is rarely good. The features are small, as are the eyes. Thin eyebrows are nicely arched.

WEAKNESSES

Sinus troubles, skin eruptions, allergies.

HOW MOON IN CAPRICORN PEOPLE
RELATE TO THE SUN SIGNS

TO SUN IN ARIES

The solar Aries is a challenge to the lunar Capricorn. It takes some time for any relationship to move into a meaningful area since the solar Aries is intrigued by Capricorn but not sure about him, and the lunar Capricorn is looking for ways to use the energy of the Aries. Friendships can blossom, fade, and blossom again almost on a seasonal basis, according to the needs of each party.

This can be a difficult relationship if the lunar Capricorn ever adopts a martyred attitude and chooses to suffer in silence. The solar Aries cannot relate to this as he always prefers to discuss matters openly. Romantically this is not an exciting relationship unless the lunar Capricorn is much older than the female Aries. It then has a chance to mature into a romance in which the Aries brings a flash of sunlight into the life of an aging man. In business this pair is only reasonably compatible since Aries moves too fast for Capricorn and has no time to waste in planning.

TO SUN IN TAURUS

The lunar Capricorn relates very well to the solar Taurean. Although they are both earth signs, there is a great difference in temperaments, but the link between them is an understanding of the meaning of loyalty and hard work. Romantically it is always better if the lunar Capricorn is male and much older than the Taurean; one can become the provider and the other homemaker. In reverse, the lunar female Capricorn can also be the provider, but the dragon of resentfulness lurks in the depths of her subconscious making her feel she is sharing too much with the Taurean male even though he, too, may be able to provide money.

The lunar Capricorn can be a militant career woman; in this role she allows nothing to get in her way, which makes it difficult for her to play the usual feminine role the solar male Taurean expects in a romantic involvement. In business, the lunar Capricorn and solar Taurean see things very much as one unit and are prepared to work well in tandem and share the rewards. The lunar Capricorn is most cooperative in this relationship; problems will arise only if the lunar Capricorn undertakes too much at one time—he cannot stand being unsuccessful.

TO SUN IN GEMINI

If the lunar Capricorn is male, there can be a good relationship with the much younger solar Geminian, but it does not work in reverse. The lunar Capricorn is best when the patriarchal qualities come out, but the maternal qualities are not very obvious. In business the lunar Capricorn can provide guidance to the Geminian but soon loses patience and then loses interest. The lunar Capricorn cannot stand the versatility of the Geminian, who is never consistent in moods. The solidarity which the lunar Capricorn can bring to a friendship is not appreciated by the mercurial Gemini.

TO SUN IN CANCER

This pair has a natural affinity and sympathy, although the physical attraction comes only when the male lunar Capricorn is older than the solar Cancerian and has established himself in life. Intuitively the solar Cancerian knows that the best can be very good and the worst can be coped with, so romantically it can be a meaningful relationship although there may be little sexual attraction. The lunar Capricorn can shoulder an enormous amount of responsibility, which delights the solar Cancerian. The saturnine Capricorn must be careful, though, not to let his dark moods inhibit the solar Cancerian and encourage the introvertedness that is always there. Youthful Capricorns and Cancerians can maintain long-term friendships. In business this relationship can be exceptionally profitable to both parties as they are shrewd enough to exploit the other with the best of intentions and then combine the hard-working talent of the lunar Capricorn with the highly intuitive qualities of the Cancerian.

TO SUN IN LEO

There is an attraction here in terms of friendship. The lunar Capricorn can cash in on the many social contacts the solar Leo has cultivated; Leo does not mind being used in this fashion provided there is proper appreciation. Romantically it is not a very strong relationship unless the lunar Capricorn is male, and even then it is a capricious romance. Leo tries to dominate the lunar Capricorn in a romantic relationship; he often fails because of the basic coldness of the Moon in Capricorn, as well as the Capricorn's sexual fears. On the positive side, the lunar Capricorn encourages Leo to take the limelight. The female lunar Capricorn can be excellent in business with a Leo; both sexes are at their best in business.

TO SUN IN VIRGO

The lunar Capricorn sees in the solar Virgo all the qualities which he longs to find in himself—dedication, loyalty, and careful concern. The solar Virgo appreciates the sound logical advice that the lunar Capricorn is always able to offer. Romantically, there are no sexual fireworks; this marriage can seem a bit dull to others, but it will last because such a high degree of companionship and understanding exist. It is also a good business relationship and can be an association in which business and marriage are merged; both parties are extremely interested in making money. Both must be careful here that they do not allow too much nervous tension to build up through too much work and too little relaxation. In a marriage relationship, the children and grandchildren thrive as they receive considerable affection as well as material goods.

TO SUN IN LIBRA

Although the lunar Capricorn can be too much concerned with material things, the moon's influence softens this characteristic and it is this which makes the lunar Capricorn interested in the solar Libran. It is a mutual attraction because the solar Libran recognizes the independence and hard-working, decisive qualities of the Capricorn. Good, solid friendships can be the result of the first awareness of each other; a romance is never based entirely on sexual attraction but rather more in terms of empathy and the need for companionship. In business it is a good association if the Capricorn takes the initiative and he is likely to do; after that he provides sensible guidance for the solar Libran who is glad to have any decision-making responsibility taken out of his hands and left to a reliable person. The lunar Capricorn is very good with a Libran mate or business partner if there are creative talents to be exposed or even exploited, but the lunar Capricorn must be careful not to allow the solar Libra to take credit for his achievements.

TO SUN IN SCORPIO

The lunar Capricorn is intrigued with the solar Scorpio because of the mystique which surrounds the personality. He does not mind if the mystique dissolves into deviousness, providing there is a basic honesty in their particular relationship. This often happens, and it is the grass roots of any meaningful friendship, romance, or business partnership because the lunar Capricorn not only insists on honesty but seems able to encourage the solar Scorpio to indulge in it. Many relationships do not get off to a good start, but an interested lunar Capricorn brings dogged determination to the pursuit of anything that interests him. In the end it pays off, and the solar Scorpio has a very good friend, lover, spouse, or business partner as long as he never deviates from the original contract set up between them. As long as this honesty exists, the lunar Capricorn will happily cater to the whims of the solar Scorpio.

TO SUN IN SAGITTARIUS

The attraction between the lunar Capricorn and the solar Sagittarian is of a hit-and-miss variety, dependent on timing. They can move in the same circles without really striking up anything of a friendship and then suddenly find each other. This relationship is often one in which senior citizens figure, and while the attraction may not be sexually inspired, it is enough to rejuvenate both parties and probably lead to marriage. As a partnership in business, it never gets off the ground unless a third party intervenes.

TO SUN IN CAPRICORN

Though the lunar Capricorn and his solar counterpart are both materialistic, this is never a happy union in terms of friendship or romance, although it can succeed in business or in certain professions such as law or medicine. The lunar and solar Capricorns cannot contribute enough to each other except possibly the sharing of depression, and this is hardly adequate to provide a good basis for love and marriage. There is a possibility of a low-key friendship since misery does sometimes crave company, but it is a temporary arrangement.

TO SUN IN AQUARIUS

This is not a good combination for any sort of personal relationship; it seems to lack all the chemistry necessary for romance or meaningful friendship. It can be very good for business providing it is of a professional nature in which both parties can respect each other.

TO SUN IN PISCES

The solar Piscean can be attracted to the capable, concerned attitude of the lunar Capricorn. Ultimately, this is an uneasy relationship because the sterner aspects of the moon in Capricorn upset the sensitive qualities of the solar Piscean. The relationship can thrive in business when the practicality of the lunar Capricorn can implement the creative ideas of the solar Piscean. There is always a danger that the lunar Capricorn will not understand the ultrasensitivity of the solar Piscean and will dismiss the Piscean's intuition as imagination.

CHARACTERISTICS OF MOON IN AQUARIUS PEOPLE

Lunar Aquarians are very imaginative; if this is translated into creative channels, it brings positive achievements in the arts, and gives the chance to extend their life-styles into a variety of interesting situations. The restlessness of the capricious moon is stabilized in this sign, but if there is not an outlet for the the lunar Aquarian's vivid imagination, it may deteriorate into gossip and rumor spreading. This is rarely done with malice, but rumors can bring some unfortunate backlashes when the source is located, and few lunar Aquarians can cope with this. They do most things with good intentions, but these are not always tempered with wisdom and judgment. They are broad-minded about the changing trends in society, while many will advocate free love and freedom of sexual activities, as they grow older they are more inclined to preach than practice.

What Moon in Aquarius people love most of all is to shock others by pronouncing definite views on subjects that were once considered taboo. They are innovators in helping change some aspects of social life, but when the same ideas are applied to their personal life, they are surprised that things fall apart. All too often the freedom which is so important to the lunar Aquarian becomes an issue when the freedom of a partner is expressed. They are a mixture of radical thought and conservative action. Male lunar Aquarians are broadminded because it suits them to be; the female is often not allowed the same freedom and generally emerges as an intellectual with firm ideas about feminine liberties. Both sexes are prone to mental anxiety and tension, becoming overstimulated by ideas and handicapped by the many parasitic people who hang on to the lunar Aquarian's bandwagon without making any real contribution to their chosen cause.

There is a genuine desire to seek out unusual relationships and to study such things as metaphysics and the occult sciences. In seeking their own freedom, lunar Aquarians long to blaze the way for others, but forget that all men are not equal. In romance they look for companionship based on mutual interests and in business they need a stable partner who knows how to bring out the best of the creative imagination but can act as a brake when the ideas are impractical.

As we move farther into the Age of Aquarius, lunar Aquarians will have a greater role to play in laying down the guidelines for a new society, but it is too soon yet for them to be totally effective.

PHYSICAL CHARACTERISTICS

Middle-sized person, well made and inclined to corpulence after middle age. Brown hair inclined to balding in the male and thin hair in the female. The skin is clear and fresh looking. The eyes are small ovals. Delicately arched brows.

WEAKNESSES

Varicose veins, eye afflictions, ulcers on lower extremities.

HOW MOON IN AQUARIUS PEOPLE
RELATE TO THE SUN SIGNS

TO SUN IN ARIES

Generally, the lunar Aquarian has little time for the reckless solar Aries, although an elderly lunar Aquarian can relate well to a youthful Aries, enjoying the fresh and unusual ideas that the Arian is capable of. In business, the lunar Aquarian can make use of the solar Arian's innovative ideas and is willing to take the necessary time to polish those ideas into small jewels. The lunar Aquarian can successfully emulate the energy and drive of the solar Aries if he is so inspired. Obviously some lunar Aquarians will be romantically attracted to a solar Aries, but it is not a meaningful relationship after the glow of attraction has passed. The solar Aries demands too much, talks too much, and generally upsets the easygoing life which the lunar Aquarian seeks.

TO SUN IN TAURUS

The older lunar Aquarian is physically attracted to the youthful Taurean; this attraction can result in marriage and a mutually agreeable life-style. When the Taurean really begins to dominate and takes over in a very subtle manner, the Aquarian's reaction is one of philosophic resignation; the Taurean domination is not enough to break up the marriage. The marriage can come to an end, however, if the lunar Aquarian directs his attention too far away from home; this is something the solar Taurean will not tolerate. As far as Taurus is concerned, charity begins and ends within the domestic circle. This marriage will always be held together by mutual concern for children.

In business, this partnership is very compatible; the solar Taurean supplies stability to the lunar Aquarian intellect.

TO SUN IN GEMINI

These two air signs have a mutual attraction in fits and starts. It is an uneasy relationship unless it is based on professional achievements; it thrives well in medicine and surgery. Neither the lunar Aquarian nor the solar Gemini expects any type of relationship to last long, and both are content to live for the day and accept whatever changes tomorrow brings. This is a workable basis for friendship, but it can be tough if a hasty marriage takes place (and this is the sort of situation that both these types are susceptible to). The "marry in haste and repent at leisure" axiom might have been coined with the lunar Aquarian and the solar Gemini in mind; both are prone to make several marriages. Their children are likely to suffer because of the endless arguments over parental rights; the division of property is not of great interest to either of them. In business, this pair works best under short-term arrangements.

TO SUN IN CANCER

This is a complicated relationship because of the basic personality conflicts; but the lunar Aquarian does have the capacity to understand the needs of the solar Cancerian, and the Cancerian has the intuition to help the Aquarian when he becomes bogged down in trivia. The lunar Aquarian appreciates the reserved nature of the solar Cancerian and understands that he sometimes needs to be left alone. This can cause problems, though, as the lunar Aquarian may carry the withdrawal too far, especially if he is annoyed or upset by the Cancerian outpourings of emotion.

In business this is not very successful unless both parties start off with a lot of money—backed up by a lot of good fortune—as neither of these types is adept at good management.

TO SUN IN LEO

There is an electrifying attraction here from the word *go,* and it lasts for a long time. The lunar Aquarian finds the solar Leo attractive in every respect; both inspire confidence in the other. The lunar Aquarian has a complete understanding of the solar Leo's need to bask in the sunshine and has no desire to compete with him in that arena. The romantic relationship based on strong sexual urges settles down into a loving and considerate companionship. The relationship deepens as the years go by, especially if there are children. It is also a strong and rewarding business relationship.

TO SUN IN VIRGO

The lunar Aquarian appreciates the finer qualities of the solar Virgo's mind and the quiet, unruffled temperament. The lunar Aquarian and solar Virgo are well matched through their intellects and can be very successfully united in projects involving money. They can be very creative together, and this is one of the best reasons for their forming a business partnership. The personal attraction they may feel seems to satisfy itself in terms of a lengthy (but platonic) friendship. Marriage can succeed here although there is very little romance; a lasting relationship may be produced by their mutual pursuits and goals.

TO SUN IN LIBRA

The mutual attraction is electrifying with plenty of physical attraction and a mutual need for sexual activity. Courtships can mature into marriages; there is every chance that this relationship will be lasting and harmonious. It can be one of the most romantic relationships in the zodiac, and it is not unusual for a previously married lunar Aquarian to find real happiness with a solar Libran. Part of the appeal here is the Aquarian's ability to be there whenever the Libran needs help, but the Aquarian must be careful not to overindulge the solar Libran's whims. This can also be a strong business relationship, especially if the intimate relationship is there as well.

TO SUN IN SCORPIO

The lunar Aquarian can be enchanted by the secretive solar Scorpion. The lunar Aquarian can sometimes direct the emotional turmoil of the solar Scorpio into an intellectual outlet. All goes well with this pair until the Aquarian follows his instincts to improve the Scorpion; then it rarely works out well. Most of all, the solar Scorpio loves to retain his secrets and hates any probing into his background, even if he has nothing to hide. The truth-loving Aquarian feels that any hint of mystery is circumstantial evidence that something is being hidden. This air of mystery is intriguing enough to start a romance, but the romance will be blighted by the Scorpion's jealousy.

A business relationship stands a better chance of success, providing that both parties start off with good intentions and a clear definition of duties.

TO SUN IN SAGITTARIUS

The fiery solar Sagittarius seems to burn up the energy of the lunar Aquarian; it is a debilitating relationship if it is romantic in nature. When the fires of passion begin to smolder, what remains is a strong friendship with a great deal of devotion and loyalty on both parts.

In business, the intellectual lunar Aquarian mergers very well with the energetic solar Sagittarian, and both receive equal rewards in terms of fame and fortune. They are better in a business partnership where they are equally involved in responsibilities.

TO SUN IN CAPRICORN

The lunar Capricorn is not likely to be enchanted by the solar

Aquarian; they seldom become more than polite friends. Marriage can be a disaster course, but it can be made palatable if money is available to bolster the relationship. A romantic relationship *can* be very good between senior citizens who have both led interesting lives and then found a common bond of companionship.

In business, the relationship is reasonably successful, depending on the age of both parties. If the two enter into a business association when young, the chances are that they will not reap rewards for many years; it must be viewed as a long-term project.

TO SUN IN AQUARIUS

This can be a delightfully comfortable relationship based on mutual interests and a reasonable amount of physical attraction, especially if both have been married before. Both parties must take care here not to spend too much time pinpointing the other's faults and overlooking his good points.

In business this can be successful if both are involved in the legal or medical professions, but in all other businesses a third party is necessary.

TO SUN IN PISCES

Amazingly, there is little physical attraction in this relationship, perhaps because the lunar Aquarian never trusts the solar Piscean when it comes to romantic overtures. Romances are short-lived, as neither type likes to feel totally committed on a personal level. When the relationship ends, it is nearly always because the solar Piscean cannot function in an unemotional relationship; the lunar Aquarian cannot stand to play the central role in the lunar Piscean's emotional life.

In business this relationship can work if the Aquarian is given free range in making decisions.

CHARACTERISTICS OF THE MOON IN PISCES PERSON

People with this position of the moon in their charts have every chance to be a few steps ahead of others if they follow their intuition; this position denotes strong psychic qualities. Unfortunately, other planets may set up fears within the lunar Piscean so that he does not follow his intuition or deliberately pushes it aside. So strong is the intuitive quality however, that even when it is pushed away, there will come a time in life when it cannot be ignored. At that point, the lunar Piscean sets out on a much more positive and secure way of life. It is a compensating factor as the lunar Piscean is not always fitted to toil in the hard, materialistic world and poor health can beset him.

Lunar Pisceans are not afraid of hard work; their humane qualities often take them into areas of work where the pay is poor such as the nursing profession or social work. Their basic instincts are to do good for as many people as possible; they often have no awareness that they should not be ashamed to do some good for themselves first. This awareness need not make them materially ambitious because doing good for themselves also relates to the care of the mind, body, and spirit. The latter is very important to lunar Pisceans but the vagaries of the unstable moon in this restless water sign seem to produce fantasies; many of these are related to the way in which lunar Pisceans will seek unorthodox spiritual experiences. In seeking they may get bogged down by fantasies. They often become the tool of much stronger types who exploit them. But once a lunar Piscean comes out of the fantasy stage to face reality (albeit through an unpleasant experience), he will pull himself together and begin to use his inner resources with excellent results. In time these inner resources lead to unexpected success in the creative arts and other professions.

Apathy is the lunar Piscean's worst enemy; he needs a strong partner who will gently guide him toward positive thinking. When this positive thought is combined with intuition the lunar Piscean has spectacular power to meet challenges.

Many Pisceans feel the world in which they live is so ill adjusted that they want to reject it, but guidance will teach them that this is part of their karmic experience, and then they adjust philosophically. Lunar Pisceans are romantic and give more affection than they generally receive; they are very dedicated to any person they make a loving commitment to. It does not seem to matter that the person may not return the affection fully; it is part of the Piscean desire to serve humanity and individuals with the one commodity they have a surfeit of: the capability to love. They can be very ambivalent in business and work better in areas where their natural creativity is given expression.

PHYSICAL CHARACTERISTICS

Rather short stature, plump figure running to obesity. Round, full face with pale complexion. The eyes are full and protruding, but with heavy lids that give a sleepy expression. Eyebrows are full but heavily arched. The light brown hair can have russet highlights.

WEAKNESSES

Relaxed tissues, weak lungs, alcoholism, constant colds.

HOW MOON IN PISCES PEOPLE
RELATE TO THE SUN SIGNS

TO SUN IN ARIES

The attraction is strong. The solar Aries dominates, but the lunar Piscean enjoys this. The psychic nature of the lunar

Piscean can easily cope with the forward-looking schemes of the solar Arian and can assess their chance for success. The lunar Piscean is very impressed by the energetic solar Aries, and the Aries in turn finds a great contrast in the lunar Piscean, who is so well versed in the art of relaxation, which the Aries finds so hard to achieve. Given time and patience, the solar Aries can develop a very romantic attitude toward the lunar Piscean. Once the romance has been initiated, marriage generally follows very quickly, and the honeymoon period is quite lengthy. On a friendly basis, the lunar Piscean is quick to respect the Aries; there is great rapport, and such friendships survive the test of time and trauma. In business the relationship is most satisfactory if there is a third partner.

TO SUN IN TAURUS

This is an emotionally charged relationship whether it is on the basis of friendship or of a more intimate nature. The creative lunar Piscean enjoys the taste of the good life which is so important to the solar Taurean. To outsiders, this relationship may seem a bit too domestic, but the lunar Piscean always has a good time with the Taurean. In the romantic context this is a very loving relationship, both sexual and sensual, with a great deal of companionship and the sharing of mutual interest. The solar Taurean must take care not to totally overindulge his Piscean companion. This is also a fine business relationship.

TO SUN IN GEMINI

Although the lunar Pisces enjoys floundering through life and the Gemini rarely seems to land in one place for more than a moment, somehow these two manage to get together. Pisces dominates the relationship, and Gemini both allows it and enjoys it. They share intellectual and creative instincts; the intuitive lunar Pisces has the good sense of timing which the Gemini lacks and somehow this intuitive force seems to transmit itself to the Gemini.

*　　*　　*

The romantic relationship is a strange combination of love, play, sex, and sensuality, with plenty of time left over for companionship. Both are likely to have been married before, and the previous experience produces a greater appreciation of each other. In friendship the rapport is great; they share many mutually creative projects.

These two should never go into business together without a third party, not because they would be unsuccessful, but because they are both careless and will miss opportunities without the guiding hand of a third person.

TO SUN IN CANCER

This is a good relationship on all levels, providing both start off with equal social and financial status. These two have a tremendous natural attraction and instinctively seek each other. Their physical attraction and psychic awareness create a strong bond that is the basis for a much longer friendship than either is capable of with other signs. Romantic engagements blossom into marriage, often despite the advice of friends. They follow their own intuitions and go ahead when they have made up their minds.

In business, the Cancerian dominates, and the union can be very successful but unpredictable, as their fortunes swing from one extreme to the other.

TO SUN IN LEO

The romantic instincts are strong. The solar Leo is inclined to dominate, but the lunar Piscean does not seem to mind, although he might be resentful if anyone else tried the same tactics. One of the reasons why this relationship can be good in terms of romance or friendship is that the lunar Piscean does not mind the solar Leo's enjoyment of the limelight. The lunar Piscean must be careful not to become too reserved in this relationship or to resist making legitimate demands on the solar Leo. The solar Leo has a great affectionate respect for the lunar Piscean and will accommodate him however possible.

In business, inevitably, the Leo dominates. This is an especially successful association if the business is related to the theater.

TO SUN IN VIRGO

This is not a relationship that has a strong sexual attraction. The emotional Piscean can be very hurt by the solar Virgo's rather heavy-handed methods; the solar Virgo is generally convinced that everything he does is as near perfect as possible. Pisceans can get along very well with others even when they recognize their faults; this is not the case with the solar Virgo. When marriages take place here, it is generally after a tryout period. It can be successful due to the greater understanding of the Piscean; the lunar Pisces can supply sensitivity to the solar Virgo.

In business this association is profitable to both, especially as they mature in years and experience.

TO SUN IN LIBRA

Libra will dominate this relationship. There will be some friction here, but it generally acts as necessary catalyst to mutual achievements. The outgoing solar Libra has a great need for reassurance, and the psychic awareness of the lunar Piscean allows him to deliver that reassurance whenever necessary. The lunar Piscean is also able to forget and forgive old hurts. The solar Libran must take care not to exploit the lunar Piscean's lack of confidence. This can be a successful business relationship if the female is Pisces and the male is Libra; it is not so strong if the sexes are reversed.

TO SUN IN SCORPIO

A strong mental and psychic attraction draws the lunar Piscean to the more dramatically inclined solar Scorpion.

When there is romance in the air, they are quick to seize opportunities to be together; this is probably the happiest time for them since they both have strong physical needs. A great deal of trust has to come into the relationship in order for it to be workable over a long period.

It is quite good, too, for a lunar Piscean to be in business with a solar Scorpio, but both resent the intrusion of anyone else at top executive levels and will use amazingly devious and successful tactics to retain their own positions.

TO SUN IN SAGITTARIUS

The robust Sagittarian comes on too strong for the more timid lunar Piscean, but they may have an attraction built on the Piscean's admiration for the solar Sagittarian; the Sagittarian, in turn, is quite capable of putting the Piscean at ease. When he succeeds in this endeavor, there is every possibility of a romance. The lunar Piscean has a strong desire to trust anyone he is in love with and does not forgive easily if he is let down.

In business the relationship is much more stable and rarely gets out of hand emotionally if the Sagittarian is in command but is able to make allowances for the intuitive instincts of the lunar Piscean.

TO SUN IN CAPRICORN

This is probably the most unlikely attraction in the entire zodiac. It generally starts with the lunar Piscean's feeling that the solar Capricorn is trustworthy. Very often this is true, but there can be highly emotional scenes when the Piscean suffers a cruel letdown which always seems to come about in a dramatic way from which there is no escape. The female Capricorn is less likely to inflict emotional hurt on the lunar Piscean, but the males are always capable of this. Romantically, when this happens, it is the end for both of them; in friendship the hurt is just as likely to occur. Yet the attraction is so strong that both parties are apt to seek another companion of the same planetary pattern and replay the whole emotional scene again. It is very likely that in this unusual attraction there is some strong Karmic tie which the lunar Piscean has experienced in a past life. If this is so, then the solar Capricorn has every chance to make up for the past wrongs in this life, but his saturnine personality makes him continue to make the same mistakes.

In business, the lunar Piscean again looks for trustworthiness and, providing there is no emotional involvement, it can work out very profitably for both.

TO SUN IN AQUARIUS

The attraction is generally on a mental level or through mutual interests in the arts, metaphysics, or any of the occult sciences. It fails on a purely pragmatic level since neither can cope with practicality. Romance can be very deceptive since neither is quite honest in his approach, and something more akin to religious fervor can be mistaken for love. Disillusion follows very quickly unless there are children of the union.

In business, if the same intellectual attraction is there to anchor the two, they can achieve some success, personal distinction, and fame.

TO SUN IN PISCES

This is a favorable relationship since both can cope with the other's eccentricities. There is a strong mutual attraction here. Both are good conversationalists, and they enjoy many of the same interests. They will have tremendous empathy for each other in times of trouble. If financial affairs are in order, marriage can survive the many emotional traumas that will result from the interference of in-laws.

A business relationship between this pair is fraught with difficulties. It can succeed spectacularly if there is a third partner who can cope with these two emotional but highly intuitive people.

CHAPTER V

Shafts of Moonbeams

The moon influences just about every facet of human emotion, and it is the emotions which set up the basic motivations for a particular life-style. Both love and hate are strong emotions, intangible forces which can make a life harmonious or discordant. They are the two dramatic polarities of the zodiac, and the moon influences both of them. In the huge amount of mail I receive every day, the majority of letters ask how to attract love and how to hold it.

HOW TO ATTRACT LOVE

MOON IN ARIES-MALE

While Sun in Aries attracts love through physical charm, the Moon in Aries male has a much more subtle approach. He himself looks for attraction in the other person and becomes like a moth to the flame. He rarely gets singed because the chosen mate falls in love with him first; then he responds and commits himself.

MOON IN ARIES-FEMALE

She can be quite a show-off, and once she has a target, she uses flamboyant, provocative remarks to attract attention. She talks him into situations he cannot refuse—enslaving him, if only temporarily, by the choice of words and instilling a feeling in him that she needs him.

MOON IN TAURUS-MALE

He sets out deliberately to evoke maternal feelings and succeeds. He writes poems and recites them aloud, sends flowers, and offers a mixture of sensuality and tenderness which is hard to resist.

MOON IN TAURUS-FEMALE

She does not mind letting a man know when she wants to be courted and after the first romantic overtures, she is quick to let her loved one know that he is THE only one for her. She never rushes and can even maintain surprise and wonder while walking down the aisle, as if she did not know that this was what was in her mind from her first awakening that she needed a mate.

MOON IN GEMINI-MALE

He is precocious and never gives too many clues that he is interested, so romance often becomes a game of "catch me if you can," but the hunted is willing to be caught when he has had enough of the game. Try to trick him or trap him and he will climb the first moonbeam and disappear.

MOON IN GEMINI-FEMALE

The thought of love makes the Gemini female very happy and it shows in her eyes; her teasing manner has a very youthful charm even if she is beyond the first flush of youth.

She can attact love by a strange type of negative salesmanship, flirting with someone else very deliberately, provoking a mild form of jealousy, and succumbing to attention just as the real target thinks all is lost. She attracts by tantalizing tactics.

MOON IN CANCER-MALE

He attracts love by being concerned about the small things in life that affect his beloved. Nothing is too much trouble and he does lovely things; he is always concerned and sympathetic. Somehow there is an intuitive feeling that despite all he does, his main interest is to give love and be loved.

MOON IN CANCER-FEMALE

Age makes a great difference as to how the Cancerian female goes about attracting love. When very young she exploits her vulnerability like a kitten asking for attention; few can resist. In middle age she manages to give the appearance of youthfulness and makes the most of her best attributes such as gentleness and a desire to be helpful. After middle age, she still manages to seem vulnerable while hiding a very determined spirit to get what she has set her heart on. Her main attraction is a special type of innocence which men find very hard to resist, as it appeals to their virility.

MOON IN LEO-MALE

He attracts love by being different, often searching out women in lower social or professional strata so that he emerges godlike to anyone who wants someone to look up to and admire. He gives the impression that if he is a god or a king, he will make his loved one into a goddess or a queen. Very often he attracts love by outlandish promises, and few women can resist the idea of having the world at her feet. His prime attraction is that he is larger than life.

MOON IN LEO-FEMALE

She attracts love with her warm and generous nature, conveying the idea that everything she has will be shared with the loved one. The more he responds, the stronger her power to attract, and power is something she loves as much as love itself.

MOON IN VIRGO-MALE

He talks of far-off places with strange, romantic sounding names and before the loved one knows it, she is willing to go dutch to share any experience with him. As he often speaks with disdain about ordinary sexual pleasures, he makes his lovemaking seem a special magical union. He attracts because he always states he is looking for perfection, and every woman knows she is perfect.

MOON IN VIRGO-FEMALE

Her distant look is her main attraction. It instills a desire to break down the reserve and see if there is any real warmth in the calm, beautiful creature who seems so self-assured (but is generally scared silly about being committed). She appeals to the mountaineer's mentality—the beautiful remote one is there, waiting to be conquered.

MOON IN LIBRA-MALE

His attraction is that of a lost boy waiting to be rescued. He is capable of raising very loving and maternal feelings; he responds to attention with great affection and gratitude. It is not a case so much of being vulnerable as being defenseless.

MOON IN LIBRA-FEMALE

She knows she has everything to offer, and her main attraction is that she can always pick and choose. Whoever is chosen knows that it is a wonderful privilege and responds with love. She is a finely tuned violin waiting for a bow—then she will make beautiful music, and every song will be of love.

MOON IN SCORPIO-MALE

His male attraction is a sensual and sexual one; it is hard to know which dominates until the clinches begin. He wants to be loved passionately and is like a starving man confronting a meal. There is generally a Good Samaritan around who is attracted to his telegraphed message of love. He has a "take me, I am all yours" attitude, but it soon changes to "you are mine and no one else can have you."

MOON IN SCORPIO-FEMALE

Her main attraction is that she appears like an offering ready to be sacrificed on the altar of love—with a keen appreciation of the high priest who will perform the act. However, she is capable of reversing the role at the last minute, and the sacrificial victim becomes the enchantress who lures men to love and sometimes to their doom. She attracts love by a strong sense of drama and a vital animal magnetism.

MOON IN SAGITTARIUS-MALE

He attracts love by treating his target as a good friend and talking of platonic friendship. His attraction is a healthy nature-loving type and he is quite capable of prefacing a statement of love by saying, "I am a rough diamond and I want to be loved for myself." He often is.

MOON IN SAGITTARIUS-FEMALE

She attracts love by being very capable, self-assured, and independent. Like her male counterpart, she offers herself by pointing out her faults, concluding that her attributes are taken for granted. She attracts love because when she is ready for it, she has already been a good and loyal companion.

MOON IN CAPRICORN-MALE

He brings a type of emotional intensity to the forefront; this has a special attraction for the woman who believes that falling in love is likely to do some good for a man. He is well aware that love is like this, and he will spend plenty of time in creating the illusion that he really needs someone to love him and arranges a sort of barter system: "Love me and I will do this for you." He always keeps his word, but he may become dull as the years go by.

MOON IN CAPRICORN-FEMALE

The main attraction is that this is a competent female not given to flighty ways; she easily convinces a prospective mate that she will never NEVER be in competition with him. She is a chameleon who adjusts easily to any environment. She has a great deal of attraction because the male still loves to think of the female as someone happy to bask in the light of his masculinity.

MOON IN AQUARIUS-MALE

His independence attracts like a knight in shining armor, and like the knights of old, he is always looking for a maiden in distress to rescue. He has plenty of clout in his chosen sphere, and this, too, attracts many women who like to share power. Unfortunately he does not share power, and he certainly does not think he needs any maiden to rescue *him!* At least that is what he *thinks,* but he attracts women who also have the power of positive thinking, and they manage to form an easy relationship.

MOON IN AQUARIUS-FEMALE

She is fiercely proud of her independence, and this is an attraction in itself. She never says, "Anything you can do, I can do better," even though she may know this is true. Her main attraction is that she does not want to enter into any illusory relationship and is quite prepared to let her mate know she will share his problems while appreciating him and enjoying mutual pleasures.

MOON IN PISCES-MALE

His main ability to attract love is that he knows an enormous amount about it; he is never lost for a fine poetic phrase or gallant gesture of consideration. He makes a female feel she is a precious thing, and he has high ideals about the woman he wants to spend his life with.

MOON IN PISCES-FEMALE

She attracts love because she sees it as a positive necessity to her life-style, but she never settles for second best. She looks around and makes a choice; it is through sympathetic concern and empathy that she attracts a love which will recognize her unspoken demands.

HOW TO KEEP LOVE

MOON IN ARIES-MALE

He may slip from grace very frequently as he is not averse to flirtations, *but* he does know when he has a good thing. Marriage and love take away a lot of his pangs of loneliness, but those flirtations are often irresistible. When everything seems as if it is about to fall apart, he will swear he has reformed. He means it when he says it....

MOON IN ARIES-FEMALE

She, too, likes to wander a bit, but hates to admit that she could make a mistake. She will go all out to keep her lover with her ability to think back to what she liked in him when they first met and then will set the scene to reenact those first idyllic moments.

MOON IN TAURUS-MALE

Once he has gone into a love affair, he never wants to jeopardize it, although he hates to apologize for any mistakes he makes. So he apologizes by offering tokens of love such as flowers or a new electric coffeepot. Few people can quarrel when a gift is proffered, and Venus, his ruling planet, makes him always conscious that love is a vital necessity in his life.

MOON IN TAURUS-FEMALE

Love is a possessive urge, and the Moon in Taurus female never likes to part with anything she has gained, including her man. She has a great sense of timing and knows how to wheedle and cajole when things go wrong. Her ability to provide an exceptionally good meal at critical times has saved many a romance from foundering. When all else fails, her way to a man's heart is still through his stomach.

MOON IN GEMINI-MALE

He maintains love by suddenly becoming hurt and vulnerable. Who wants to kick a man out of the love nest at such a time? Then he really exerts himself to be nice and uses his considerable conversational gifts to talk himself back into favor.

MOON IN GEMINI-FEMALE

She hates to spend time counting her worries. When times are bad, she has the good sense to count her blessings, and generally love comes out on the credit side. She encourages her mate to express himself and talk things out and will find herself agreeing with him so all is well that ends well.

MOON IN CANCER-MALE

When love begins to cool, the Moon in Cancer male goes through feelings of hurt but rallies to do all he can to please his lover (even if he has the private reservations that she may be unreasonable). Generally he understands her even better than he understands himself, and he is quick to suggest a second honeymoon in some romantic place if only to talk things over, confident he can turn it into a love feast.

MOON IN CANCER-FEMALE

Provided there is no other female on the horizon, the Moon in Cancer woman is very clever at reviving and maintaining love. She sets out to keep her mate interested in her through being excessively interested in him. As she likes plenty of attention herself, she appreciates that her mate will respond to this tactic. The old slippers-by-the-chair-and-a-loving-kiss is still an ancient formula for maintaining love.

MOON IN LEO-MALE

The Moon in Leo male is quick to recognize danger signals in his love affairs. He is also wise enough to tackle the danger before it gets too serious, doing it with outrageous gestures of affection and a whirlwind courtship with lots of personal attention. He may want to growl, but he manages to purr.

MOON IN LEO-FEMALE

She maintains love by keeping herself from losing her grip on the situation and sets out to restore the balance at the first sign of trouble. Love is an honorable emotion to her, and she reveres honor in everything. She is especially good at reviving old memories. If she has to bring in reinforcements to help her, out comes the family photograph album with the wedding pictures and she will use her children or relations as her aides. It is very difficult to leave a Leo female because what Madame Leo wants she gets.

MOON IN VIRGO-MALE

He maintains love by doing more to help his mate whether it is by sharing mutual chores or getting her to a psychologist. He will go to a marriage counselor as a last resort, but generally he can maintain love by devoted service and sweet reason.

MOON IN VIRGO-FEMALE

She is inclined to panic at first if she thinks love is flying out of the window, but with her usual prudence, she will close the window. She makes herself very attractive and takes an increased personal interest in the things her mate likes to do. If she suspects there is another woman, she keeps close to his side but never lets him think she is policing his activities. She retains love by her subtle insistence that they share much of their time together.

MOON IN LIBRA-MALE

When a Libra man feels that love is wilting, he needs a friend to push him into action. Without this extra shove, he will simply go away and brood; if he has a creative mind, he will write a melancholy poem to a lost love. In matters of love, the Libran will always rely on the advice of someone else.

The next step will be to take a shot of Dutch courage and return to his mate, very abject and apologetic. He will profess that it was all his fault and win her back in that way.

MOON IN LIBRA-FEMALE

She is utterly dedicated to preserving love, using everything within her power, including feminine guile, basic intuition, and tremendous attention to personal appearance. Rather than go to a marriage counselor she will resort to tears or seek sympathy through nonexistent sickness. She might also try acting out passionate love scenes which have first come to her as dreamlike fantasies.

MOON IN SCORPIO-MALE

He maintains love with the same dramatic methods that he used during courtship. If there was an excess of sexual activity, then sex is likely to be the answer. And no one can outdo his passionate declarations of love. He becomes more considerate if she is not feeling well. He also takes care to systematically eliminate anything in her life which is a danger to him.

MOON IN SCORPIO-FEMALE

She uses her native cunning to maintain love and is generally one step ahead of her mate in understanding what makes him tick. She stays in the driver's seat at all times and makes herself very necessary to her mate.

MOON IN SAGITTARIUS-MALE

He maintains love by taking more and more responsibilities from the shoulders of his mate, causing her to become more and more reliant on him. Generally he likes to take her away from the domestic scene into new exotic surroundings, and together they share new experiences. It works like magic.

MOON IN SAGITTARIUS-FEMALE

She may have to fight depression if she feels love is fading, but she puts on a very good mask to hide her feelings. She never initiates quarrels and will walk away from them to allow time for her mate to cool off. She is capable of returning as if nothing has happened, and there are no recriminations likely to issue from her. At all times she acts as a companion and friend.

MOON IN CAPRICORN-MALE

Life falls apart for the Moon in Capricorn male when he feels love is fading, but he knows it is his duty to try to maintain it. Generally he makes pathetic mistakes in trying to maintain love, and these very mistakes are often the thing which enable the love to survive. Because he seeks perfection, his admission of failure is likely to generate feelings of sympathy.

MOON IN CAPRICORN-FEMALE

She is very capable at settling for a lesser degree of love without feeling too annoyed about it; her approach to love is philosophical, accepting many changes. She perseveres and never lets up on attention to her mate, giving him a great feeling of security.

MOON IN AQUARIUS-MALE

All too often, he does not recognize danger signals until it is too late. Then he will pull out all stops to maintain a balance of love through expressions of devotion. He will seek a marriage counselor, if necessary, or psychological aid. Most of all he will point out how necessary he is in her life and ask what would she do without him. He is smart enough to know that once a need is pointed out that love can be revived.

MOON IN AQUARIUS-FEMALE

Because she is independent to a much greater degree than many of the other women in the zodiac, the Moon in Aquarius woman is her own worst enemy when it comes to maintaining love. She cannot make the first effort on her own. She will first use friends and relations as arbitrators and then make a sincere but not passionate declaration of love at a strategic moment. Because she is so independent, such a declaration seems like capitulation and a small victory for the mate.

MOON IN PISCES-MALE

He hates to think he is not maintaining love and so builds fantasies into which he can safely retreat. What he does not choose to see he can hardly acknowledge, and this enables him to behave as if everything is still perfect. Such dreams can produce a new form of happiness in which a still-perfect love is realized in the mind. Never destroy the dreams of a male Pisces because that is when love really goes away. He saves himself a lot of heartache by rationalizing that love was a dream in the first place.

MOON IN PISCES-FEMALE

The Moon in Pisces female is much more down-to-earth than her male counterpart when it comes to maintaining love. She uses her intuition, not as a weapon but as a tool of defense, sensing difficulties before they happen and so being prepared for them. She spruces herself up, becomes more alert to her partner's needs, and works on the premise that her partner will recognize that she is doing it all for him. She maintains love by putting as much of herself as possible into living, making her inherent weaknesses less noticeable.

CHAPTER VI

How to Trap a Mate

If you trap the moment before it's ripe,
The tears of repentance you'll certainly wipe;
But if once you let the ripe moment go,
You can never wipe off the tears of woe.

—William Blake

There comes a time in the lives of most people when they consider trapping a mate. The reasons are not often analyzed but they can be physical, mental, or financial. There is a season for hunting, and the astrological one shows itself by the position of the moon in your natal horoscope.

Some people are born to be hunted, others to be the hunter. We can gloss over the basics by saying we are waiting for the right mate to come along, and we disguise basic motivations by referring to love as a necessary part of acquiring a mate. This is when the hunter and the hunted find the best relationship, but hunting for a sexual companion is a modern variation of the old primeval instinct of finding a mate. The long courtship is a thing of the past, although once it was thought to be the way two people got to know each other before embarking on wedded bliss. Weddings are not quite so popular as they were, but the need for companionship is still one of man's most basic needs. Celibacy has its place in the world, but even that provides for substitutes in terms of companionship. One can be "married to Christ," "wedded to work," or sexually frigid enough to want to enjoy the other sex in every way other than in the bedroom. Many people have loneliness forced upon them by a society that does not find it easy to relate to old age. Losing one's mate through death can either kill the hunting instincts or hone them to a keenness that was never felt in the original search for companionship. While we have free will, circumstances, causes, and effects will indicate in the horoscope how real the needs, wants, and desires for companionship are likely to be. The position of the moon in the natal horoscope is the first indicator, but as we get older and perhaps have had one or more experiences of companionship at any of several levels, then we have to progress the chart to find the position of the progressed moon. New needs, wants, and desires manifest themselves from year to year. These influences are calculated from the position of the natal moon.

MOON IN ARIES-FEMALE

Once having sighted the potential mate, move in to gain his confidence. After the first encounter, all the best and brightest ideas must seem to be his, with you as the placid, adoring acolyte. Any idea of marriage should come from him. Without appearing to be overly eager, do not let the grass grow under your feet. He may belong to a sign noted for its impatience and while you know you are "made for him," even your best friend could be edging in on the action. It is not too hard for you to get a mate, but holding him is more difficult. Spend a few months sifting through those pseudoemotions you had to use to get him to the point of marriage, and then surprise him by a rapid maturity act. Tell him you want to share everything in his life—even his worries—and you will be surprised how many men are delighted to shift responsibilities. The next step is to be sure you live up to your words . . . accept the responsibilities with as few moans as possible. In time he will know he made a wonderful decision, and you will know you can twist him round your little finger.

MOON IN ARIES-MALE

You have to work hard at seeing each female first as an individual and second as a potential victim of your aggressive charm. Play the field when you are young, but get down to being discriminating before the age of twenty-five. What do you want in your mate? If you are looking for a twin soul who likes everything you like, then you may get the girl of your choice only to find that she has changed her mind about some of the things you thought she enjoyed. Be ardent but considerate, aggressive without being a bully, and remember that twin soul though she may have been, she also has an identity of her own, and it will assert itself once she has the security of marriage. You are more inclined to want a companion nicely delivered to the marital bed complete with legal documents than you want a relationship with too much freedom for the other person to walk out. The Moon in Aries does not indicate emotional security, and while you talk about freedom, you really mean YOUR freedom, not the other person's. Tie the knot with marriage.

MOON IN TAURUS-FEMALE

A mate with money will make you feel secure, and to get him you have to use a few wiles. Never project the image of poverty and, if you hunt the wealthy, most of them want to believe that someone is going to love them for themselves alone. You are capable of this, but there is some inner voice telling you it is just as easy to love where there is money as there is to love without it. Start the relationship as you mean it to go on; let him know you do not feel it is cute to eat at a hamburger joint and would prefer a French restaurant. Dress well enough for any special occasion, but give the impression that although you enjoy dressing up to please yourself, you are happy he likes to see you well groomed since you want to complement his good looks. Making a companion feel good is easy for you, but to others it may seem that you are paying compliments. You are going to enjoy sharing all the good things of life; expect him to make his contribution with as much faith as you make yours.

MOON IN TAURUS-MALE

No one is going to try to assess your bank balance because you can carry off grand occasions with charm and the subtle idea that you were born with a silver spoon in your mouth and were weaned on caviar. There will always be enough females around you to have a charming companion on your arm; the difficulty comes when you want to settle down. You know someone is going to be lucky, but will she realize it? Two cannot always live in the same style as one—how much are you prepared to share your life-style? Generally, you are able to marry someone with substance, and this turns out well for you because with a bit of help you can really turn a tiny nest egg into a miniature Fort Knox. If you cannot live happily ever after, it will not be because you are short of money.

MOON IN GEMINI-FEMALE

Getting your potential mate is going to impose some disciplines on you, because as one of the great talkers of the zodiac, it is not easy for you to listen. You attract men with your sparkle and vivacity, but how is your mate going to be sure he can impress you if you always place him in the role of listener? Keep up with whatever sports or hobbies he likes and express concern for any strain he may feel at work. Instill confidence in him by letting him know you are sure he can succeed at just about anything he wants to do and how proud you are of him. Never become gushing because, while you may be quite sincere, it does not always appear like that to others. No long courtship for you—once you have the first ring on your finger, the wedding ring goes on very quickly afterward.

MOON IN GEMINI-MALE

There are still many bright young ladies who enjoy a flashy companion, and you are capable of giving any of them a very good time. The trouble may be that they cannot keep up with your perpetual motion. Look for a woman who has a natural zest for living and is not going to get into a flap when you decide you want to go away for the weekend and give her only a couple of hours' notice. Your spontaneity is half your charm. It is wonderful, too, that with a companion who can move at your own rapid pace, you turn into a good husband and provider. You have to make your views very plain from the start of any relationship because if you meet a woman who thinks she can reform you and make you move at a slower pace, neither of you will be happy. Lay your cards right on the table and do not gamble on love's making everything right after marriage. For you, things have to show signs of being right from the first meeting.

MOON IN CANCER-FEMALE

Finding a mate brings out your best maternal instincts, and this is fine if you can find someone who wants to be mothered. There are many such men around, but it is going to be difficult if you fall in love with someone who wants affection but does not want to be smothered by consideration. You will be more satisfied with the one who enjoys being mothered, and it will be frustrating if you fall in love with any other type. You are very sensitive and can be hurt easily; any rebuke from a lover or husband may make you feel rejected. You cannot maintain a good balance between being maternal and even understanding that some people are very self-sufficient and can manage very well without so much obvious concern. At your best, you are the ideal "total woman," putting her mate first. At your worst, you are bossy, and some men simply cannot stand a domineering woman. Care in getting deeply involved in any relationship is your best insurance for a happily married life with mutual companionship.

MOON IN CANCER-MALE

She will love the care and consideration you show for her, but if you start off by catering to her every whim, she will expect it for the rest of her life. The whims of a young woman are not likely to be the same whims as she gets older . . . and older. Also, there will be times when something unexpected happens and you have to become concerned about others, perhaps children. Look for a mate who can understand these changes in relationships; the lover's becoming the husband and then a father can put a big strain on the very thing some women admire more than anything—the feeling that *she* is the sun, moon and all the planets in your firmament. You are not likely to suffer in silence, either, when you change from being sweetly solicitious to making noises like a wolf baying at the moon. Her opinion of you may suffer.

MOON IN LEO-FEMALE

The moon in this position softens some of the domineering spirit of the personality and takes off the rougher edges. When you make a compliment, you do so sincerely. Your companion can have a shortage of good looks and manners, but you will see what you want to see. So, if you have made up your mind you want a good rough diamond with enough toughness to stand up for you and protect you, then ugliness and poor manners will not mean a thing at first, because you think you can reform your man. What were once thought of as idiosyncracies during courtship can become faults during marriage. The tendency of women with this placement of the moon in the natal chart is to seek the companionship of men much younger than yourself. This might have been a problem a generaion ago, but it is not too much of a hazard in these enlightened days. You will love him and never want

126

to leave him, so that may mean making compromises—
something that is never easy for you.

MOON IN LEO-MALE

You know your own shortcomings and can live with them,
but you are smart enough to disguise them when you are
seeking a companion. Try to make a secondary plan for the
days when some of the faults surface because it is hard to
play a part twenty-four hours a day after you are married. Of
course you can retaliate by pointing out that she may not be
perfect, but that upsets your own standards as much as hers
because everyone knows that you have always looked for
perfection in others. With an understanding companion, it
will be easier for you to smooth out some of those faults and
gradually eliminate them, and then you can be really proud
of yourself. If a Moon in Leo male indulges well beyond
social drinking, when he gives it up he is not afraid to declare
to the world that he made it and expect congratulations on a
remarkably fine achievement. Well, all your faults may not
be as dramatic as being a reformed drinker but the same
desire to acknowledge any reformation will always appeal to
you.

MOON IN VIRGO-FEMALE

You are very critical of the opposite sex and must learn to
take criticism yourself. It is too easy for you to make a male
companion feel inferior when he wants to impress you with
his manliness; give him a chance to show off a little;
otherwise, forming a romantic attachment becomes a
herculcan task. You have enough discipline to curb your
analytical qualities, remember that it is not often that love of
any kind stands up to constant criticism or a scathing
tongue. Use these qualities in your working life and it will
probably pay dividends. Seek a companion away from your
work environment, preferably in a good financial bracket or
with good social contacts. If he has high standards, they will
be a challenge which you will enjoy meeting. Never get

depressed if you do not marry early; the position of the Moon in Virgo seems to lead to lengthy courtships and late marriages. Most of all, have a little fun in your relationship and try not to bring your briefcase to meetings with your prospective lover; it is all too often your obvious badge of authority. Let him talk about his work—intelligent listening will work wonders in developing a sympathetic rapport.

MOON IN VIRGO-MALE

You can frighten many women away by being too coolly intelligent at the first meeting. Let her discover this attribute slowly. You do not need to play dumb, but give her the chance to do a little peacock preening because it is a sign she wants you to be sufficiently impressed to ask for a second date. No matter how intelligent a woman is, she still likes to be treated as a female, and a little follow-up with a phone call or some flowers after the first meeting never hurt any romance. It is the sort of thing you always intend to do but forget when you get involved with work. Because you have a natural admiration for a well-groomed, attractive girl, give her the chance to express an interest in literature, the arts, or her opinion of the political scene. Try to get some fun in your dates, play the role of the lover instead of the teacher. You cannot help being blunt, but a few compliments can soften this. Be tolerant of mistakes and aware of the tension which women go through. She will admire your practical approach to problems, but never talk down to any woman; it breeds resentment.

MOON IN LIBRA-FEMALE

Seeking companionship is never going to be difficult. You have to spend a lot of time sorting people out, and it is awfully difficult for you to make decisions. So you find yourself in the dilemma of wishing that Frank, who is so handsome, had some of the tenderness of Bob, who could have more style like Eddie. In short, you need a companion who is a composite of everything you have set as a standard since you were a romantic girl hoping that a knight in shining armor would come along and rescue you. Set yourself a goal, and then zoom in on the most likely target with the greatest number of attributes, including enough money to keep you in the style you have already decided is necessary for happiness. Moon in Libra females often find the best companion in an older man in a stable profession. He can be relied upon to earn a steady income, and you can be relied upon to help him spend it graciously.

MOON IN LIBRA-MALE

You look for Siamese-twin type of companionship, doing everything together with plenty of close warm attention. You are capable of giving it and you wonder why it should not be reciprocal. It is not a bad idea, but it is becoming more difficult to have long-standing relationships in which closeness in all things is the cement holding it together. Make allowances for the unpredictable qualities of a woman who at first adores the idea of liking all the same things and doing them. She will be the first to insist that you share the household chores as if you like them, and be hurt if you do not, because togetherness to her also means sharing some of the things which in your heart you really need a woman to help you with. Building togetherness into a marriage contract can be a tricky business because you probably see togetherness only as sharing the fun things of life.

MOON IN SCORPIO-FEMALE

The temptations to probe into his past love affairs can become an obsession and a bone of contention between you. Be wise . . . allow him a few secrets in his past because you are sure to have some in your own. You can foul up the relationship after the first few dates if you want to know if he loves you as much as he did the last girl. If you feel that you must know, take the plunge while you are still in your courtship stage, because it will be much worse to squeeze information out of him when you are married. Besides, you are likely to hurt yourself as much as him. Old loves are best forgotten, and it is not your business to resurrect them unless they creep back into your relationship. Then you are justified in zapping them with the famous scorpion sting. When you have gotten your mate, cheer yourself up by realizing that no matter how many loves he may have had in the past, you are the one in his life now. He probably wants to develop amnesia about the past, anyway, if you are as smart and charming as you know yourself to be. Most men know instinctively when they have made a good match, but they hate jealousy.

MOON IN SCORPIO-MALE

If you go through life hinting that you must marry a virgin, be prepared to meet a lady who tells you the facts of life. If you are a great lover—and most of you are—she may presume you have had some experience to bring you up to this expertise, so forget the original game plan. Virgins can be more than you can rightfully expect once you have reached the stage of wanting a meaningful relationship leading to marriage. Those timid, shy girls are perfect victims for men of your sign, but remember that they can become clinging vines, too, and in time the clinging vine can strangle even a Scorpio. Psyching out the other sex is one of your favorite occupations, but be prepared for the female of the species to be just as dangerous as the male—two can play this game. Once you really fall in love, you are sunk; it is much better for you if the lady of your choice returns your love without timidity.

MOON IN SAGITTARIUS-FEMALE

Because you love freedom above anything, you may be reluctant to enter into any relationship likely to lead to marriage. Well, take your time—sort out the potentials, but try to get your timing right. Sometimes you can delay the marriage action too long and become accepted as a career girl who likes a bit of fun but has no inclination to get married or share her life with a permanent partner. Fine, if this is really what you want; but you have a natural love of companionship, so you have to begin plans early in life to reconcile this with love, sex and marriage. The alternative is a series of loose relationships. Although you love freedom, you are not promiscuous and do not relate a series of free love adventures to the idealistic companionship you seek.

MOON IN SAGITTARIUS-MALE

You are not likely to be dragged screaming to the altar because you are as wary as a rabbit of a trap when it comes to any possibility of a relationship deepening into marriage. You can think of numerous reasons not to get tied down and generally can manage to extricate yourself gracefully even if you have to resort to the old "Darling, you deserve something better than me." When all else fails, you turn your face to the west and walk into the sunset—only to meet someone else just as you reach the horizon, and the scene starts all over again. Responsibilities of an aged parent may prevent you from getting married, or at least supply a decent enough excuse to anyone who wants to rush your fences. Then the day comes when the tender trap is sprung so subtly you scarcely know what has hit you, but you passionately want to be married. You keep on swearing that you must both have freedom and that a marriage contract is not bondage. When you reach this stage, you are set to be a delightful companion, kind, considerate, and are capable of working hard to make your marriage work.

MOON IN CAPRICORN-FEMALE

You love to be the power behind the throne—always there when needed, always solicitous, always ready to lend a helping hand. If you have an affair or live with anyone, you can be very self-effacing; you will not intrude or become too pushy if your mate is already married. You are almost too good to be true and can lull such mate into a state of false security so that he believes he is the luckiest man on the earth; a wife at home and a mistress who knows her place. But as you grow older, the position changes and you become concerned about your future. Who is going to look after you in old age? Has he made provision for you in his will? Suppose the devoted lover of so many years has a coronary? At this stage, it is not unusual for anyone born with the Moon in Capricorn to leave the mistress status and seek a regular relationship, leaving the old lover wondering why it all came to an end. The opportunity to get married young is rare, but if you do, it is generally to someone mature, in a good position, and older than you. Loyalty and the instincts for long-lasting relationships are your natural attributes. Whether mistress, wife, or mother, you can be faithful to your ideals and the people around you. However, you take it very hard if a lover or husband walks out on you.

MOON IN CAPRICORN-MALE

You are inclined to devote a lot of time to your chosen profession, and it is generally easier for you to look for companionship with someone who will work with you or even for you. You can handle this sort of practical arrangement from an early age. If you miss out on marrying in your youth, you seem able to go on until well after middle life without seeking any deep emotional relationship, but you compensate with dedication to your work. Your chosen companion must always be in a position to offer you something beyond affection. If you gain executive position, it helps to have a wife who can entertain and be diplomatic. If you are not in a robust financial situation, then you look for someone who understands that keeping an eye on the cents helps accumulate dollars. If you are ambitious and want to get to the top quickly, you are capable of marrying the boss's daughter and discreetly using the relationship to advance your career.

MOON IN AQUARIUS-FEMALE

If you start your family before you are married, you are one of the few signs who can cope with all the responsibility this entails. You are extremely idealistic and want your mate to share your goals. You may believe it when you tell him you and he can save the world but be sure he is not agreeing only to take advantage of you. If there is one thing that is likely to ruin any relationship for you, it is to discover your companion in a lie. You can be very literal and will always remember if someone says, "I love you forever," and believe it is really true. On the other hand, you can get out of relationships very neatly yourself by saying, "We have grown apart... I am more mature now. I think we must always be friends... it has been a beautiful experience." You can walk away from a relationship firmly believing that a few words have healed any possible wounds. Discovering that this is not true can become a nightmare for you. Make sure that you get the ground rules straightened out before you embark on any relationship. You can hurt your friends just as easily as those you have been more intimate with.

MOON IN AQUARIUS-MALE

Be realistic in your relationships. The bright little girl who appeals to you may not want to be treated like your daughter once the early stages of courtship have been achieved. Study your attitudes and try to have a realistic approach to the relationships. If you want a daughter so that you can present a father image, it is safer to adopt a child than take a child-bride and discover that she has enough wisdom to be your grandmother. Start out with a totally honest appraisal of the relationship and you are just the person to sustain it; as it starts in the beginning, so it will be through married life— give or take a few exceptions. You are inclined to give the impression that you are a knight in shining armor ready to rescue any maiden in distress. If you are married, the desire

133

to rescue members of the opposite sex can cause complications, or at least put you in a position where you have to do a lot of explaining.

MOON IN PISCES-FEMALE

It does not matter if your search for a companion does not make sense to anyone else but yourself. You will always go on a ruthless search for beautiful people, hoping to sort out one who is the epitome of perfection. The moon in this position produces some extremes of deception, and the awakening from the dream that love, sex, and marriage are one glorious adventure can be very upsetting to your psyche. It is not easy to reconcile the best thing within you (the idealism of love, for instance) with the cruel realities of the world and the fact that even beautiful relationships can change from contact with mundane things like money. The way to companionship is fraught with dangers, but you will always continue the pursuit. Happiness comes when someone recognizes the subtle undertones of your sensitivity and has a tender regard for you rather than full-blooded passion. Settle for this type of relationship and it will gradually build you up into a position of strength in which all your major attributes shine like a good deed in a naughty world. You can so easily be taken advantage of by those types who enjoy playing with your emotions and walk away when they have achieved destruction. Run like the wind away from any companion who seems to enjoy emotional cruelty.

MOON IN PISCES-MALE

You look for all the finest qualities in anyone you want as a companion. Once you have a glimpse of even one attribute that interests you, there is a tendency to weave a fabric of dreamy idealism around her. The not-so-perfect seems to be the perfect, you dust the pedestal you have kept waiting for this occasion, and put her on it. All too often the pedestal is too small for the figure, she has only to make a slight move, and she topples to the floor. Even then you are capable of picking up the pieces and tenderly trying to put them together, then finding that something is missing. At this stage, you search for the missing part outside the original relationship and you are very adept at handling two romantic relationships. This can go on for a long time until the time of reckoning comes—one or the other discovers the deception, and guess who is sent out into the cold hard world to begin all over again? You can take up the search several times when you are young, but it is not easy after middle age. Many people with the Moon in Pisces in the natal horoscope find themselves lonely at the age of fifty unless they profit from their early experiences and try to change their attitudes toward the other sex. Try loving a person while knowing their imperfections, just as you must try to love yourself.

CHAPTER VII

Moon Mates—
For Women Only

How lonely we shall be.
What can we do,
You without me,
I without you?

"Midnight Lament"
—Harold Munro

So you know the birthdate of the man in your life and think you understand him through his sun sign. Then why does the old romantic glow get tarnished and seem as if it will rust away altogether? You have let him be the aggressive lover if he is an Aries, or accepted the fact that he must work hard if he is a Capricorn. Still there seems something missing; maybe it is a lack of ease in communication, a deterioration of sexual activities, or somehow the idea that two can live as cheaply as one has now been proved a myth. More romances fall apart and more divorces occur from small things, molehills grow into mountains, and before you really understand what went wrong, the whole thing has blown up and you are sorting out the property.

The solution may be easier than you think. Know where the moon is in the natal chart of your man and you will be more able to understand what goes on in his mind and how it influences his emotions. That Leo who wooed you so majestically and promised to share the world with you turned out to be a damp firecracker. Did you really go for all that macho act and then discover that the lion was a timid pussycat when he had to face the landlord and tell him he would be late with the rent?

Dear heart, know his moon, and while you may have to cope with all his weaknesses, you may find that you have enough strength to supplement them. Certainly you will understand him better as a whole person. If you can love a person knowing his faults instead of being overpowered by his virtues, then you have a better chance of staying in love.

MOON IN ARIES

He wants to do nice things for you, but he likes to think of them himself. Give him time and he will get around to them. He intends to send you flowers for your birthday but will forget the date. He will enjoy his nights out with the boys or going away on his own. Be suspicious if he brings you a super present after these occasions, and you will never get another one. While he enjoys possessing you, he will never want to be tied to your apron strings. He craves variety, thrives on it, and hates to have the same breakfast every Wednesday. If he has any need to be jealous, then you have a dangerous creature on your hands. His ideas of freedom do not extend to your teasing him. If he says he is going to one place for dinner and then changes his mind, it is not because he is deceitful. Underneath the aggressiveness he has to show the world, and especially if he is in a job where he has authority, he is really very sensitive. When things go wrong, he expects you to have ESP and understand him. Pet him, try to please him, and he will never leave you. When you have a scrap, be the first to offer the kiss of reconciliation.

MOON IN TAURUS

Do not be taken in by too many romantic candlelit dinners. This man is a home lover and likes to be waited on in his own home. He will provide the financial means but expect you to use his money wisely. He can justify his own extravagances but will appreciate you more if you do the same. Hurt his pride and he will show his temper. His name and reputation are valuable assets to his ego. Dust a good substantial pedestal, put him on it, and the chances are he will not fall off it. The solid faithful stability you admired when you were young and insecure may give way to a dull ponderous middle age, but count your blessings—he can be the major one. He loves flattery but can see through insincerity. In his youth he may have sown a few wild oats, but never remind him of them or he will begin to look for faults in you and never hesitate to get in a gentle dig about them.

Praise him, but be sure to make a comfortable place for him. He always knows when he has a good home, and nothing will budge him from it.

MOON IN GEMINI

He talks a lot and can stretch a little learning into what appears to be deep philosophical thought. Living up to it is what he is not likely to do because he does not practice what he loves to preach. He feels insecure with older people, and the thought of aging is a perpetual worry. Let *him* find the first white hair on his head—there is no need for you to point it out, even in fun, because it is not going to be a joke with him. Never compete with him when he is remembering the joys of childhood or holding the limelight; beneath all that talk is a childlike quality, an innocence which cannot always cope with everyday affairs. He can be as persistent as a mosquito in money matters, but only when money is due to him; hates to be reminded about anything he has borrowed. Most of all, try to understand his neuroses—he needs them to function. If he smokes too much, don't bother pointing out the dangers to him. He knows and has come to terms with them and rationalizes that since the air is polluted, anyway, he may as well enjoy his cigarettes.

Never try to get him away from youthful companions; he needs to relate to youth because aging is his secret fear. Laugh at his subtle, slick jokes even if you have heard them before. Be grateful that he wants to share most things with you even though he is prepared to push away the unpleasant things of everyday life. Try to reform him and you'll lose him.

MOON IN CANCER

He is morbidly sensitive. Hard words may not break bones, but they will bruise his tender skin and wound his even more delicate psyche. He needs lots of time to himself, but if you suggest he should be on his own, he will feel rejected. And that breeds depression. He loves to be protective even though he is the one who often needs it much more than you do. Even though he may not have much money, never suggest going dutch with him when courting.

He is idealistic about the opposite sex and will often talk of his mother. Think twice about saying even one tiny wrong word about her; otherwise it is you who will fall short of the ideal. Keep him waiting and he will become upset; not because he is angry, but because he has gone through agonies of wondering if you were abducted or hurt. In any emergency, his imagination will generally see the worst of the situation. When children arrive, he may cease to be the lover and become a dutiful husband and devoted—even doting— father. When he buys you candy, it is generally the brand he likes best, and he is likely to eat half of it. Not to worry—he will buy some more.

For all his desires to be protective, he is really another child for you to look after. Coax him, coddle him, and he will share even his shell with you.

MOON IN LEO

Laugh at him for wearing a flamboyant tie and he may try to strangle you with it. Compare him to your best friend's husband and you are likely to ruin that foursome for bridge. He will be curious about your past love affairs and go into fits of remorse if he feels inadequate. Often he is, but the age-old wiles of women can cope with this. He has to believe in himself before he can get around to believing in you, much less appreciating you. Flaunt your charms in public and he will be a raging king of the forest, but flaunt them in the privacy of your own home and he will eat out of your hand for days afterward.

He is as curious as a cat, and if he thinks you have a secret, he will do all he can to wheedle it out of you. Deny him this and he becomes dangerously suspicious and jealous. Love him passionately, but remember—he expends a lot of energy on other things than sex. Even the great lover of the zodiac has to have his eight hours' sleep.

MOON IN VIRGO

He is very sensitive to noise and such things as other people smoking. He will never cease to cast a disapproving glance or give a quick lecture on virtues and vices—*His* virtues and *your* vices, of course. Attempt to live up to his high standards and he will give you brownie points for trying. He is always struggling to be efficient, and this can make him irritable. He will walk away from arguments if you start them, but will stand his ground forever if he initiates one. He does not like to make quick decisions but when he has come to a

141

conclusion, that is it and there is no more to be said. He will have the last word in most things. His sense of humor is limited, and if you try to play jokes on him, he gets an inferiority complex. He will be fastidious about food and cleanliness; togetherness for him does not mean sharing the same toothbrush. Keep him busy and, most of all, keep healthy. Even if he understands sickness, he will not be comfortable living with someone who "enjoys" bad health, although he will always be dutiful and considerate.

MOON IN LIBRA

He is likely to think that art is more important than kitchen utensils, he is not concerned with the mundane things of life. In many ways you have to be a buffer between him and nasty intrusive things, such as bills. He will file them away—in the wastepaper basket. Get financial affairs sorted out as soon as the ring is on the appropriate finger; he will love to have this burden taken from him. His zodiacal sign is the scale of justice, and it is always slightly tilted—in his favor, not yours. He hates arguments and will agree verbally·but keep his real feelings smoldering for ages.

You will always have rivals because he enjoys looking at members of the opposite sex but is often too timid to be promiscuous. Your biggest danger is an intellectual type, though, rather than prettier than a picture type. If you see him getting too intense about a friend who is overpoweringly intellectual, be ruthless and take a quick course in whatever subject he thinks she excels at. He will switch his attention back to you. Make decisions for him but not in an obvious manner because he will know immediately if you are developing into the one thing he cannot stand: a bossy female. If you have children, he will always be your adoring mate with the children coming a close second in his life but never surpassing you in his affections. Guard him like a precious jewel and he will never allow anyone to borrow him, much less steal him.

MOON IN SCORPIO

Beneath the sarcasm and the sting of the scorpion's tail there is a desperate human being longing to be loved but not always sure how to respond. The moon in this sign becomes very complex. You can never be quite sure when a black mood will hit or when passionate demands will be made on you. It is no use having a headache; otherwise he will go through guilt pangs of rejection.

Everything with Scorpio is a matter of timing—you have to be synchronized with him. Let your own clock run down and he is likely to run away. He can be morbidly sensitive and intensely introverted one moment only to surprise you with a flash of gregariousness. He enjoys many acquaintances but has few friends; do not remind him of this, since he will see it as a rebuke.

If you have scraps, he will generally return to you—but leave him and you'll never get back into the house, much less into his heart. Because he knows his weaknesses so well, he cannot stand having weak people around him; it is up to you to be strong enough to stand up to his moods and tantrums. Love him passionately but maintain your own identity; he will respect you for it.

MOON IN SAGITTARIUS

He has many childlike qualities (ranging from asking too many questions to extreme naïveté) but hates to be thought infantile. Those constant, often inappropriate, questions can be irritating, but he will never understand why you become brusque with him. He likes to be thought chivalrous and generous and acknowledged as such. Although he talks a lot about freedom, he has many inner fears about being alone, especially as he approaches middle age. With lots of nervous energy to get rid of, he generally adopts a sporting image but

143

he hates to be beaten. He can be very macho, seeking out male companions for pleasure, but he also loves to feel he is a ladies' man. Rely on him, be a clinging vine, but know when to let go. Give him the iron hand in the velvet glove treatment, and he will love it.

MOON IN CAPRICORN

He will try to keep unpleasant things from you and expect you to do the same, but when anything unpleasant is exposed, he will blame everyone but himself. He has a tremendous inferiority complex and tries to compensate by gaining social status. Acceptance by groups of people is important to him. Although he can take rejection on a personal basis, it will bring on moods of deep depression. He will never admit his faults to you, but he knows them all too well and carries a big load of guilt most of his life. He is not likely to be demonstrative in public and is embarrassed if you are.

Always have plenty of time to spare when he needs to talk about himself and his plans for the future. He sees himself as a perfectionist, but he is really afraid of making mistakes. Keep him busy, praise his work, and cater to his material needs.

MOON IN AQUARIUS

He wants to spread himself over as much ground as possible, and although this involves sharing his time with groups of people who may not appeal to you, he will expect you to share his interests. He can break up relationships just as quickly as he makes them and this could include severing the marriage ties, although he will tell you it is for your own good. He knows all about the Age of Aquarius and sees himself as one of the leaders of the age—but his being king does not necessarily mean that you will be queen.

*   *   *

He can be very patient but should never be taken for granted. He hates to give in to illness. He will expect you to keep his intellectual pace. He has strong ideas about how children should be educated. A fierce spirit of independence enables him to overcome many obstacles in life, but he is likely to give up *anything* if he feels a principle is involved. He likes his wife to have an identity of her own; respect and caring through actions means more to him than protestations of love. He may forget most anniversaries but never the time when you first met.

Look after his physical well-being, be concerned with his concern for other people, and you will have a long-lasting marriage.

MOON IN PISCES

Try to get him to see life in terms of practicality and he will run away—his dream world and neuroses are as important to his lifestyle as breathing. He learns through personal experiences, never vicariously. He is ultrasensitive and intuitive; never expect him to take what appears to be the logical course of action.

If you want to create a scene, tell him he is ungrateful. He may seem to drift through life in a nebulous manner, but his inherent intuition generally gets him out of trouble. If he seems to flatter you, never be embarrassed—he means it. His secret fear is being left to grow old on his own; he will cling to children and grandchildren all through his life. When he behaves mysteriously, play the game with him; he will never be able to keep a secret for any length of time. He loves to be inquisitive about your friends.

Pamper him, but never be condescending; he can sense ulterior motives. The more he is loved, the more he responds and gives of himself.

CHAPTER VIII

Moon Parents

Just as the moon influences your choices in love and marriage, it affects the kind of parent you are or will be. The placement of the moon in any natal horoscope will be a deciding factor in whether parents give tender loving care to their offspring, whether they dote to the point of spoiling the child, or whether they can temper good judgment and their own experiences to the needs of their particular child.

With so much spoken about the generation gap between parents and children in the last ten years, I think that astrology can be a vital guide to erase and explain many of the mistakes which parents either accept reluctantly and painfully or resentfully or with abject self-pity. Family counselors have begun to play a big part in trying to sort out difficulties between parents and children, but when a relationship goes wrong, many parents are ashamed to discuss it, much less be honest with a stranger. This rarely applies to an astrologer who is called on to explain the difficulties because he is able to produce the visual image of the natal chart and show lines of cause and event. I feel it is terrible that so many parents and children carry unnecessary loads of guilt simply because they do not understand that their basic nature at a certain time was geared to their not being able to understand certain specific sets of circumstances. By explaining the position of the moon in the natal chart, astrologers can ease the burden of guilt, thus enabling all concerned to start on a new cycle in life with a more positive attitude toward making it successful. Some may even shrug their shoulders philosophically as they find that not all parents are to blame for their children and, equally so, children can no longer get into trouble and then shrug off their responsibility for their own actions.

MOON IN ARIES

Filled with independence, you are likely to want these qualities in your own children, but remember how sad it is to see a child expected to act out the frustrations of an overly ambitious parent. The idea of a son first and a daughter afterward seems to dominate those born with the moon in Aries. A pair in reverse can lead to a firstborn girl being expected to adopt a male-oriented life-style, while the boy may be granted so many favors that he is quite spoiled.

MOON IN TAURUS

With this position of the moon in the natal horoscope, you want your child to appreciate its home and you as the focal point in it; that makes it hard on you when the time comes to cut the apron strings. Some of you can never do this and thus build up some difficult psychological conditions. It is easier for these people to have daughters if the old saying has any meaning: "A son is a son until he gets a wife, but a daughter is a daughter all of her life." Learning to cope with sons is a tough challenge for many Moon in Taurus mothers, and sometimes this is combated by having a large family. This way they stand a chance of one child being tied to the household for a longer period.

MOON IN GEMINI

It is providential that this sign is noted for its capacity of multiple births since this solves a lot of problems. One day

Moon in Gemini people admire having a son and then change to adoring a daughter, but the main thing is that whatever the sex, they appreciate alert and lively children. Gemini parents thoroughly enjoy being like a brother or sister to their own children. The tough part comes when the alert children grow up and age while the Moon in Gemini parent remains youthful. And an aging child often throws a reflection on its parents who generally like to think they are not only young in spirit but physically youthful as well.

MOON IN CANCER

The moon is at home in its own bailiwick, and just about all the basic traits of Cancer magnify themselves to a point where there is some distortion of facts. Moon in Cancer people are sympathetic, eager to please and, most of all, far too easygoing with their children. It is fine when the children are young and all the protective forces of the moon can be expressed in kissing a bruised knee better or wiping away tears. Once this phase has passed, there is a huge gap in the life of the moon in Cancer parents; they are likely to adopt another child or become excellent foster parents because that need to be wanted is an essential part of their life-style. Deprive them of being needed and the life force itself begins to dry up. Moon in Cancer types are the best grandparents in the zodiac.

MOON IN LEO

The feminine qualities of the moon are dominated by the ultramasculinity of the zodiac sign ruled by the sun. A son is an essential part of life to Moon in Leo people, and the male parent sees the child as an extension of himself. If the son makes mistakes, the patriarchal father spirit is hurt. If a girl makes a mistake, the Moon in Leo woman wonders what she did wrong. It is not easy for children with Moon in Leo parents to obtain and sustain their own identity, a point which has contributed to some family splits in recent years as more and more children leave the home rather than remain subject to heavy parental control.

MOON IN VIRGO

This position accentuates the Virgoan love of beauty associated with the idea of cleanliness. In many families it is still acceptable for the boys to be messy and dirty while girls are little angels in clean dresses. While others know that nothing is farther from the truth, Moon in Virgo people cling to this idea. They believe that little girls are made of sugar and spice and all that's nice and girls are generally treated better than boys. When the little girl proves she can be a tomboy, the Moon in Virgo person becomes ruthlessly reproachful, and girls may develop a sense of guilt if this goes on too long.

MOON IN LIBRA

This produces a well-polished person with a great love of the arts and a feeling for all the word "culture" brings into focus. Moon in Libra people are not so interested in the sex of their first child as the hope that it will grow up to appreciate the good things of life; they take pains to prepare him for them according to their own experience. It is not unusual for Moon in Libra mothers to go to symphony concerts during pregnancy not merely to enjoy the music but firmly believing that they are exposing the unborn child to one of the better things of life. All children born to Moon in Libra parents have a chance to explore the arts; difficulties come when a child is born in a birth sign which prefers manual work and could not care less for the creative arts.

MOON IN SCORPIO

Having a baby is intensely personal to Moon in Scorpio parents, so beware of offering congratulations too soon; wait until the birth has taken place. Moon in Scorpio people are jealously possessive and rarely appreciate doting grandparents or other relations expressing opinions about the upbringing and welfare of their children.

MOON IN SAGITTARIUS

People with the moon in this position rarely fret over trivialities and take to parenthood with both emotional pleasure and an inner resolution to fulfill their responsibilities. If a defective child is born, you can bet he will be loved even more than any other perfect children in the family. There is not likely to be any thought of sending him away from the family circle or hiding him from friends. He belongs to the family and will always remain so.

MOON IN CAPRICORN

In this position, the moon struggles to sustain the good-citizen image which Capricorns love and it often presents problems because the Moon in Capricorn wants to show its more wayward side and is hemmed in by tradition and existing cultural mores. Children born to a Moon in Capricorn parent are always encouraged to "better themselves," and education starts very early in life. The harder the child works, the more his parents like him; but it can be hard for a child who is not astrologically suited to the pressure of getting ahead. Something has to give, and generally the child gets away from home, leaving a lonely spot in parents who may forgive shortcomings with difficulty but can never wholeheartedly forget.

MOON IN AQUARIUS

A child born to a Moon in Aquarius parent is in for some conflict from the moment of his birth. The parent wants to guide him, but also insists that he become independent at an early age. This is something which is not easy to regulate. Some children may be born independent by nature, others need much more guidance, and the trouble is that Aquarians are not good at timing. The result is that they muddle along in a constant state of surprise at the problems their children create, and they are not adept at helping them find solutions. But what they lose in well-timed guidance they make up for in providing companionship to their children which continues long after the child has reached adolescence; it is then the child begins to appreciate the spontaneous qualities of his parent. Parents with the Moon in Aquarius always try to fulfill their responsibilities.

MOON IN PISCES

Once the children are on their feet, the Moon in Pisces parent is inclined to lean on them. This goes on well into the adult life of the son or daughter. They love family consultations and try to involve even their young children in discussions. Sometimes there is a tendency to make the child appear too knowing and adult for his years but with his vast capacity for love, the Moon in Pisces parent can achieve wonders and when called up in an emergency will always be there. They thrive on memories complete with baby photos and memorabilia of the days when they, too, were young. They are always concerned with the spiritual welfare of the child as much as they are in giving physical help.

CHAPTER IX

The Practical Moon—
Guide Your Day the Lunar Way

The daily position of the moon can have a great impact on your life in some unexpected areas. Taking daily notice of the moon's position can make your day a good deal more productive and pleasant.

HOUSEKEEPING

Housekeeping is no longer the perogative of the female as more and more bachelors cope with such work and modern marriages are almost contracts for sharing domestic work. All those nasty janitorial activities which go into maintaining a home will work best when the moon is in a specific sign. Use the good transits, knowing you can tackle the work with more ease, and declare an unofficial holiday when Lady Luna becomes a tyrant. Working in harmony with the moon can be a project for the entire family. An ephemeris giving the daily position of the moon is a great present to give to yourself, but make sure everyone else in the family sees it. Put it in a prominent position, such as the kitchen or bathroom. Once you have the knack of moonbeam housekeeping, you will find you expend less energy on tedious chores and have more time for leisure.

MOON IN ARIES

You will be ready to get into action for just about anything connected with the house. You can tackle several jobs at once, and have enough energy to cope with what seems to be chaos. Declare certain areas of the house as disaster areas and off-limits to anyone likely to get in your way as you work. It is a time when your enthusiasm will be catching, so accept the best offers for cooperation. Rapidly changing from one active job to another will get your adrenaline running, and at the end of the day you will feel very satisfied. The danger is that you will not know when to stop, so remember that the transit of the moon in each sign is only a little over two days. Create the chaos which may involve moving furniture around, getting a room ready for decorating, and cleaning out all the closets—but do it on the first day of transit. Mopping-up operations have to be done the next day and should enter a state of détente by the end of the second day. The last few hours of the transit can be used to put the finishing touches on your work. Then collapse after taking a bow and a round of applause for all you have achieved.

MOON IN TAURUS

Getting into top gear for household work is not possible, but if you realize you are capable of working only in low gear, you can still get through by determined plodding aided by some preplanning. Just getting started during this transit of the moon is half the battle—procrastinate, and the pile of dishes and washing will get larger. This is not a time to consider a major domestic project, so choose some routine chore that is begging for attention. If you watch television and feel tempted to try that wonder cleanser which seems to have magical qualities, this is no time to try it; stick with the old Brand X that you know. This is not a good time for purchases, as the household budget is not likely to be robust during this transit. The Spaniards have a very good word which really expresses how you feel about getting to grips with work—*mañana*. Energy and willpower will catch up with you tomorrow or the next day.

MOON IN GEMINI

This transit of the moon makes you ultraconscious of the untidiness of others. In fact, you will be so busy organizing the family that you will forget that setting a good example is also necessary. Take the plunge and see that your own personal possessions are not scattered all around the house because no one else is likely to want to follow you around. You may have to cajole, bribe, or yell to get the family into action, but whatever approach you use will bring results. Tidying up papers in your desk will remind you that you really should answer letters and pay bills. Do this—it will make you look busy while actually getting rid of a chore.

MOON IN CANCER

When the moon is transiting in its own sign, this is the time to stay at home, enjoy your surroundings, and think of how you can improve them. You won't even want to leave the house for a trip to the supermarket, so have meals planned around what you have already stored away in the freezer. Cast your eyes around and even if the silver is not a family heirloom, it will look more valuable if you use this time for cleaning. Brighten the house by cleaning the windows, framed pictures, and china and crystal that have been stored away. Put your feet up in the morning after breakfast, read the paper, and reminisce about the latest snapshots in the family photograph album. As the moon moves into the last part of its transit, you may feel like having a party so that others can enjoy your home. If you come out with the old cliché that it is so much nicer to entertain friends at home rather than take them out to dinner, you will really mean it and know it is true.

MOON IN LEO

You will feel manic and inclined to show off, but how do you relate this to tackling housework? Rearrange things, use the best china, prepare gourmet meals, and don't sit down to any meal feeling like a slob. It's a good time to go through clothes, give away anything not up to your ideas of grandeur, and then find that you have really tidied out the closets; now you have room for other clothes or shoes you have been thinking of buying. The Moon in Leo makes you feel generous, so it will not be so painful to part with things. You will have enough self-confidence to know you can replace everything in due time, provided that you do not receive unexpected bills.

MOON IN VIRGO

This is a time to get lots of work done; your energy level is high enough to get through some marathon tasks without feeling as if you have been put through a chopping machine. Heavy work tackled now will convince you that there is something of a superman or superwoman instinct in it. Since the Moon in Virgo accents the critical nature as well as instincts for ultracleanliness, tackle the bathrooms and medicine cupboards. Throw out all outdated stock without worrying about how much they cost. Last year's antibiotics are not going to cope with this years' viruses. While you can be critical about the state of your house, try to keep from criticizing members of the family. Get them involved in helping, but keep supervision on a pleasant level so that the extra work is fun as well as practical.

MOON IN LIBRA

It is never difficult for you to take pride in beautifying your surroundings, but it is not easy for you to make earthshaking decisions at this time. Don't overtax yourself by worrying whether you should change the drapes or rehang the pictures in the bedroom. Do the minimum of work so that you have plenty of time for relaxation and, while sitting in a comfortable chair, you can let your imagination run riot about those disturbing drapes and pictures. If you cannot stand them any longer, get a member of your family to help while you supervise operations from your favorite chair. If you cannot stand the sight of someone else working, invent a reason for taking a trip out even if it is only to window-shop, but resist the temptation to buy things you will not need immediately.

MOON IN SCORPIO

No matter how large your living quarters may be, you still feel as if you are living in a telephone booth. Cast your eyes around and move things around. It is not so much a case of tidying as getting large furniture into a position where there is enough room for it. You have plenty of energy to put up extra shelves, getting things on the wall will help the floor space. Potted plants which normally clutter up side tables often look more attractive when hung from wall brackets or the ceiling. The moon in this transit makes you feel creative, so sewing can be both practical and relaxing. Throw away those old magazines which have accumulated into mountains; tidy up the bookshelves and get the goods in the freezer systematically arranged and check for depleted stock. Start any heavy work in the morning rather than afternoon because anything you start and finish in one day will be more successful and satisfying. Getting up the next day to finish off a job somehow quells the intense interest you felt when you started.

MOON IN SAGITTARIUS

You may not get the local award for the parent of the year or the best housekeeper, but in this two-and-a-quarter-day transit, you feel that someone should appreciate and recognize your talent for homemaking. Do some crafty chores to draw attention to yourself. Junior wanted some new cushions for his room? Right—he has them even if you have to make them yourself. Keep up doing the extra things and someone is sure to notice. Working a lot harder than usual, you can still get through the day with enough energy to spare for an evening out, going to Little League with one of the children, or a visit to the bowling alley. Try to remember to exchange the library books because when this transit is over you are going to want to collapse on Junior's new cushions, curl up with a book, and yell for someone to bring you a coffee. Was the whirlwind worthwhile? Definitely yes, because you thrive well on contrasts. Making the cushions was a good feeling, and those who make them should definitely be allowed to lie on them.

MOON IN CAPRICORN

Efficiency is the keynote for your activities when the moon is in Capricorn, the opposite sign to its normal bailiwick of Cancer. During the Capricorn transit you will look for ways to make improvement. Feel you are spending too much time in the kitchen preparing foods? Then think of ways to streamline the preparation; there are lots of things which can be prepared for meals several days ahead. Next to the invention of the washer and dryer, the inventor of refrigeration should receive a few hallelujahs. Besides, conservation appeals to your nature. With plenty of physical energy, you also have more than enough mental energy to spare for critizing just about everything in your home—and that includes the people living in it. If you live on your own, the criticism will turn inward on yourself but—for goodness' sake—please let the criticism be constructive. The mental energy will also turn to doing some serious thinking about how to stretch the dollar.

MOON IN AQUARIUS

No matter how pleasant your home life is or how much you love the house and people in it, this transit of the moon breeds ideas that you are in a tender trap and, in the interests of survival, you have a desire to get away for as many hours as possible. Try and make it possible because if you have to stay at home with this brain fever steaming up inside you, any housework you do will be done like a zombie. If you stay home, you will do the routine jobs like a robot. Break the tense atmosphere with music while you work, or deliberately contrive coffee breaks beyond the normal times. Cheat a bit and stretch those coffee breaks. Everything is much easier on your nerves if indeed you can slip out into the bustling world for a few hours each day—a lunch date can work wonders and is worth the expense because you will come home more able to face housework. The Aquarian moon makes you loquacious, and if there is no one to talk to, then talk to yourself—but don't expect too many sensible answers!

MOON IN PISCES

Pulling yourself together from pleasant daydreams may be necessary because daydreams do not get the regular chores done. Buying magic wands to wave over a pile of dishes or loads of laundry no longer seems to work. Compromise. Give yourself half the day for dreaming, but get the basics out of the way before you dive into whatever dream suits your mood. Since you are a water sign and the moon influences all liquid, bring the laundry up to date and see that the kitchen is basically tidy. Then get on with your daydreaming because if you push yourself to keep in the world of reality, you will end up stuffing things in drawers just to get rid of them. If this happens, once the moon has gone through this transit, you will spend the rest of the month doing major detective work tracking things down. If you have any creative ability, this is a time to play around with ideas to put into action in the future. Most of all, keep cheerful when you are with other members of the family despite the feeling that you are floating on Cloud Nine. Let yourself slide down easily and gently to earth as the moon in Pisces transit runs out. Crashing the barrier between daydreams and reality can shock the psyche.

*　　*　　*

Moonbeam housekeeping is likely to grow in popularity. For those who normally enjoy housekeeping without feeling they have to go the route of the "Total Man" or "Total Woman," understanding the transits of the moon and their influence on the approach to routine household jobs can explain why even the "Total" person has days when she or he casts a malicious look at work. No one is that perfect. For those who enjoy goofing off, it is an ideal escape route, since a period of what seems like laziness can be explained as merely the fault of the wayward moon.

> The innocent moon, which nothing does but shine
> Moves all the laboring surges of the world.
>
> —Francis Thompson, "Sister Songs"

MOON MAGIC IN THE KITCHEN

As we've discovered, of all the celestial bodies, none has more influence on domestic life than the moon. It has moments when it helps romances, flirts with sexual activities and, if these are not enough, lurks over the kitchen. All you have to do is tune into your moon calendar and use the good vibes to get the best results from your culinary efforts. Poetry inspired by the moon is all very well, but as many love affairs have flourished through the influence of the moon in the kitchen as by providing moonstruck sonnets.

Away with the idea that "the way to a man's heart is through his stomach"—moon magic in the kitchen is effective for both sexes, and it is now no secret that women visit men who promise to cook a meal for them, a prelude to memorable seduction scenes. Cooking can be a means of uniting a family who say "ooh" and "aah" as astrological moon magic produces an essentially different meal in tune with the position of the moon. As the moon moves from sign to sign every two and a quarter days, each movement releases different kinds of energies and influences. Catch the moonbeams and get the best out of cooking. Knowing where the moon is can take the pain out of catering for a large party; and when all you want is to grab a snack and sit down to ease your aching feet, then you can blame the moon. In short, knowing how to use astrological moon magic in the kitchen can help you physically and mentally so that you can enjoy cooking without its being a chore.

MOON IN ARIES

Be prepared for some blunt member of the family suggesting to you that he has had enough of some old favorite which has made encore appearances for too long. With the moon in this position, you will not be hurt or uptight that anyone dares to criticize the meat loaf you prepared for three days in a row, relying on a succession of vegetables to augment it. Discard the idea of the old family favorite and go all out for a new project. Be daring—scatter spices around, and if the Indian curry does not look quite like the one you once had in a genuine Indian restaurant, you can be sure no one else will complain about it. Throwing a seemingly spontaneous party will be easy when the moon is in Aries, but aim at numerous quick-to-prepare dishes in which you use your imagination.

MOON IN TAURUS

If you are wise, this transit of the moon will encourage you to pace yourself, planning meals for two days and thus allowing time to get on with other work in the kitchen. According to the season, you might like to can some vegetables or fruits or even stock up the deep freeze. It is not a good time to try new dishes—you will not feel like being creative, but sometimes there is pressure from other members of the family bringing friends home and hoping to impress them with Mom's or Dad's prowess as a cook. Stick to well-tried traditional dishes and save your temper from getting out of hand by tactfully suggesting that many hands make light work in the kitchen.

MOON IN GEMINI

It's delicious snack time, and the tendency will be to skimp on regular meals, substituting things like canapés or unusual open-top sandwiches. It will be hard to resist the temptation to send out to the local deli for carry-out food and if it is convenient and relaxes you, then it can't do any harm. After all, the transit is only for a little more than two days; and no one is going to starve in that time. If you have studied your moon calendar and noted this transit, it is not a bad idea to have a few easy dishes in the freezer and bring them out as required. It is generally cheaper than bringing home carry-out dishes. This is not a transit when you want to feel that you are chained to the kitchen stove.

MOON IN CANCER

If you have an old family recipe, this is the time to parade it and then sit back waiting for the applause, and then surprise everyone with coming up with an encore. Take a bow when people tell you this or that dish is just as good as when Grandma or Auntie Flo made it. You are not likely to make any mistakes during this transit if you keep to recipes you know well. It is also a good time to trade recipes with smug satisfaction, knowing that your neighbor will never quite achieve the perfection you have managed. After all, years of experience have taught you a thing or two about that old recipe, and you know intuitively the right amount of spice or herb to give any dish a masterly touch.

MOON IN LEO

This is gourmet time for you, with a chance to become a raconteur at the table, telling everyone about the first time you ate this spicy dish; you can bet it will conjure up a few romantic memories. Go foreign at this period of the moon's transit; think back to vacations when a few dishes really seemed to round off a perfect day. When you re-create them you will be doing more than cooking, you will be creating and sharing a mood. Remember one thing, though: this transit comes around frequently. Try not to tell the same story the next time around, otherwise the good food may be ruined by boredom. Do not forget the right wine for the special dish; that can be another conversation piece.

MOON IN VIRGO

Health will be on your mind, and this inevitably leads to discontent with run-of-the-mill food. Wary of trying to prepare health-food meals if you have guests; it is just about the time when unexpected company is likely to surprise you. Compromise with a pure health-food dish and one jazzed up a bit to make it super-palatable. You have plenty of energy at this time which can be as well used in the kitchen as anywhere else, so be ingenious in your preparation for meals and do not get stuck on soybean soup or bran muffins. You can do much better. Health-food cookbooks are a great help, but a dash of imagination will improve most of the basic recipes. Take courage in one hand, but be sure to have a goodly bunch of herbs in the other. It will be quite easy to give an extra touch of interest by setting the table with special care.

MOON IN LIBRA

You do not need to read any book on etiquette or how to be the gracious hostess or host since charm comes naturally to you at this time. You may not want to impress on people that you are the super cook of the world, but you can serve even simple dishes at this time and if you have guests they will go away thinking they have had a memorable meal. Don't reserve the charm for guests—use it in the family circle as well. Try to balance meals so that everyone has a chance to enjoy his special favorite with plenty to spare for a second helping. Try to think in terms of more people than you actually have in the house, for there will be a tendency to underestimate other people's appetites.

MOON IN SCORPIO

Time to use up all the leftovers, but you need not produce spartan meals if you have kept the herb and spice rack stocked up. The family may remark they have never tasted anything so good before, and they probably never will until the next Scorpio transit of the moon. Somehow it brings out a secret urge to be creative and penny-pinch at the same time, and that is quite an achievement for you. The feeling will not last, but make the best of it while you can. Try to have some energy left over to create a dessert from scratch rather than pile on the ice cream and topping. Or if your taste does not run to desserts, go for a hearty soup. If you have any skill in breadmaking, now is the time to do it. If you have never tried it before, go into action and bake a practice loaf or some rolls. Great with that homemade soup—and a change from crackers.

MOON IN SAGITTARIUS

It is strike time for you as far as the kitchen is concerned. Down with the tools, away with the pots and pans, and out with the instant foods. You can cheat a little if you know when to expect this transit. Prepare something in advance, but the main thing is to feel that you can have a couple of days with the minimum amount of kitchen work. Family and guests will learn the meaning of pot luck, but you will sure enjoy the rest. When the transit is over, a few guilt feelings will be the spur to make you outdo yourself, and the family will heave a sigh of relief. The best way to get through this period is to eat out if finances permit. If they do, you have it made—and the kitchen will always be there when the transit has passed.

MOON IN CAPRICORN

Guard against letting your moodiness affect your cooking. Even simple dishes can get fouled up, and this will only add to your blue mood. If it is practical at all, get someone skillfully maneuvered into the kitchen and let him take over the menus. It is even likely to cheer you up when you are eating to think, albeit a bit sourly, that you might have done better yourself but, after all, it is only likely to be a few meals. To offset this bit of cloudiness in your thinking, which affects your palate, think how clever you were to have conned someone else into the kitchen. Be sure to find something to keep you busy after a meal in case you get corralled into cleaning up. Plan your escape routes with diplomacy.

MOON IN AQUARIUS

Crazy recipe time in the kitchen and if you have someone who will help you create a few mad dishes, you will enjoy it all the more. Green bread may not be your usual favorite, but it fits into the moon madness that creeps into the kitchen. The difficulty will be not to mix your drinks if you go out, or for that matter if you stay at home. Start the day with a good breakfast and it will give you strength to whiz through kitchen gadgets you have always meant to try. Since the moon madness is a passing phase, resist the temptation to prepare too much food for any one meal. Nothing can be more horrible than green bread two days later, and it can even be a shock to your own system as you wonder why you ever got involved with anything so silly.

MOON IN PISCES

Take a bit of this, a dash of that, and a pinch of something else, and whether it is a rare omelet or a soufflé, you will have created something in tune to your mood which is likely to be flippant and longing for variety. This is a good time to ask lots of friends to come around with a covered dish to contribute to the menu; you can have fun exchanging recipes. Go easy with any dishes needing to be cooked in wine, and prepare only enough to eat in a single meal. Leftovers will depress you because your whimsical mood lasts only as long as the two-day transit. Then it is back to the sensible meals and probably time to start a diet.

It is a good idea to hang an astrological calendar in your kitchen so that you can catch the phases of the moon and its transits. The unique feelings these transits evoke as far as kitchen work and cooking are concerned can throw you off your balance if they creep up on you and take you by surprise. If you have a family, they will also be prepared for the variations on the cooking theme which occur during these transits. It is only fair to let them have a chance to make their own arrangements if they feel a particular phase of the moon is too much to cope with. The influence of the moon brings variety, emotion, and many moods into our lives, and we are not exempt from them even in ordinary kitchen work. Use the transits to advantage and you will have more fun in the family circle and quite a bit of harmonious exhilaration.

CHAPTER X

Full Moon, Barometer of Emotions

Emotion is the chief source of all becoming-conscious. There can be no transforming of light and of apathy into movement without emotion.

—Carl Jung, *Psychological Aspects of the Modern Archetype*

Astrologers have always associated the moon with emotion, and poets have been quick to express many of the characteristics of this luminary in their verse. Dreamy, ephemeral, wayward, inconstant, and mystical are only a few of the adjectives used. Beyond these romantic characteristics is a full quiver of moonbeams which strike right into the heart of less likable emotions such as irrational behavior, the mesmeric quality to influence masses, and the changes of mood which turn a seemingly placid person into one beset by any number of mental abberations or character disorders.

The word "lunacy" is derived from the root word "luna" (the moon); for centuries man has associated the vagaries of luna with lunacy—not always meaning idiocy but a time of agitation. We find this agitation in love as much as in hate, two extremes of emotion. In the course of a year, the moon becomes full in each of the twelve signs of the zodiac. At this time, the moon is always in opposition to the position of the sun. This opposition of the two luminaries accounts for the waywardness of emotions and moods which occur at the time of the full moon. It brings about a higher incident of violence, lunacy in its many forms, and exaggerated emotions.

When the sun is in a fire sign, the moon is full in an air sign:

Sun in Aries brings a full moon in Libra.
Sun in Leo gives a full moon in Aquarius.
Sun in Sagittarius gives a full moon in Gemini.

These are the times when the full moon exerts its weakest influence because the sun, as the life giver, is strong in the fire signs of the zodiac and the influence of the moon is undetermined. The full moon in August is the harvest moon, a time for celebration and rejoicing; emotions are strong, of a happy, carefree nature. The emotion of happiness is at a higher octave than when the full moon is in Libra and the sun in Aries. It is equally as debilitated when the full moon is in Gemini and the sun in Sagittarius, although this can be the time when creative people feel a rush of inspiration.

The reverse happens when the full moon is in a fire sign and the sun in an airy one. The full moon in Aries happens when the sun is in Libra, and the full moon in Leo occurs when the sun is in Aquarius. The third full moon in a fire sign happens in Sagittarius when the sun is in Gemini. At these times, anger is the dominant emotion; relationships become difficult because the full moon in a fire sign creates fiery explosions of emotion. When the full moon is in Aries, the quarreling is generally restricted to two people and can be bad for marital relationships. At the time of a full moon in Leo, electrical appliances are more apt to break down and

170

cause irritation because of the inconvenience and temper because of the expense and necessity of getting them fixed. When the full moon occurs in Sagittarius, well-made plans go astray, time is wasted, people sulk, thump the table in anger, hurt others, and end up feeling paranoid. The full moon has its greatest impact on these violent emotions when the moon is just on the horizon after sunset. It is not a good time to plan a cocktail party.

The full moon is in an earth sign when the sun is in a watery sign. The sun in Cancer has a full moon in Capricorn, the sun in Pisces has the Virgo full moon, and the sun in Scorpio has its full moon in Taurus. These are the times when emotions are strong but positive. They are times when actions taken in a positive manner can yield good results because the earth signs stabilize the wayward and erratic influences of the full moon. The sun in its position in the watery signs is less harsh and demanding. Unusual health patterns occur with the full moon in Virgo, and business matters will be demanding. Guard possessions against loss when the full moon is in Taurus; many of these losses are due to personal carelessness. It is a time to check the insurance and double-check that doors are locked. On a more emotional level, it is also a time when your heart should not be worn on your sleeve.

The most depressing full moons are those that occur when the sun is in an earth sign and the full moon in the watery ones. The full moon in Cancer occurs when the sun is in Capricorn, in Pisces when the sun is in Virgo, and in Scorpio when the sun is in Taurus. Since a full moon occurring in Cancer has a double impact because it is in its own sign, emotions are doubly depressing during this period. In fact, it is a time when a person should be prepared for the advent of the full moon and deliberately struggle against depression. If you are given to apathy and self-pity, try to keep occupied or arrange for an extra flurry of companionship. The full moon in Cancer can be very depressing to those who live alone or feel the world has treated them badly. Know the symptoms and take precautions against the worst influences. This is not always easy unless one can approach the full moon with determination to beat the worst effects by doing something different and, most important of all, by seeking companionship.

A full moon in Pisces creates some very dramatic feelings, often associated with self-destruction. The suicide rate is higher at this time than at any other period, but fortunately every person feeling self-destructive does not commit suicide. This is a period of self-hate which is destructive to the psyche and a lack of appreciation for the quality of life. Keeping busy is one way to combat this depression, but I realize it is not as easy as it seems. When the full moon is in Pisces, anyone working in black magic seems to be particularly powerful because all the emotional energy goes into a single act of destruction whether it is by sticking pins in dolls or casting an evil eye on a neighbor.

The full moon in Scorpio seems to be the catalyst to homicide, and again statistics support this. While not everyone will want to go out and commit murder, it definitely gives rise to feelings of revenge and recklessness. A person highly affected by the full moon in Scorpio in a particular cycle of planetary aspects could find himself involved in vengefulness such as destroying material things. This is a time when riots and looting are most likely to happen. When the moon is in a water sign, it is at its most dramatic and powerful. A full moon in Pisces brings about health problems; in all the water signs there is always an intense emotion which can cloud logic and reason.

About one-third of the people born in the world have a full moon in their natal chart. You can easily determine this if you have your own natal chart set up. If the moon in your chart is directly opposite the natal sun, then the moon was full, or nearly full, at the time of birth. This can have a profound effect on the personality, bringing into play a higher degree of sensitivity; you are likely to be the victim of your own highly inflammable emotions. Everyone born at the time of the full moon reacts to each full moon very intensely, especially when it comes into your own sign again. It is particularly hard on women who tend to have trouble in childbirth and a tendency to miscarriages. According to Dr. Eugene Jonas of the Astra Research Center for Planned Parenthood in Nitra, Czechoslovakia, women born during a sun-moon opposition have a higher incident of miscarriage than others if they are pregnant when this aspect reoccurs.

In the synthesis comparison of horoscopes, people tend to be attracted to those who have their natal sun in opposition to the other person's natal moon. Richard Burton and Elizabeth Taylor have a variation on this theme which accounts for their on-off romantic relationship. They seem as if they cannot live together for very long, but then they cannot bear to be parted. Burton has his sun in Scorpio and moon in Virgo, while Elizabeth has her sun in Pisces, reacting to Burton's moon in the opposing sign of Virgo, but she also has her moon in Scorpio. There must never be a day in their lives when high emotions and resultant tension do not build up. Burton, with his outward weaknesses, is actually a very strong force capable of influencing Elizabeth who, with the sun and moon both in water signs, is ultrasensitive. The moon in Virgo in Burton's horoscope brings a toughness into his makeup and, while the sun in Scorpio adds to his drinking problem, he always knows what he is doing.

The moon is the celestial body which is concerned with the shaping of human relationships for better or for worse, according to the sign and house it is associated with. Although all emotions and moods are intensified at the time of the full moon, the drama may not last long, although circumstances and motivation before and after the full moon will always play their part. The secret of coping with the explosive impact of the full moon is to be ready for it and take a positive attitude in trying to combat its worst influences. The full moon, in some of the signs of the zodiac, can be as destructive as the atom bomb, or it can be no more than a Chinese firecracker being set off at a party. Within yourself you have the means of controlling at least some of the action. You can sail into the full moon period and let it toss you around like a piece of seaweed in the ocean or you can build a dam of reason to hold back the emotional tides. We can never completely master the influence of the moon because emotion is one of the most exciting influences on mankind. What we can do is to develop a philosophy for living that enables us to weather the ebb and flow and gradually eliminate the more negative qualities.

GUIDE TO THE FULL MOON
IN THE ZODIACAL SIGNS

FULL MOON IN ARIES

Watch your temper and do not let your naturally aggressive nature run riot or go about looking for trouble.

FULL MOON IN TAURUS

Take more than normal care in looking after your possessions. This is especially important when traveling or leaving your home for a vacation at this time.

FULL MOON IN GEMINI

Try to have a realistic approach to everything whether you are in love or just having a good time. You can overdo the "hail-and-well-met" type of living; there is a tendency to become manic.

FULL MOON IN CANCER

Avoid depression and self-pity by deliberately seeking out friends, even if it is only to have a shoulder to cry on. If possible, listen to their advice and, more important still, take the advice if you have reason to respect your friends' wisdom.

FULL MOON IN LEO

Not a time to be adventurous in trying out new electrical appliances or even buying them. See that your list of service people is up to date with phone numbers; do not get upset if they cannot come at once.

FULL MOON IN VIRGO

A good time to have a physical checkup. Go with the positive feeling that it is better to be reassured you are in good condition than to neglect symptoms and allow them to get worse.

FULL MOON IN LIBRA

If you have to make life-and-death decisions, this is no time to do it. You find it easy enough to procrastinate; this is the time to put off decision making until a more propitious time.

FULL MOON IN SCORPIO

If you really cannot resist hating someone, don't go out and buy a gun or resort to black magic. Both have a habit of backfiring on you, so why take the risk? Think before you act, and try to put vengeful feelings at the back of your mind, even though you may smolder a bit. Keep busy, in a creative—not destructive—manner.

FULL MOON IN SAGITTARIUS

Be philosophic enough to know that if your seemingly well-made plans have gone astray, you have enough energy to adapt to existing circumstances. Use the time for second thoughts about your venture; they will produce new motivations.

FULL MOON IN CAPRICORN

Study you budget or, if you are in the big-time money business, this is a great time to appraise your stock portfolio or consider real estate potentials.

FULL MOON IN AQUARIUS

You do not need a party to raise your spirits, but it is a good time to celebrate because you feel happy and want your friends to share in it.

FULL MOON IN PISCES

Keep away from anything likely to add to your depression. If you go to a movie, play, or merely watch a television show, steer clear of those with highly emotional contents. You will not cheer yourself up by taking an extra drink; the way to quell those depressed feelings is generally through seeking the companionship of younger people.

CHAPTER XI

The Ephemeris

The ephemeris is nothing more than a specialized calendar issued by the Naval Service. Not only are the months and days delineated, but the position of each planet is noted for each day of the year. The sale of ephemerides has increased in the last ten years until they are best sellers (although they never make *The New York Times* list of best-selling books). The escalating interest in astrology as a serious and personal subject accounts for the increased sales and they will continue to climb as more people become moon-conscious and refuse to settle for the more usual sun-sign astrology.

Many libraries stock ephemerides, which are very reasonably priced, if you do not want to buy one for the year of your birth. Although most people buy them only for the year of their own birth, it is possible to get ephemerides which cover tcn- and fifteen-year periods, although these are more expensive. It is no more complicated to find the position of your moon at birth than looking through any other calendar, and it will provide a special insight to the emotions. Consulting an ephemeris, finding the moon position and studying its characteristics, enables many people to steer clear of the psychiatrist's couch. Understanding your own motivations and what makes you tick will ultimately enable you to understand other people. Once you begin to study moon signs, you are less likely to be deceived by other appearances, which are what sun-sign astrology presents. To determine your moon position from the simplified ephemeris that follows, turn to the year of your birth. This ephemeris gives only the odd-numbered days of the year. If your birthday falls on an even day, remember that each sign of the zodiac has thirty degrees and that the moon moves at a rate of one degree for every two hours that elapse, or twelve degrees in each day. If your birthday is January 7, 1940, your moon was at approximately fifteen degrees Sagittarius (15 in the ephemeris). If your birthday is January 8, 1940, you should read the sections on both Sagittarius and Capricorn. You'll be able to determine very easily which one is your moon sign. Because the moon is such a fast-moving body, it is hard to estimate exactly where it was at the moment of your birth. A professional astrologer will have to do your chart to determine your precise moon placement.

♈ = Aries	♎ = Libra
♉ = Taurus	♏ = Scorpio
♊ = Gemini	♐ = Sagittarius
♋ = Cancer	♑ = Capricorn
♌ = Leo	♒ = Aquarius
♍ = Virgo	♓ = Pisces

1900	Jan.	Feb.	Mar.	April	May	June	July	Aug.	Sep.	Oct.	Nov.	Dec.
1	2	25	3	27	4	22	25	9	23	27	16	25
3	2	25	4	26	1	17	19	2	18	23	15	24
5	1	24	3	23	26	11	12	27	14	21	15	23
7	0	22	1	18	21	4	7	23	13	21	15	22
9	28	18	27	12	15	29	2	20	13	22	14	19
11	25	12	22	6	8	24	28	19	13	20	12	15
13	21	7	16	0	3	20	26	19	11	16	8	10
15	15	1	9	24	28	17	25	17	7	11	2	4
17	10	24	3	19	24	15	24	14	2	6	26	28
19	4	18	27	14	21	13	23	10	27	29	20	22
21	27	12	22	10	18	12	21	5	20	23	14	17
23	21	8	17	7	17	10	17	0	14	17	8	13
25	16	4	14	6	15	7	13	23	8	11	4	10
27	12	4	12	6	14	4	8	17	2	6	0	8
29	10	3	11	5	12	0	3	11		3	7	6
31	10		12		9		27					4

1901	Jan.	Feb.	Mar.	April	May	June	July	Aug.	Sep.	Oct.	Nov.	Dec.
1	♉ 18	♋ 10	♋ 20	♍ 7	♎ 10	♏ 24	♐ 27	♒ 15	♈ 7	♉ 16	♋ 9	♌ 15
3	♊ 16	♌ 6	♌ 15	♎ 1	♏ 4	♐ 18	♑ 23	♓ 13	♈ 6	♊ 15	♌ 6	♍ 11
5	♋ 14	♍ 1	♍ 10	♏ 25	♏ 27	♑ 13	♒ 19	♈ 11	♉ 4	♋ 13	♍ 2	♎ 6
7	♌ 10	♍ 26	♎ 4	♏ 18	♐ 21	♑ 9	♒ 16	♉ 9	♊ 2	♌ 9	♍ 27	♏ 0
9	♍ 6	♎ 20	♎ 28	♐ 12	♑ 16	♒ 6	♓ 14	♊ 8	♋ 29	♍ 5	♎ 21	♏ 23
11	♎ 0	♏ 13	♏ 22	♑ 7	♒ 12	♓ 4	♈ 13	♋ 5	♌ 25	♎ 24	♏ 15	♐ 17
13	♏ 24	♐ 7	♐ 16	♒ 7	♓ 9	♈ 2	♉ 10	♌ 3	♍ 21	♏ 18	♐ 8	♑ 11
15	♐ 17	♐ 3	♑ 11	♓ 30	♈ 8	♉ 1	♊ 7	♍ 29	♎ 15	♐ 11	♑ 26	♒ 6
17	♑ 12	♑ 0	♒ 7	♈ 29	♉ 7	♊ 29	♋ 4	♎ 25	♏ 9	♑ 5	♒ 22	♓ 2
19	♒ 8	♒ 28	♓ 6	♉ 0	♊ 5	♋ 26	♌ 29	♏ 19	♐ 3	♒ 0	♓ 19	♈ 28
21	♓ 5	♓ 28	♈ 6	♉ 0	♋ 5	♌ 21	♍ 23	♐ 13	♑ 27	♓ 26	♈ 17	♉ 26
23	♈ 4	♈ 27	♉ 6	♊ 29	♌ 0	♍ 15	♎ 17	♑ 7	♒ 22	♈ 24	♉ 17	♊ 25
25	♉ 3	♉ 26	♊ 6	♋ 26	♍ 25	♎ 9	♏ 11	♒ 1	♓ 18	♉ 24	♊ 17	♋ 25
27	♊ 1	♊ 23	♋ 3	♌ 22	♍ 19	♏ 3	♐ 6	♓ 27	♈ 16	♊ 24	♊ 17	♌ 23
29	♋ 29		♌ 29	♍ 16	♎ 12	♐ 3	♑ 2	♈ 24	♉ 16	♋ 24		♍ 20
31	♌ 26		♍ 25					♉ 22				

1902	Jan.	Feb.	Mar.	April	May	June	July	Aug.	Sep.	Oct.	Nov.	Dec.
1	2	16	24	7	10	28	5	28	22	28	15	18
3	26	10	18	2	6	26	4	28	20	24	9	12
5	20	4	12	28	3	25	4	27	16	19	3	5
7	14	29	7	25	2	26	4	25	11	13	27	29
9	8	25	3	24	2	26	3	21	5	7	21	25
11	3	22	29	28	1	24	0	15	1	1	16	21
13	29	19	28	23	29	21	25	9	5	26	13	20
15	25	17	26	21	24	16	19	3	23	22	12	20
17	22	15	24	18	19	10	13	27	18	19	12	20
19	19	14	22	15	13	4	6	22	14	18	12	18
21	19	12	18	10	7	28	1	18	11	17	11	14
23	17	9	13	4	1	22	26	15	8	16	8	9
25	14	5	8	28	25	16	21	12	7	14	4	3
27	10	0	2	22	19	11	18	10	5	7	29	27
29	4		25	16	15	7	15	9	3	3	24	20
31							14	7	1			

1903	Jan.	Feb.	Mar.	April	May	June	July	Aug.	Sep.	Oct.	Nov.	Dec.
1	♒ 2	♓ 18	♓ 27	♉ 17	♊ 25	♌ 19	♍ 27	♏ 16	♐ 1	♒ 3	♈ 17	♈ 20
3	♒ 26	♈ 13	♓ 23	♊ 15	♊ 24	♍ 17	♎ 23	♐ 11	♑ 25	♒ 27	♓ 12	♉ 17
5	♓ 21	♈ 10	♈ 20	♊ 13	♋ 24	♎ 14	♏ 19	♐ 5	♒ 19	♓ 22	♈ 9	♊ 15
7	♈ 17	♉ 7	♉ 18	♋ 11	♍ 20	♎ 9	♏ 13	♑ 28	♒ 13	♈ 17	♉ 6	♋ 14
9	♉ 14	♉ 7	♉ 16	♌ 10	♍ 17	♏ 4	♐ 8	♒ 22	♓ 8	♉ 13	♉ 4	♌ 13
11	♉ 13	♊ 6	♊ 16	♌ 7	♎ 13	♏ 4	♐ 1	♒ 16	♈ 3	♊ 10	♊ 3	♍ 12
13	♊ 13	♋ 5	♋ 15	♍ 4	♏ 8	♐ 29	♑ 25	♓ 11	♈ 29	♋ 8	♋ 1	♎ 9
15	♋ 14	♌ 1	♌ 12	♎ 0	♏ 2	♐ 23	♒ 19	♈ 6	♉ 27	♌ 6	♍ 29	♏ 6
17	♌ 13	♍ 26	♍ 9	♏ 24	♐ 26	♑ 16	♒ 14	♈ 3	♉ 25	♍ 5	♎ 26	♐ 2
19	♍ 10	♎ 20	♎ 4	♐ 18	♐ 20	♒ 10	♓ 10	♉ 1	♊ 24	♎ 3	♏ 23	♑ 27
21	♎ 6	♏ 14	♏ 28	♐ 12	♑ 14	♒ 5	♈ 7	♉ 1	♋ 23	♏ 28	♐ 19	♒ 22
23	♏ 0	♐ 8	♐ 22	♑ 6	♒ 10	♓ 29	♈ 8	♊ 1	♋ 20	♐ 23	♑ 13	♓ 15
25	♐ 24	♑ 2	♑ 16	♒ 2	♓ 7	♈ 29	♉ 8	♋ 28	♌ 15	♑ 18	♒ 7	♓ 9
27	♑ 17		♒ 11	♓ 28	♈ 5	♈ 29	♉ 6	♌ 25	♍ 10	♒ 11	♓ 1	♈ 3
29	♒ 11		♓ 6	♈ 26	♉ 5	♉ 29	♊ 3	♎ 19		♓ 5	♓ 25	♉ 28
31	♓ 6		♈ 3		♊ 4							♉ 24

1904	Jan.	Feb.	Mar.	April	May	June	July	Aug.	Sep.	Oct.	Nov.	Dec.
1	♊ 9	♌ —	♌ 24	♎ 17	♏ 24	♈ 12	♒ 15	♓ 29	♉ 13	♊ 18	♌ 9	♍ 17
3	♋ 8	♍ —	♍ 24	♏ 16	♐ 21	♉ 6	♓ 8	♈ 22	♊ 9	♋ 15	♍ 7	♎ 16
5	♋ 8	♎ 29	♎ 24	♐ 13	♑ 16	♓ 0	♈ 2	♉ 17	♋ 5	♌ 13	♎ 6	♏ 14
7	♌ 8	♎ 26	♏ 22	♑ 8	♒ 11	♓ 24	♈ 26	♊ 13	♌ 4	♍ 12	♏ 5	♐ 12
9	♌ 8	♏ 21	♐ 18	♒ 3	♓ 4	♈ 24	♉ 21	♋ 11	♍ 4	♍ 12	♐ 4	♑ 10
11	♍ 6	♐ 15	♑ 12	♒ 26	♓ 28	♉ 13	♊ 18	♋ 10	♍ 4	♍ 12	♑ 28	♒ 5
13	♎ 3	♑ 9	♒ 6	♓ 20	♈ 23	♊ 10	♋ 17	♌ 10	♎ 4	♎ 10	♒ 22	♓ 0
15	♏ 29	♒ 3	♒ 0	♈ 14	♉ 18	♋ 8	♋ 16	♍ 9	♏ 28	♏ 7	♓ 16	♈ 23
17	♐ 24	♓ 26	♓ 23	♉ 9	♊ 15	♋ 7	♌ 15	♎ 6	♐ 23	♐ 26	♈ 9	♉ 17
19	♑ 18	♓ 21	♈ 18	♉ 5	♊ 13	♌ 6	♍ 12	♏ 26	♐ 17	♑ 19	♉ 4	♊ 12
21	♒ 12	♈ 15	♉ 12	♊ 2	♋ 9	♍ 4	♎ 9	♐ 20	♑ 11	♒ 13	♉ 29	♋ 7
23	♓ 6	♉ 9	♊ 8	♋ 0	♌ 7	♎ 2	♏ 4	♑ 14	♒ 4	♓ 7	♋ 25	♌ 4
25	♈ 29	♉ 3	♋ 5	♋ 28	♍ 5	♏ 29	♐ 29	♒ 7	♓ 28	♈ 2	♋ 22	♍ 2
27	♉ 24	♊ 26	♋ 3	♌ 27	♎ 3	♐ 25	♑ 23	♓ 1	♈ 23	♉ 28	♌ 19	♎ 0
29	♊ 19	♊ 21	♌ 3	♍ 26	♏ 29	♑ 20	♒ 17	♈ 1		♉ 25		♏ 28
31	♋ 16		♍ 3		♐ 29		♓ 17			♊ 25		♏ 26

1905	Jan.	Feb.	Mar.	April	May	June	July	Aug.	Sep.	Oct.	Nov.	Dec.
1	♍ 10	♑ 1	♏ 11	♒ 27	♈ 0	♉ 14	♊ 18	♌ 6	♍ 28	♏ 7	♐ 0	♒ 6
3	♐ 8	♒ 27	♐ 6	♓ 21	♈ 24	♊ 9	♋ 14	♍ 4	♎ 27	♐ 6	♑ 27	♓ 1
5	♑ 5	♒ 27	♑ 0	♈ 15	♉ 18	♋ 4	♌ 11	♎ 3	♏ 26	♑ 4	♑ 23	♈ 26
7	♒ 1	♓ 16	♒ 24	♉ 9	♊ 12	♌ 1	♍ 8	♏ 2	♐ 24	♒ 1	♒ 17	♉ 20
9	♓ 25	♈ 9	♓ 18	♊ 3	♋ 7	♍ 28	♎ 6	♐ 0	♑ 21	♓ 26	♓ 11	♊ 13
11	♈ 19	♉ 3	♈ 12	♋ 28	♌ 4	♎ 25	♏ 5	♑ 27	♒ 16	♈ 20	♈ 5	♋ 7
13	♉ 13	♉ 27	♉ 6	♌ 24	♍ 1	♏ 24	♐ 3	♒ 24	♓ 11	♉ 14	♉ 28	♋ 2
15	♊ 7	♊ 23	♊ 1	♍ 21	♍ 29	♐ 23	♑ 1	♓ 20	♈ 5	♊ 8	♊ 23	♌ 27
17	♋ 2	♋ 20	♋ 28	♎ 20	♎ 29	♑ 20	♒ 28	♈ 15	♉ 29	♋ 2	♋ 17	♍ 23
19	♋ 28	♌ 19	♋ 27	♏ 20	♏ 29	♒ 16	♓ 24	♉ 9	♊ 23	♌ 26	♌ 13	♎ 20
21	♌ 26	♍ 19	♌ 27	♐ 20	♐ 28	♓ 11	♈ 19	♊ 2	♋ 17	♍ 21	♍ 10	♏ 18
23	♍ 25	♎ 18	♍ 27	♑ 20	♑ 28	♈ 5	♉ 13	♋ 26	♌ 12	♎ 17	♎ 8	♐ 17
25	♎ 24	♏ 15	♎ 25	♒ 17	♒ 21	♈ 28	♊ 6	♌ 21	♍ 8	♏ 15	♏ 8	♑ 16
27	♏ 23	♐ ...	♏ 21	♓ 12	♓ 15	♉ 23	♋ 1	♍ 17	♎ 7	♐ 14	♐ 8	♒ 13
29	♐ 21		♐ 21	♈ 6	♈ 8		♋ 26	♎ 14	♎ 6	♑ 15	♐ 8	♓ 9
31	♑ 18		♒ 15		♉ 2		♌ 22	♏ 13		♐ 15		

184

1906	Jan.	Feb.	Mar.	April	May	June	July	Aug.	Sep.	Oct.	Nov.	Dec.
1	♓ 22	♉ 6	♉ 13	♊ 27	♌ 0	♍ 19	♎ 27	♐ 20	♒ 13	♓ 19	♉ 5	♊ 8
3	♓ 16	♉ 29	♊ 7	♊ 22	♌ 26	♎ 17	♏ 26	♐ 19	♓ 10	♈ 14	♊ 0	♋ 2
5	♈ 10	♊ 24	♋ 27	♋ 18	♎ 24	♎ 17	♏ 26	♑ 18	♓ 6	♈ 9	♊ 23	♋ 26
7	♉ 4	♋ 19	♋ 23	♌ 16	♎ 23	♏ 17	♐ 25	♒ 15	♈ 1	♉ 3	♋ 17	♌ 20
9	♊ 28	♌ 15	♌ 22	♍ 15	♏ 23	♐ 17	♑ 23	♓ 11	♉ 25	♊ 27	♌ 11	♍ 15
11	♊ 24	♍ 13	♍ 21	♎ 15	♐ 24	♑ 15	♒ 20	♈ 5	♊ 19	♊ 21	♍ 6	♎ 12
13	♋ 20	♎ 11	♎ 20	♏ 15	♐ 23	♒ 12	♓ 15	♉ 29	♋ 13	♋ 15	♎ 4	♏ 11
15	♌ 17	♏ 10	♏ 19	♐ 13	♑ 20	♓ 6	♈ 9	♊ 23	♌ 8	♌ 12	♏ 3	♐ 11
17	♍ 15	♐ 8	♐ 17	♑ 10	♒ 15	♈ 1	♉ 3	♋ 17	♍ 4	♎ 10	♐ 3	♑ 11
19	♎ 13	♑ 6	♑ 13	♒ 6	♓ 10	♉ 24	♉ 27	♌ 12	♎ 1	♏ 9	♐ 2	♑ 11
21	♏ 12	♒ 3	♒ 9	♓ 0	♈ 4	♊ 18	♊ 21	♍ 9	♎ 0	♏ 9	♑ 29	♒ 9
23	♐ 10	♓ 0	♓ 4	♈ 25	♉ 27	♋ 12	♋ 16	♎ 6	♏ 29	♐ 8	♒ 25	♓ 5
25	♑ 8	♓ 25	♈ 28	♉ 21	♊ 21	♌ 7	♌ 12	♏ 4	♐ 28	♑ 6	♓ 20	♈ 29
27	♒ 4	♈ 20	♉ 22	♊ 12	♋ 15	♍ 2	♍ 9	♐ 2	♑ 25	♒ 3	♈ 14	♉ 23
29	♓ 29		♊ 15	♋ 6	♌ 10	♍ 29	♎ 7	♑ 1	♒ 23	♓ 28		♊ 17
31	♈ 24		♊ 15		♍ 5		♏ 6	♑ 29		♈ 23		♋ 11

185

1907	Jan.	Feb.	Mar.	April	May	June	July	Aug.	Sep.	Oct.	Nov.	Dec.
1	♋ 23	♍ 9	♍ 18	♏ 9	♐ 17	♒ 11	♓ 18	♉ 6	♊ 21	♋ 23	♍ 7	♎ 10
3	♌ 17	♎ 5	♎ 15	♐ 7	♐ 16	♓ 8	♈ 15	♊ 1	♋ 15	♌ 17	♍ 2	♏ 7
5	♍ 12	♏ 2	♏ 12	♐ 6	♑ 14	♈ 5	♉ 10	♊ 25	♋ 9	♍ 12	♎ 29	♐ 6
7	♎ 8	♐ 0	♐ 11	♑ 4	♒ 12	♉ 0	♉ 4	♋ 18	♌ 3	♎ 7	♏ 27	♑ 5
9	♏ 5	♐ 28	♐ 9	♒ 1	♓ 8	♉ 25	♊ 28	♌ 12	♍ 28	♏ 4	♐ 26	♒ 5
11	♐ 4	♑ 28	♑ 7	♓ 28	♈ 3	♊ 19	♋ 21	♎ 7	♎ 24	♐ 2	♑ 25	♓ 4
13	♑ 4	♒ 27	♒ 5	♈ 24	♉ 28	♋ 13	♌ 15	♎ 1	♏ 21	♑ 0	♒ 23	♈ 1
15	♒ 4	♓ 25	♓ 3	♉ 20	♉ 22	♋ 6	♍ 9	♏ 27	♐ 19	♒ 28	♓ 21	♉ 28
17	♓ 3	♈ 21	♈ 29	♊ 14	♊ 16	♌ 0	♎ 4	♐ 25	♐ 17	♓ 26	♈ 18	♊ 23
19	♈ 0	♉ 16	♉ 24	♊ 8	♋ 9	♍ 25	♏ 1	♐ 23	♑ 16	♈ 24	♉ 14	♋ 18
21	♉ 26	♊ 10	♊ 18	♋ 1	♋ 4	♍ 22	♏ 19	♑ 22	♒ 15	♉ 22	♊ 9	♌ 12
23	♊ 20	♋ 4	♋ 12	♋ 26	♌ 0	♎ 20	♐ 28	♒ 22	♓ 13	♊ 18	♋ 3	♍ 5
25	♋ 14	♋ 28	♋ 6	♌ 21	♍ 27	♏ 20	♑ 28	♓ 21	♈ 10	♋ 13	♌ 27	♎ 29
27	♌ 7	♌ 22	♍ 0	♍ 19	♍ 26	♐ 20	♒ 28	♈ 19	♉ 5	♌ 7	♍ 21	♏ 23
29	♍ 2		♍ 27	♎ 18	♎ 26	♐ 20	♓ 27	♉ 15	♊ 1	♎ 1	♎ 15	♐ 18
31	♍ 26		♎ 24		♏ 26		♈ 24	♊ 9		♏ 25		♏ 15

186

1908	Jan.	Feb.	Mar.	April	May	June	July	Aug.	Sep.	Oct.	Nov.	Dec.
1	♏ 29	♐ 21	♒ 15	♈ 8	♉ 15	♋ 2	♌ 4	♍ 19	♏ 4	♐ 9	♒ 0	♓ 10
3	♐ 28	♑ 22	♒ 15	♉ 6	♊ 11	♋ 26	♌ 28	♎ 13	♏ 0	♐ 6	♒ 29	♈ 8
5	♐ 29	♒ 20	♓ 14	♊ 3	♋ 6	♌ 20	♍ 22	♏ 7	♐ 26	♑ 4	♓ 28	♉ 6
7	♒ 27	♓ 17	♈ 12	♊ 28	♌ 0	♍ 14	♎ 16	♏ 3	♐ 24	♒ 3	♈ 27	♊ 3
9	♓ 25	♈ 12	♉ 8	♋ 22	♍ 24	♎ 8	♏ 12	♐ 1	♑ 24	♒ 3	♉ 25	♋ 0
11	♈ 20	♉ 6	♊ 2	♋ 16	♎ 18	♏ 4	♐ 9	♐ 1	♒ 25	♓ 1	♊ 22	♋ 25
13	♉ 15	♊ 29	♋ 26	♌ 10	♏ 13	♐ 1	♑ 8	♑ 1	♓ 24	♈ 27	♋ 17	♌ 19
15	♊ 9	♋ 23	♋ 19	♍ 4	♐ 9	♐ 29	♒ 7	♒ 1	♈ 23	♉ 22	♌ 11	♍ 13
17	♋ 2	♋ 17	♌ 14	♎ 0	♐ 6	♑ 28	♓ 7	♓ 0	♉ 19	♊ 15	♍ 5	♎ 7
19	♋ 26	♌ 11	♍ 8	♏ 27	♑ 4	♒ 28	♈ 7	♈ 27	♋ 13	♋ 9	♎ 29	♏ 1
21	♌ 20	♍ 7	♎ 4	♐ 24	♒ 3	♓ 26	♉ 4	♉ 22	♌ 7	♌ 3	♏ 24	♐ 27
23	♍ 14	♎ 3	♏ 0	♐ 22	♓ 1	♈ 24	♊ 0	♊ 16	♍ 1	♎ 28	♐ 19	♑ 24
25	♎ 10	♏ 1	♐ 27	♑ 20	♈ 29	♉ 20	♋ 25	♋ 10	♎ 25	♏ 23	♑ 16	♒ 23
27	♏ 7	♐ 0	♑ 25	♒ 19	♉ 27	♊ 16	♌ 19	♌ 4	♎ 19	♐ 20	♒ 13	♓ 22
29	♐ 6		♒ 24	♓ 17	♊ 24	♋ 10	♍ 13	♍ 28	♏ 14	♑ 17	♓ 11	♈ 21
31			♓ 24		♊ 19		♎ 7	♎ 22				♉ 19

1909	Jan.	Feb.	Mar.	April	May	June	July	Aug.	Sep.	Oct.	Nov.	Dec.
1	♉ 3	♊ 22	♋ 2	♌ 18	♍ 20	♏ 4	♐ 7	♑ 26	♓ 19	♈ 28	♊ 20	♋ 25
3	♊ 0	♋ 17	♋ 27	♍ 11	♎ 14	♏ 29	♑ 4	♒ 25	♈ 19	♉ 28	♋ 17	♌ 21
5	♊ 26	♌ 12	♌ 21	♎ 5	♏ 8	♐ 25	♒ 2	♓ 25	♈ 18	♊ 25	♌ 13	♍ 16
7	♋ 21	♌ 6	♍ 14	♏ 29	♏ 3	♑ 22	♓ 0	♈ 24	♉ 16	♋ 22	♍ 8	♎ 10
9	♋ 15	♍ 29	♎ 8	♏ 24	♐ 29	♑ 20	♓ 29	♈ 22	♉ 12	♌ 17	♎ 2	♏ 3
11	♌ 9	♍ 23	♎ 2	♐ 19	♑ 25	♒ 18	♈ 27	♉ 19	♊ 7	♍ 11	♎ 25	♐ 27
13	♍ 3	♎ 18	♏ 27	♐ 15	♑ 23	♓ 16	♈ 25	♊ 15	♋ 2	♎ 4	♏ 19	♑ 22
15	♎ 27	♎ 13	♏ 22	♑ 12	♒ 21	♓ 15	♉ 22	♋ 10	♋ 26	♏ 28	♐ 13	♒ 18
17	♎ 22	♏ 10	♐ 19	♑ 11	♓ 20	♈ 13	♊ 18	♌ 5	♌ 19	♏ 22	♑ 8	♓ 15
19	♏ 18	♐ 9	♐ 17	♒ 11	♈ 18	♈ 10	♋ 14	♌ 29	♍ 13	♐ 16	♒ 4	♈ 12
21	♐ 17	♑ 10	♑ 18	♒ 10	♉ 15	♉ 6	♋ 8	♍ 22	♎ 7	♑ 11	♓ 2	♉ 10
23	♑ 16	♒ 9	♒ 18	♓ 7	♊ 10	♊ 0	♌ 2	♎ 16	♏ 2	♒ 8	♈ 0	♉ 9
25	♒ 16	♓ 6	♓ 18	♈ 2	♊ 4	♋ 24	♍ 26	♏ 11	♐ 29	♓ 6	♉ 29	♊ 8
27	♓ 15		♈ 15	♉ 26	♋ 28	♋ 18	♎ 20	♐ 7	♑ 27	♈ 6	♊ 29	♋ 6
29	♈ 13		♉ 11		♌ 22	♌ 12	♏ 15	♑ 4	♒ 27	♉ 6	♋ 28	♌ 3
31	♉ 10		♊ 6				♐ 12	♒ 4		♊ 6		♌ 29

1910	Jan.	Feb.	Mar.	April	May	June	July	Aug.	Sep.	Oct.	Nov.	Dec.
1	♍ 12	♎ 25	♏ 3	♐ 17	♑ 21	♓ 10	♈ 19	♊ 12	♌ 4	♍ 10	♎ 26	♏ 28
3	♏ 6	♏ 19	♏ 27	♑ 12	♒ 17	♈ 9	♉ 18	♋ 10	♍ 1	♎ 5	♏ 20	♐ 22
5	♎ 29	♐ 13	♐ 21	♒ 8	♓ 15	♈ 8	♊ 17	♋ 8	♍ 26	♎ 29	♐ 13	♑ 16
7	♏ 23	♐ 9	♐ 16	♓ 6	♓ 14	♉ 7	♊ 15	♌ 5	♎ 21	♏ 23	♑ 7	♒ 11
9	♐ 18	♑ 6	♑ 14	♈ 6	♈ 14	♉ 5	♋ 13	♍ 0	♏ 15	♐ 16	♑ 1	♓ 6
11	♑ 11	♒ 4	♑ 13	♈ 6	♉ 13	♊ 2	♌ 10	♍ 25	♏ 8	♑ 10	♒ 27	♈ 3
13	♒ 9	♓ 2	♒ 12	♉ 4	♊ 10	♋ 27	♍ 5	♎ 18	♐ 2	♒ 5	♓ 24	♉ 2
15	♓ 7	♈ 0	♓ 11	♊ 1	♋ 6	♌ 21	♎ 29	♏ 12	♐ 27	♓ 2	♈ 24	♊ 1
17	♈ 6	♉ 28	♈ 8	♋ 27	♌ 0	♍ 14	♏ 22	♐ 7	♑ 24	♈ 0	♉ 24	♊ 2
19	♉ 4	♊ 24	♉ 4	♋ 21	♌ 24	♎ 8	♐ 16	♑ 2	♑ 22	♉ 0	♊ 23	♋ 1
21	♊ 1	♋ 20	♊ 0	♌ 15	♍ 17	♏ 2	♐ 11	♒ 0	♒ 21	♊ 0	♋ 21	♌ 2
23	♋ 28	♌ 15	♋ 24	♍ 9	♎ 6	♐ 28	♑ 7	♒ 28	♓ 20	♋ 28	♌ 16	♍ 29
25	♌ 24	♍ 10	♌ 18	♎ 2	♏ 1	♑ 24	♒ 4	♓ 26	♈ 17	♌ 24	♍ 11	♎ 25
27	♍ 19		♍ 12	♏ 26		♒ 21	♓ 0	♈ 25	♉ 14	♎ 19	♎ 5	♏ 20
29	♎ 13		♎ 5		♐ 27		♈ 28	♉ 23		♏ 14	♏ 5	♐ 13
31			♐ 5					♊ 20				♑ 7

189

Astronomical ephemeris table for 1911 (Moon's sign and degree). Zodiac symbols are read as: ♈ Aries, ♉ Taurus, ♊ Gemini, ♋ Cancer, ♌ Leo, ♍ Virgo, ♎ Libra, ♏ Scorpio, ♐ Sagittarius, ♑ Capricorn, ♒ Aquarius, ♓ Pisces.

1911	Jan.	Feb.	Mar.	April	May	June	July	Aug.	Sep.	Oct.	Nov.	Dec.
1	♐ 13	♓ 0	♓ 9	♉ 0	♊ 8	♋ 2	♍ 9	♎ 27	♐ 11	♑ 13	♒ 27	♈ 0
3	♑ 8	♓ 27	♈ 6	♉ 29	♋ 8	♍ 0	♎ 5	♏ 21	♑ 5	♒ 7	♓ 22	♈ 27
5	♒ 3	♈ 24	♉ 4	♊ 28	♋ 6	♍ 26	♏ 0	♐ 15	♑ 29	♓ 2	♈ 19	♉ 26
7	♈ 0	♉ 22	♊ 3	♋ 26	♍ 3	♎ 21	♏ 24	♐ 8	♒ 24	♓ 28	♉ 18	♊ 26
9	♈ 27	♊ 20	♋ 1	♌ 23	♍ 29	♏ 15	♐ 18	♑ 3	♓ 19	♈ 25	♊ 18	♋ 27
11	♉ 26	♋ 19	♋ 29	♍ 19	♎ 24	♏ 9	♑ 12	♒ 27	♈ 16	♉ 24	♋ 16	♌ 26
13	♊ 25	♌ 17	♌ 27	♎ 15	♏ 18	♐ 3	♒ 6	♒ 23	♉ 13	♊ 22	♌ 13	♍ 23
15	♋ 25	♍ 15	♍ 23	♏ 10	♐ 12	♐ 27	♓ 0	♓ 19	♋ 11	♋ 21	♎ 9	♎ 19
17	♌ 23	♎ 11	♎ 19	♐ 4	♑ 6	♑ 21	♈ 26	♈ 16	♌ 10	♌ 19	♏ 4	♏ 14
19	♍ 20	♏ 6	♏ 14	♐ 27	♒ 0	♒ 16	♉ 22	♉ 15	♍ 8	♍ 16	♐ 29	♐ 8
21	♎ 16	♐ 0	♐ 7	♑ 21	♒ 24	♓ 13	♊ 20	♊ 14	♎ 6	♎ 13	♑ 23	♑ 2
23	♏ 10	♐ 23	♑ 1	♒ 16	♓ 20	♈ 10	♋ 19	♋ 13	♏ 4	♏ 8	♒ 17	♒ 26
25	♐ 3	♑ 17	♑ 25	♓ 12	♈ 18	♉ 11	♌ 19	♌ 12	♐ 0	♐ 3	♓ 11	♓ 19
27	♑ 27	♒ 13	♒ 21	♈ 9	♉ 17	♋ 11	♍ 17	♍ 9	♑ 25	♑ 27	♈ 5	♈ 14
29	♒ 22		♓ 17	♉ 8	♊ 17	♋ 11	♎ 14	♏ 5	♒ 19	♒ 20		♉ 9
31	♒ 17		♈ 15		♋ 17		♏ 14	♏ 29		♓ 14		♊ 5

190

1912	Jan.	Feb.	Mar.	April	May	June	July	Aug.	Sep.	Oct.	Nov.	Dec.
1	♉ 19	♋ 12	♌ 6	♍ 29	♏ 5	♐ 22	♑ 25	♉ 9	♈ 25	♊ 1	♋ 23	♌ 2
3	♊ 19	♋ 13	♌ 6	♎ 27	♐ 1	♐ 16	♒ 18	♈ 3	♉ 21	♊ 28	♌ 21	♍ 0
5	♋ 20	♍ 13	♍ 5	♏ 23	♐ 26	♑ 10	♓ 12	♈ 28	♊ 18	♋ 26	♍ 20	♎ 28
7	♌ 20	♎ 11	♎ 2	♏ 18	♑ 20	♒ 4	♈ 6	♉ 24	♋ 16	♌ 25	♎ 18	♎ 24
9	♍ 19	♏ 7	♏ 28	♐ 12	♑ 13	♒ 28	♉ 2	♊ 22	♋ 16	♍ 24	♏ 15	♏ 20
11	♍ 16	♐ 26	♐ 22	♐ 6	♒ 8	♓ 23	♊ 29	♋ 22	♌ 16	♎ 23	♐ 12	♐ 15
13	♎ 11	♐ 19	♐ 16	♑ 0	♓ 3	♈ 21	♋ 28	♌ 22	♌ 15	♏ 20	♐ 7	♑ 9
15	♏ 5	♑ 13	♑ 10	♒ 25	♈ 29	♉ 20	♌ 29	♍ 21	♎ 13	♐ 16	♑ 1	♒ 3
17	♐ 29	♒ 8	♒ 4	♓ 21	♉ 27	♊ 20	♍ 29	♎ 17	♏ 9	♑ 11	♒ 25	♓ 26
19	♐ 23	♓ 2	♓ 29	♈ 18	♊ 26	♋ 20	♎ 28	♏ 12	♐ 3	♒ 5	♓ 19	♈ 21
21	♑ 16	♈ 28	♈ 25	♉ 16	♋ 25	♋ 18	♏ 25	♐ 7	♑ 27	♓ 29	♈ 13	♉ 17
23	♒ 11	♉ 25	♉ 22	♊ 14	♋ 24	♌ 15	♏ 21	♐ 0	♒ 21	♈ 23	♉ 9	♊ 15
25	♓ 5	♊ 23	♊ 19	♋ 13	♌ 22	♍ 11	♐ 16	♑ 24	♓ 15	♉ 18	♊ 7	♋ 14
27	♈ 1	♊ 23	♋ 18	♌ 11	♍ 18	♎ 6	♑ 10	♒ 18	♈ 9	♊ 14	♋ 5	♌ 13
29	♉ 28		♋ 16	♍ 8	♎ 14	♏ 1	♒ 3	♓ 13	♉ 5	♊ 11	♋ 4	♍ 11
31	♊ 27		♍ 15		♏ 9		♓ 27			♋ 9		♎ 1

191

1913	Jan.	Feb.	Mar.	April	May	June	July	Aug.	Sep.	Oct.	Nov.	Dec.
1	♎ 25	♐ 13	♐ 22	♒ 8	♓ 10	♈ 24	♉ 27	♋ 17	♍ 10	♎ 18	♐ 10	♑ 16
3	♏ 21	♑ 8	♑ 17	♓ 25	♈ 4	♉ 19	♊ 24	♌ 16	♎ 10	♏ 18	♐ 8	♒ 11
5	♐ 16	♒ 26	♒ 11	♓ 19	♈ 28	♊ 16	♋ 23	♍ 16	♎ 9	♐ 16	♑ 3	♓ 5
7	♑ 11	♒ 20	♓ 5	♈ 14	♉ 24	♋ 14	♌ 22	♎ 16	♏ 7	♐ 12	♒ 28	♈ 29
9	♒ 5	♓ 13	♈ 29	♈ 10	♊ 20	♋ 12	♍ 21	♎ 14	♐ 3	♑ 7	♒ 21	♈ 23
11	♒ 29	♈ 8	♈ 23	♉ 7	♋ 17	♌ 10	♍ 19	♏ 10	♐ 28	♒ 1	♓ 15	♉ 17
13	♓ 23	♉ 4	♉ 17	♊ 4	♌ 15	♍ 9	♎ 17	♐ 6	♑ 22	♒ 25	♈ 9	♊ 13
15	♈ 17	♊ 0	♊ 13	♋ 3	♍ 14	♎ 6	♏ 13	♐ 1	♒ 16	♓ 18	♈ 4	♋ 9
17	♉ 12		♋ 10	♋ 2	♎ 12	♏ 4	♐ 9	♑ 25	♓ 9	♈ 12	♉ 0	♌ 7
19	♊ 9	♋ 0	♋ 9	♌ 2	♏ 10	♐ 0	♑ 4	♒ 19	♈ 3	♉ 7	♊ 26	♍ 7
21	♋ 7		♌ 9	♍ 0	♏ 8	♑ 26	♒ 28	♓ 12	♉ 28	♊ 3	♋ 24	♎ 5
23	♌ 7	♌ 0	♍ 9	♎ 27	♐ 5	♒ 20	♓ 22	♈ 6	♊ 23	♋ 0	♋ 22	♏ 3
25	♍ 8	♍ 0	♍ 8	♏ 22	♐ 0	♓ 14	♈ 16	♉ 1	♋ 20	♌ 28	♍ 21	♐ 1
27	♎ 7	♎ 0	♎ 6	♐ 22	♑ 24	♓ 8	♉ 10	♊ 27	♌ 18	♍ 27	♎ 20	♐ 29
29	♏ 5	♏ 27	♏ 2	♐ 16	♒ 18	♈ 2	♊ 5	♋ 25	♍ 18	♎ 27	♏ 18	♑ 27
31	♐ 1		♐ 26		♓ 12		♋ 3	♌ 25		♏ 26		♒ 24
												♓ 19

192

1914	Jan.	Feb.	Mar.	April	May	June	July	Aug.	Sep.	Oct.	Nov.	Dec.
1	♓ 1	♈ 15	♈ 23	♊ 8	♋ 12	♍ 2	♎ 11	♐ 4	♑ 26	♓ 1	♈ 16	♉ 19
3	♓ 25	♉ 9	♉ 17	♊ 3	♌ 8	♍ 0	♏ 9	♑ 2	♒ 21	♒ 25	♉ 10	♊ 13
5	♈ 19	♊ 3	♊ 11	♋ 29	♍ 6	♎ 29	♐ 8	♑ 29	♒ 16	♈ 19	♊ 4	♋ 7
7	♉ 13	♊ 29	♋ 7	♋ 29	♍ 5	♏ 29	♑ 6	♒ 25	♓ 11	♉ 13	♊ 28	♌ 2
9	♊ 8	♋ 26	♋ 4	♌ 27	♎ 5	♐ 28	♑ 4	♒ 20	♈ 4	♊ 7	♋ 22	♍ 28
11	♋ 4	♋ 25	♌ 3	♍ 26	♏ 4	♐ 26	♒ 0	♓ 14	♈ 28	♋ 1	♌ 18	♎ 25
13	♌ 1	♌ 25	♍ 3	♎ 27	♏ 1	♑ 22	♓ 24	♈ 8	♉ 22	♌ 26	♍ 15	♏ 23
15	♍ 29	♍ 24	♎ 2	♏ 25	♐ 26	♒ 16	♈ 18	♉ 2	♊ 18	♍ 22	♎ 14	♐ 23
17	♍ 28	♎ 22	♏ 0	♐ 22	♐ 20	♓ 10	♉ 12	♋ 27	♋ 14	♎ 21	♏ 14	♑ 22
19	♎ 26	♏ 20	♐ 26	♑ 17	♑ 14	♈ 4	♊ 6	♋ 22	♌ 13	♏ 21	♐ 15	♒ 19
21	♏ 23	♐ 16	♑ 20	♒ 12	♒ 8	♉ 28	♋ 2	♌ 20	♍ 13	♐ 21	♑ 14	♓ 15
23	♐ 19	♑ 11	♑ 14	♓ 5	♓ 2	♉ 23	♋ 28	♎ 19	♎ 12	♑ 19	♒ 11	♈ 10
25	♑ 15	♒ 6	♒ 8	♈ 29	♈ 27	♊ 19	♌ 25	♏ 18	♏ 9	♒ 15	♓ 7	♉ 3
27	♒ 9	♓ 29	♓ 2	♉ 23	♉ 22	♋ 16	♍ 23	♐ 17	♐ 6	♓ 10	♈ 1	♉ 27
29	♓ 3		♈ 26	♊ 17	♊ 19	♋ 13	♍ 22	♑ 15		♈ 4	♈ 25	♊ 21
31							♏ 20	♑ 12				

1915	Jan.	Feb.	Mar.	April	May	June	July	Aug.	Sep.	Oct.	Nov.	Dec.
1	4	21	29	21	0	23	29	16	1	2	17	20
3	29	18	27	21	0	21	26	11	24	26	12	18
5	25	16	26	20	28	17	20	5	18	21	10	17
7	22	14	25	18	25	12	14	28	13	18	9	17
9	19	13	24	15	20	6	8	23	10	16	9	18
11	18	11	21	11	15	29	2	18	7	15	9	17
13	17	8	18	5	9	23	26	14	5	14	7	14
15	16	5	14	0	2	17	21	11	7	13	4	10
17	14	1	9	24	26	12	17	9	2	11	0	4
19	10	25	3	17	20	7	14	4	0	7	25	28
21	5	19	27	11	15	4	12	6	27	3	20	22
23	29	13	21	6	11	2	11	4	24	28	13	16
25	23	7	15	2	8	1	10	2	20	23	7	10
27	17	3	10	0	7	2	9	29	15	17	1	4
29	12		7	29	8	1	7	24	9	10	25	0
31	8		6		8		4	19		4		27

194

1916	Jan.	Feb.	Mar.	April	May	June	July	Aug.	Sep.	Oct.	Nov.	Dec.
1	♏ 11	♑ 4	♑ 28	♓ 20	♈ 26	♊ 12	♋ 15	♌ 29	♎ 16	♏ 23	♑ 15	♒ 24
3	♐ 10	♒ 4	♒ 27	♈ 17	♉ 21	♋ 6	♌ 8	♍ 24	♏ 12	♐ 20	♒ 14	♓ 22
5	♑ 11	♓ 3	♓ 25	♉ 13	♊ 16	♋ 0	♍ 2	♎ 19	♐ 10	♑ 19	♓ 12	♈ 19
7	♒ 11	♈ 1	♈ 22	♊ 7	♋ 9	♌ 23	♍ 27	♏ 16	♑ 8	♒ 17	♈ 9	♉ 15
9	♓ 9	♈ 27	♉ 17	♋ 1	♌ 3	♍ 18	♎ 23	♐ 14	♒ 7	♓ 15	♉ 6	♊ 11
11	♈ 6	♉ 22	♊ 12	♋ 25	♍ 27	♎ 14	♏ 20	♑ 13	♓ 6	♈ 14	♊ 2	♋ 5
13	♉ 1	♊ 16	♋ 5	♌ 19	♎ 22	♏ 11	♐ 19	♒ 13	♈ 5	♉ 1	♋ 27	♌ 29
15	♊ 25	♋ 9	♌ 29	♍ 14	♏ 18	♐ 11	♐ 19	♓ 11	♉ 3	♊ 7	♌ 21	♍ 22
17	♋ 19	♌ 3	♍ 24	♎ 9	♐ 17	♑ 11	♑ 20	♈ 8	♊ 29	♋ 1	♍ 14	♎ 16
19	♌ 13	♌ 28	♎ 19	♏ 8	♑ 17	♒ 10	♒ 19	♉ 3	♋ 23	♌ 25	♎ 8	♏ 1
21	♍ 7	♍ 23	♏ 16	♐ 7	♒ 16	♓ 7	♓ 16	♊ 27	♌ 17	♍ 18	♏ 3	♐ 7
23	♍ 1	♎ 20	♐ 14	♑ 6	♓ 13	♈ 2	♈ 12	♋ 20	♍ 11	♎ 13	♐ 0	♑ 5
25	♎ 27	♏ 17	♑ 12	♒ 5	♈ 10	♉ 27	♉ 6	♌ 14	♎ 5	♏ 8	♐ 27	♒ 5
27	♏ 23	♐ 15	♒ 10	♓ 3	♉ 5	♊ 21	♊ 0	♍ 8	♏ 0	♐ 5	♑ 26	♓ 5
29	♏ 20	♑ 14	♓ 8	♈ 0	♊ 0		♋ 24	♎ 3	♐ 26	♑ 3	♒ 26	♈ 4
31	♐ 19		♈ 6				♌ 17			♒ 1		♈ 3

1917	Jan.	Feb.	Mar.	April	May	June	July	Aug.	Sep.	Oct.	Nov.	Dec.
1	♈16	♊4	♉13	♋28	♌29	♎14	♏18	♐7	♓1	♈9	♊1	♋6
3	♉12	♊29	♊8	♋21	♍23	♏10	♐15	♑7	♈1	♉9	♊28	♌1
5	♊7	♋22	♋1	♌15	♎18	♐7	♑14	♒7	♈1	♊7	♋23	♌25
7	♋2	♌16	♋25	♍10	♏14	♑5	♒13	♓7	♉28	♋3	♌17	♍19
9	♋26	♌10	♌19	♎5	♐12	♒4	♓13	♈7	♊24	♋27	♍11	♎13
11	♌19	♍4	♍13	♏2	♑9	♓3	♈12	♉5	♋18	♌21	♎5	♏7
13	♍13	♎29	♎9	♐29	♒7	♈1	♉9	♊2	♌12	♍15	♏29	♐3
15	♎7	♏24	♏5	♑27	♓6	♉28	♊5	♋27	♍6	♎9	♐25	♐0
17	♏2	♐22	♐2	♒25	♈4	♊25	♋0	♌21	♎0	♏3	♑21	♑28
19	♐29	♑21	♑0	♓24	♉2	♋21	♌24	♍15	♏24	♐28	♒18	♒27
21	♑28	♒21	♒0	♈23	♊29	♌16	♍18	♎9	♐19	♑24	♓16	♓25
23	♒28	♓21	♓29	♉20	♋25	♍10	♎12	♏3	♑14	♒21	♓0	♈23
25	♓28	♈20	♈28	♊17	♌20	♎3	♏6	♐27	♒11	♓19	♈28	♉21
27	♈26	♉18	♉26	♋12	♍14	♏27	♐0	♑22	♓9	♈18	♉27	♊18
29	♉22		♊22	♋6	♎1	♐22	♑26	♒18	♓9	♉18	♉25	♋14
31			♋16		♎7		♐23	♒15		♉17		♌9

1918	Jan.	Feb.	Mar.	April	May	June	July	Aug.	Sep.	Oct.	Nov.	Dec.
1	♌ 21	♎ 5	♎ 13	♏ 29	♐ 3	♒ 24	♈ 4	♉ 27	♋ 17	♌ 21	♎ 7	♏ 9
3	♍ 15	♎ 29	♏ 7	♐ 24	♐ 0	♓ 22	♈ 2	♊ 24	♌ 12	♍ 16	♏ 0	♐ 3
5	♎ 8	♏ 23	♐ 2	♐ 20	♒ 28	♈ 21	♉ 0	♊ 20	♍ 7	♎ 10	♏ 24	♑ 28
7	♏ 3	♐ 19	♐ 27	♑ 18	♓ 27	♉ 20	♊ 27	♋ 15	♎ 1	♏ 3	♐ 18	♒ 23
9	♐ 28	♑ 16	♑ 24	♒ 17	♈ 26	♊ 18	♋ 24	♌ 10	♎ 24	♐ 27	♑ 13	♓ 19
11	♑ 25	♒ 16	♒ 24	♓ 18	♉ 26	♋ 16	♌ 19	♍ 4	♏ 18	♑ 21	♒ 9	♈ 17
13	♒ 23	♓ 16	♓ 24	♈ 18	♊ 24	♋ 11	♍ 14	♎ 28	♐ 12	♒ 16	♓ 6	♉ 15
15	♓ 22	♈ 16	♈ 25	♉ 16	♋ 21	♌ 6	♎ 8	♏ 22	♐ 7	♓ 13	♈ 5	♊ 14
17	♈ 21	♉ 14	♉ 24	♊ 13	♌ 16	♍ 0	♏ 2	♐ 16	♑ 4	♈ 12	♉ 5	♋ 13
19	♉ 20	♊ 11	♊ 21	♋ 8	♍ 10	♎ 24	♏ 26	♑ 13	♑ 3	♉ 12	♊ 4	♌ 12
21	♊ 18	♋ 7	♋ 16	♌ 2	♎ 4	♏ 18	♐ 21	♒ 11	♒ 4	♊ 12	♋ 1	♍ 9
23	♋ 14	♌ 2	♌ 11	♍ 25	♏ 28	♐ 13	♑ 18	♓ 10	♓ 4	♋ 10	♌ 27	♎ 5
25	♌ 10	♍ 26	♍ 5	♎ 19	♐ 22	♑ 11	♒ 16	♈ 9	♈ 3	♌ 6	♍ 21	♏ 29
27	♍ 5	♍ 20	♎ 28	♏ 13	♑ 17	♒ 7	♓ 15	♉ 7	♉ 1	♍ 1	♎ 15	♐ 23
29	♎ 29		♎ 22	♐ 8	♒ 13	♓ 5	♈ 14	♊ 4	♊ 27	♎ 25		♑ 17
31	♏ 23		♏ 16		♓ 10		♉ 13					♒ 11

197

1919	Jan.	Feb.	Mar.	April	May	June	July	Aug.	Sep.	Oct.	Nov.	Dec.
1	♐ 24	♒ 12	♒ 20	♈ 12	♉ 21	♋ 13	♌ 19	♎ 6	♐ 20	♐ 22	♒ 7	♓ 11
3	♑ 19	♓ 10	♓ 19	♉ 12	♊ 20	♌ 11	♍ 16	♏ 0	♏ 14	♐ 16	♓ 3	♈ 9
5	♒ 16	♈ 8	♈ 18	♊ 10	♊ 19	♍ 7	♎ 10	♏ 24	♐ 8	♒ 11	♈ 0	♉ 8
7	♓ 14	♉ 7	♉ 17	♋ 6	♋ 16	♎ 2	♏ 4	♐ 18	♒ 3	♓ 8	♉ 0	♊ 8
9	♈ 12	♊ 5	♊ 16	♌ 1	♌ 11	♎ 26	♏ 28	♐ 12	♓ 28	♈ 7	♊ 0	♋ 7
11	♉ 10	♋ 2	♋ 13	♍ 26	♍ 5	♏ 20	♐ 22	♑ 8	♈ 27	♉ 6	♋ 0	♌ 5
13	♊ 8	♋ 29	♌ 9	♍ 20	♎ 29	♐ 13	♑ 17	♒ 5	♉ 26	♊ 6	♌ 0	♎ 1
15	♋ 7	♌ 25	♍ 4	♎ 14	♎ 23	♐ 8	♒ 12	♓ 3	♊ 24	♋ 5	♍ 29	♎ 25
17	♌ 4	♍ 21	♍ 29	♏ 7	♏ 16	♐ 3	♓ 9	♈ 1	♋ 22	♌ 3	♍ 26	♏ 19
19	♍ 0	♍ 15	♎ 23	♏ 1	♐ 11	♑ 29	♈ 6	♉ 29	♌ 19	♍ 29	♎ 21	♐ 12
21	♍ 25	♎ 9	♏ 17	♐ 26	♐ 6	♑ 26	♉ 4	♊ 28	♍ 15	♎ 24	♏ 16	♑ 6
23	♎ 19	♏ 3	♏ 11	♐ 22	♑ 2	♑ 24	♉ 3	♋ 25	♎ 10	♏ 19	♐ 10	♒ 0
25	♏ 13	♐ 27	♐ 5	♑ 20	♒ 0	♒ 23	♊ 2	♌ 23	♏ 5	♐ 13	♐ 4	♒ 25
27	♐ 7	♐ 22	♑ 0	♒ 20	♓ 29	♒ 22	♋ 0	♍ 19	♏ 28	♑ 7	♑ 27	♓ 21
29	♐ 2		♒ 28		♓ 29	♓ 21	♌ 28	♎ 14		♒ 0	♒ 21	♈ 18
31	♑ 28		♓ 27		♈ 29		♍ 24	♎ 8		♓ 24	♓ 16	

198

1920	Jan.	Feb.	Mar.	April	May	June	July	Aug.	Sep.	Oct.	Nov.	Dec.
1	♉ 2	♋ 25	♋ 20	♍ 11	♎ 17	♐ 2	♏ 5	♒ 20	♈ 8	♉ 15	♋ 7	♌ 17
3	♊ 1	♌ 24	♌ 18	♎ 8	♏ 11	♑ 26	♐ 29	♓ 15	♉ 4	♊ 13	♌ 6	♍ 14
5	♋ 1	♍ 23	♍ 16	♏ 3	♐ 5	♒ 20	♑ 23	♈ 11	♊ 2	♋ 11	♍ 4	♎ 11
7	♌ 1	♎ 21	♎ 12	♐ 27	♑ 29	♓ 14	♒ 18	♉ 7	♋ 0	♌ 9	♎ 1	♏ 6
9	♍ 0	♏ 17	♏ 7	♑ 21	♒ 23	♈ 9	♓ 14	♊ 5	♋ 29	♍ 7	♏ 27	♐ 1
11	♍ 26	♐ 11	♐ 1	♒ 15	♓ 17	♉ 4	♈ 10	♋ 4	♌ 28	♎ 5	♐ 22	♑ 25
13	♎ 21	♑ 5	♑ 25	♓ 9	♈ 13	♊ 2	♉ 10	♌ 4	♍ 26	♏ 1	♑ 16	♒ 19
15	♏ 15	♑ 29	♑ 19	♈ 4	♉ 10	♋ 1	♊ 9	♍ 3	♎ 23	♏ 26	♒ 10	♓ 13
17	♐ 9	♒ 23	♒ 14	♉ 0	♊ 8	♌ 2	♋ 9	♎ 1	♏ 18	♐ 20	♓ 4	♈ 7
19	♑ 3	♓ 18	♓ 10	♉ 29	♋ 8	♍ 1	♌ 7	♏ 28	♐ 13	♑ 14	♈ 28	♉ 1
21	♑ 27	♈ 15	♈ 7	♊ 27	♌ 8	♎ 28	♍ 2	♐ 23	♑ 6	♒ 8	♉ 23	♊ 28
23	♒ 22	♉ 12	♉ 5	♋ 25	♍ 7	♏ 23	♎ 26	♑ 17	♒ 0	♓ 3	♊ 20	♋ 26
25	♓ 18	♊ 9	♊ 4	♌ 21	♎ 5	♐ 17	♏ 20	♒ 10	♓ 25	♈ 28	♋ 18	♌ 25
27	♈ 15	♋ 7	♋ 2	♍ 21	♏ 1	♐ 11	♐ 14	♓ 4	♈ 20	♉ 26	♌ 17	♍ 26
29	♉ 12	♌ 6	♌ 0		♐ 26		♑ 8	♈ 29	♉ 17	♊ 24	♍ 17	♎ 26
31	♊ 11		♍ 28		♑ 20		♒ 8	♉ 25		♋ 23		♏ 24

199

1921	Jan.	Feb.	Mar.	April	May	June	July	Aug.	Sep.	Oct.	Nov.	Dec.
1	♎ 8	♏ 25	♐ 3	♈ 17	♒ 19	♈ 4	♉ 8	♊ 28	♌ 22	♎ 0	♏ 21	♐ 25
3	♏ 3	♏ 19	♐ 27	♒ 11	♓ 13	♈ 29	♊ 5	♋ 28	♍ 22	♎ 29	♐ 17	♑ 21
5	♏ 28	♐ 13	♑ 21	♓ 5	♈ 8	♉ 27	♊ 4	♌ 29	♎ 21	♏ 26	♐ 13	♒ 15
7	♐ 22	♑ 6	♒ 15	♈ 0	♉ 5	♊ 26	♋ 5	♍ 28	♏ 18	♐ 22	♑ 7	♓ 8
9	♑ 16	♒ 0	♓ 9	♈ 26	♊ 2	♋ 25	♌ 5	♎ 26	♐ 14	♑ 17	♒ 1	♈ 2
11	♒ 9	♓ 25	♈ 4	♉ 23	♋ 0	♌ 25	♍ 3	♏ 23	♐ 9	♒ 11	♓ 24	♈ 27
13	♓ 3	♈ 20	♈ 0	♊ 21	♌ 28	♍ 23	♎ 0	♐ 18	♑ 2	♓ 5	♈ 19	♉ 23
15	♈ 28	♉ 16	♉ 26	♊ 19	♍ 26	♎ 20	♏ 26	♐ 12	♒ 26	♈ 29	♉ 15	♊ 21
17	♉ 23	♊ 13	♊ 24	♋ 17	♎ 23	♏ 16	♐ 21	♑ 6	♓ 20	♉ 24	♊ 12	♋ 20
19	♊ 20	♋ 12	♋ 22	♌ 16	♏ 19	♐ 11	♑ 15	♒ 29	♈ 15	♊ 19	♋ 10	♌ 19
21	♋ 18	♌ 12	♌ 21	♍ 14	♐ 15	♑ 6	♒ 9	♓ 23	♉ 10	♋ 16	♌ 9	♍ 18
23	♌ 19	♍ 12	♍ 21	♎ 11	♑ 9	♒ 0	♓ 2	♈ 18	♊ 6	♌ 14	♍ 7	♎ 16
25	♍ 19	♎ 11	♎ 19	♏ 6	♒ 3	♓ 24	♈ 26	♉ 13	♋ 3	♍ 12	♎ 5	♏ 12
27	♎ 19	♏ 8	♏ 16	♐ 1	♓ 27	♈ 17	♉ 21	♊ 9	♌ 1	♎ 10	♏ 2	♐ 9
29	♏ 17		♐ 11	♑ 25	♈ 21	♈ 12	♊ 16	♋ 7	♍ 1	♏ 9	♏ 29	♑ 4
31	♐ 12		♑ 6		♓ 21		♋ 14	♌ 7		♐ 7		♒ 29

Ephemeris table for the year 1922 — daily positions (zodiac sign and degree) by month.

1922	Jan.	Feb.	Mar.	April	May	June	July	Aug.	Sep.	Oct.	Nov.	Dec.
1	♒ 11	♓ 25	♈ 4	♉ 19	♊ 25	♌ 17	♍ 26	♏ 18	♐ 8	♒ 12	♓ 27	♈ 28
3	♓ 5	♈ 19	♈ 28	♊ 15	♋ 22	♍ 15	♎ 24	♐ 15	♑ 3	♓ 6	♈ 20	♉ 23
5	♈ 28	♉ 13	♉ 22	♋ 11	♌ 20	♎ 13	♏ 21	♑ 11	♒ 27	♈ 0	♉ 14	♊ 18
7	♈ 22	♊ 9	♊ 18	♍ 9	♍ 18	♏ 11	♐ 18	♒ 6	♓ 21	♈ 23	♊ 9	♋ 15
9	♉ 18	♋ 7	♋ 15	♎ 9	♎ 17	♐ 9	♑ 14	♓ 0	♈ 14	♉ 17	♋ 5	♍ 12
11	♊ 15	♌ 7	♌ 15	♏ 8	♏ 16	♑ 6	♒ 10	♈ 24	♉ 8	♊ 12	♌ 1	♎ 9
13	♋ 14	♍ 7	♍ 15	♐ 6	♐ 14	♒ 1	♓ 4	♈ 18	♊ 3	♋ 8	♍ 28	♏ 7
15	♌ 13	♎ 6	♎ 14	♑ 3	♑ 11	♒ 26	♈ 28	♉ 12	♊ 28	♌ 5	♎ 27	♐ 6
17	♍ 12	♏ 2	♏ 11	♒ 28	♒ 6	♓ 20	♉ 21	♊ 7	♋ 25	♍ 3	♏ 26	♑ 4
19	♎ 9	♐ 28	♐ 7	♒ 22	♓ 0	♈ 13	♊ 16	♋ 3	♍ 24	♎ 3	♐ 26	♒ 3
21	♏ 6	♑ 22	♑ 1	♓ 15	♈ 23	♉ 8	♋ 11	♌ 1	♎ 24	♏ 3	♑ 24	♓ 1
23	♐ 1	♒ 16	♒ 25	♈ 9	♉ 17	♊ 3	♌ 9	♍ 1	♏ 25	♐ 2	♒ 21	♈ 29
25	♑ 25	♓ 10	♒ 19	♉ 4	♊ 12	♋ 0	♍ 8	♎ 1	♐ 24	♑ 0	♓ 17	♉ 25
27	♒ 19		♓ 13	♈ 29	♋ 8	♋ 29	♎ 7	♏ 1	♐ 22	♒ 26	♈ 11	♊ 19
29	♓ 13		♈ 7		♌ 5	♌ 27	♏ 6	♏ 29	♑ 18	♓ 21	♉ 5	♋ 13
31					♍ 3		♐ 5	♐ 25		♈ 15		♌ 6

1923	Jan.	Feb.	Mar.	April	May	June	July	Aug.	Sep.	Oct.	Nov.	Dec.
1	♊ 14	♌ 2	♌ 10	♎ 2	♏ 11	♐ 4	♒ 10	♓ 26	♉ 10	♊ 12	♋ 27	♍ 3
3	♋ 10	♍ 1	♍ 9	♏ 3	♐ 11	♈ 2	♓ 6	♈ 20	♉ 4	♋ 6	♌ 23	♎ 0
5	♌ 8	♎ 0	♎ 9	♐ 3	♐ 10	♒ 28	♈ 0	♉ 14	♊ 28	♌ 1	♍ 21	♎ 29
7	♍ 6	♎ 28	♎ 9	♏ 1	♒ 6	♓ 22	♉ 24	♊ 8	♋ 23	♍ 28	♎ 20	♏ 29
9	♍ 4	♏ 27	♏ 8	♐ 27	♓ 1	♈ 16	♉ 18	♋ 3	♌ 20	♎ 27	♏ 21	♐ 29
11	♎ 2	♐ 24	♐ 5	♐ 22	♈ 25	♉ 9	♊ 12	♌ 29	♍ 19	♏ 27	♐ 21	♑ 28
13	♏ 0	♐ 21	♑ 1	♑ 17	♉ 19	♊ 4	♋ 7	♍ 26	♎ 18	♐ 27	♑ 20	♒ 25
15	♐ 28	♑ 16	♒ 25	♒ 10	♊ 13	♋ 28	♌ 3	♎ 24	♏ 18	♑ 24	♒ 17	♓ 21
17	♐ 25	♒ 11	♓ 20	♓ 4	♋ 7	♌ 23	♍ 0	♏ 23	♐ 17	♒ 20	♓ 12	♈ 15
19	♑ 20	♓ 5	♈ 13	♈ 28	♋ 2	♍ 20	♎ 28	♐ 22	♑ 14	♓ 15	♈ 6	♉ 9
21	♒ 15	♈ 28	♉ 7	♉ 22	♌ 27	♎ 17	♏ 26	♑ 20	♒ 10	♈ 9	♉ 0	♊ 2
23	♓ 9	♉ 22	♊ 1	♊ 17	♍ 23	♏ 15	♐ 25	♒ 17	♓ 6	♉ 3	♊ 24	♋ 27
25	♈ 2	♊ 17	♋ 25	♋ 13	♎ 21	♐ 14	♑ 23	♓ 14	♈ 0	♊ 27	♋ 18	♌ 21
27	♉ 26	♋ 13	♌ 21	♌ 11	♏ 20	♐ 14	♒ 21	♈ 9	♈ 24	♋ 21	♌ 12	♍ 17
29	♊ 22		♍ 18	♍ 11	♐ 20	♑ 12	♒ 18	♉ 4	♉ 18	♌ 15	♍ 7	♎ 13
31	♋ 18		♎ 17		♐ 19		♓ 13	♊ 28		♍ 15		♏ 10

Ephemeris table for 1924. Columns are days (odd-numbered) of each month; each cell gives the zodiac sign and the degree.

Month	1	3	5	7	9	11	13	15	17	19	21	23	25	27	29	31
Jan.	♎24	♏23	♐22	♐21	♑20	♒16	♓11	♈5	♉29	♊23	♋18	♌13	♍10	♎7	♏5	♐3
Feb.	♐17	♑16	♒14	♓11	♈6		♉25	♊19	♋13	♌9	♍5	♎3	♏1	♐0	♐28	
Mar.	♑12	♒10	♓6	♈2	♈27	♉21	♊14	♋9	♌0	♍28	♍27	♎26	♏25	♐23	♑20	
April	♓3	♓28	♈23	♉17	♊11	♊5	♋29	♌24	♍20	♎21	♎21	♏19	♐17	♑12		
May	♈7	♉2	♉26	♊19	♋12	♋7	♌3	♍0	♎29	♎29	♏29	♐29	♑26	♒22	♈17	♉11
June	♉23	♊16	♋10	♌4	♍29	♍25	♎23	♏22	♐23	♑23	♒22	♓18	♈14	♉8	♊2	
July	♊25	♋19	♌14	♍9	♎5	♏3	♐2	♑1	♑1	♒0	♓27	♈22	♉16	♊10	♋4	♋28
Aug.	♋11	♌6	♍2	♎29	♏27	♐26	♑25	♒24	♓21	♈17	♉12	♊6	♋0	♌24	♍19	♍15
Sep.	♍29	♎26	♏24	♐22	♑21	♒19	♓16	♈13	♉8	♊2	♋26	♌20	♍15	♎10	♎8	
Oct.	♎6	♏5	♐4	♑2	♒29	♒25	♓21	♈16	♉10	♊4	♋28	♌22	♍18	♎16	♏15	♐15
Nov.	♈0	♑28	♒26	♓22	♈18	♉12	♊7	♋1	♌24	♍18	♎13	♏10	♐8	♑8	♒9	
Dec.	♒8	♓6	♈2	♈27	♉22	♊15	♋9	♌3	♍27	♎22	♏18	♐16	♑16	♒17	♓17	♈15

Moon ingress table for 1925 (zodiac sign and date). Columns read left-to-right in the image: Dec., Nov., Oct., Sep., Aug., July, June, May, April, Mar., Feb., Jan., and the day column (1925).

1925	Jan.	Feb.	Mar.	April	May	June	July	Aug.	Sep.	Oct.	Nov.	Dec.
1	♓ 28	♉ 15	♉ 23	♋ 7	♌ 9	♍ 23	♎ 28	♐ 19	♒ 13	♓ 21	♉ 12	♊ 16
3	♈ 24	♊ 9	♊ 17	♌ —	♍ 3	♎ 20	♏ 26	♑ 19	♓ 12	♈ 19	♊ 8	♋ 10
5	♉ 19	♋ 3	♋ 11	♌ 25	♍ 28	♏ 18	♐ 25	♑ 19	♈ —	♉ 17	♋ 2	♌ 4
7	♊ 12	♋ 27	♌ 5	♍ 20	♎ 25	♐ 17	♑ 26	♒ 19	♈ 9	♊ 12	♋ 26	♍ 28
9	♋ 6	♌ 21	♍ 29	♎ 17	♏ 24	♑ 17	♒ 26	♓ 17	♉ 4	♋ 7	♌ 20	♎ 22
11	♋ 0	♍ 16	♍ 25	♏ 13	♐ 23	♑ 15	♓ 24	♈ 13	♉ 29	♌ 0	♍ 14	♏ 17
13	♌ 24	♎ 11	♎ 21	♏ 11	♑ 22	♒ 12	♈ 21	♈ 8	♊ 22	♌ 24	♎ 9	♐ 13
15	♍ 19	♏ 8	♏ 19	♐ 12	♒ 21	♓ 7	♉ 17	♉ 2	♋ 16	♍ 19	♏ 6	♑ 12
17	♎ 14	♐ 6	♐ 16	♑ 10	♒ 18	♈ 2	♊ 11	♋ 26	♋ 10	♎ 14	♐ 3	♑ 11
19	♏ 11	♐ 4	♑ 15	♒ 7	♓ 15	♉ 26	♋ 5	♌ 19	♌ 5	♏ 11	♑ 2	♒ 10
21	♐ 10	♑ 3	♑ 13	♓ 5	♈ 10	♊ 20	♋ 29	♍ 14	♍ 1	♐ 8	♑ 1	♓ 7
23	♑ 10	♒ 3	♒ 11	♈ —	♉ 5	♋ 13	♌ 22	♎ 8	♎ 28	♒ 6	♒ 29	♈ 4
25	♒ 9	♓ 1	♓ 9	♉ 27	♉ 29	♌ 9	♍ 16	♏ 4	♏ 25	♓ 4	♓ 27	♉ 0
27	♓ 7	♈ 28	♈ 6	♉ 21	♊ 23	♍ 2	♎ 11	♐ 1	♐ 23	♈ 2	♈ 24	♊ 25
29	♈ 3		♉ 1	♊ 15	♋ 17		♏ 7	♐ 29	♑ 22	♉ 0	♉ 20	♊ 19
31			♊ 25		♌ 11		♐ 5	♑ 28		♊ 28		♋ 19

1926	Jan.	Feb.	Mar.	April	May	June	July	Aug.	Sep.	Oct.	Nov.	Dec.
1	1 ♌	15 ♍	24 ♍	10 ♏	17 ♐	9 ♒	18 ♓	10 ♉	29 ♊	2 ♌	16 ♍	18 ♎
3	24 ♌	9 ♎	18 ♎	7 ♐	14 ♑	7 ♓	16 ♈	7 ♊	23 ♋	26 ♌	10 ♎	13 ♏
5	18 ♍	4 ♏	13 ♏	3 ♑	12 ♒	5 ♈	14 ♉	2 ♋	17 ♌	20 ♍	5 ♏	9 ♐
7	12 ♎	0 ♐	9 ♐	1 ♒	10 ♓	3 ♉	10 ♊	26 ♋	11 ♍	14 ♎	0 ♐	6 ♑
9	8 ♏	28 ♐	7 ♑	0 ♓	9 ♈	0 ♊	5 ♋	20 ♌	5 ♎	8 ♏	26 ♐	3 ♒
11	5 ♐	27 ♑	6 ♒	29 ♓	7 ♉	26 ♊	0 ♌	14 ♍	29 ♎	3 ♐	23 ♑	1 ♓
13	4 ♑	27 ♒	6 ♓	28 ♈	5 ♊	21 ♋	24 ♌	8 ♎	24 ♏	29 ♐	20 ♒	0 ♈
15	4 ♒	28 ♓	6 ♈	26 ♉	1 ♋	15 ♌	17 ♍	2 ♏	19 ♐	26 ♑	19 ♓	28 ♈
17	4 ♓	27 ♈	5 ♉	23 ♊	25 ♋	9 ♍	11 ♎	27 ♏	16 ♑	24 ♒	18 ♈	26 ♉
19	4 ♈	23 ♉	2 ♊	17 ♋	19 ♌	3 ♎	6 ♏	23 ♐	15 ♒	24 ♓	17 ♉	23 ♊
21	1 ♉	19 ♊	27 ♊	11 ♌	13 ♍	28 ♎	2 ♐	22 ♑	15 ♓	24 ♈	15 ♊	19 ♋
23	27 ♉	13 ♋	21 ♋	5 ♍	7 ♎	24 ♏	29 ♐	22 ♒	16 ♈	23 ♉	11 ♋	14 ♌
25	22 ♊	6 ♌	15 ♌	29 ♍	2 ♏	21 ♐	28 ♑	22 ♓	15 ♉	21 ♊	7 ♌	8 ♍
27	16 ♋	0 ♍	9 ♍	24 ♎	29 ♏	20 ♑	22 ♒	22 ♈	12 ♊	16 ♋	1 ♍	2 ♎
29	9 ♌		3 ♎	20 ♏	26 ♐	19 ♒	28 ♓	20 ♉	8 ♋	11 ♌	24 ♍	26 ♎
31	3 ♍		28 ♎		24 ♑		27 ♈	16 ♊		5 ♍		21 ♏

1927	Jan.	Feb.	Mar.	April	May	June	July	Aug.	Sep.	Oct.	Nov.	Dec.
1	♐ 4	♑ 23	♒ 0	♓ 23	♉ 2	♊ 24	♋ 0	♍ 16	♎ 0	♐ 2	♈ 18	♒ 24
3	♐ 1	♑ 22	♒ 0	♈ 24	♊ 0	♋ 21	♌ 25	♎ 10	♏ 23	♐ 26	♑ 14	♓ 22
5	♑ 29	♒ 22	♓ 1	♉ 24	♋ 26	♌ 17	♍ 20	♏ 3	♐ 18	♑ 22	♒ 12	♈ 20
7	♑ 28	♓ 21	♈ 29	♊ 22	♋ 26	♍ 12	♎ 13	♏ 27	♑ 13	♒ 19	♓ 11	♉ 20
9	♒ 26	♈ 18	♉ 26	♋ 18	♌ 21	♎ 6	♏ 7	♐ 22	♒ 11	♓ 18	♈ 12	♊ 20
11	♓ 25	♉ 16	♉ 21	♋ 13	♍ 15	♎ 29	♐ 2	♑ 19	♓ 10	♈ 18	♉ 10	♋ 18
13	♈ 22	♊ 12	♊ 16	♌ 7	♎ 9	♏ 24	♐ 27	♒ 17	♈ 10	♉ 19	♊ 7	♍ 15
15	♉ 19	♋ 7	♋ 10	♍ 1	♎ 3	♐ 19	♑ 24	♓ 16	♉ 9	♊ 18	♋ 2	♎ 11
17	♊ 15	♌ 1	♌ 4	♎ 24	♏ 27	♐ 15	♒ 22	♈ 15	♊ 6	♋ 15	♌ 27	♎ 5
19	♋ 10	♍ 25	♍ 27	♎ 18	♐ 22	♑ 12	♓ 20	♉ 14	♋ 1	♌ 11	♍ 20	♏ 29
21	♌ 4	♍ 19	♎ 21	♏ 13	♐ 18	♒ 10	♈ 19	♊ 12	♌ 26	♍ 6	♍ 14	♐ 23
23	♍ 28	♎ 12	♎ 16	♏ 8	♑ 15	♓ 8	♉ 17	♋ 9	♌ 21	♎ 0	♎ 8	♑ 17
25	♍ 22	♏ 7	♏ 12	♐ 5	♒ 13	♈ 7	♊ 15	♌ 4	♍ 15	♎ 24	♏ 3	♒ 10
27	♎ 16	♐ 3	♐ 9	♑ 3	♓ 12	♉ 5	♋ 12	♍ 0	♎ 8	♏ 17	♐ 28	♓ 8
29	♏ 12		♈ 9	♒ 2	♈ 11	♊ 3	♌ 8	♍ 24		♐ 11		♈ 5
31	♑ 8		♓ 8		♊ 10		♍ 3	♎ 18		♑ 5		♈ 2

206

Ephemeris table of daily positions (zodiac sign and degree) for 1928.

1928	Jan.	Feb.	Mar.	April	May	June	July	Aug.	Sep.	Oct.	Nov.	Dec.
1	♈ 16	♊ 9	♋ 4	♌ 24	♍ 28	♏ 13	♐ 15	♒ 1	♓ 20	♈ 28	♊ 21	♋ 29
3	♉ 15	♋ 7	♌ 1	♍ 19	♎ 22	♏ 7	♑ 9	♒ 27	♓ 18	♉ 27	♋ 20	♌ 27
5	♊ 14	♌ 5	♌ 27	♎ 13	♏ 16	♐ 1	♑ 4	♓ 24	♈ 17	♊ 26	♌ 17	♍ 23
7	♋ 12	♍ 1	♍ 22	♏ 7	♐ 10	♑ 25	♒ 0	♈ 22	♉ 15	♋ 24	♍ 14	♎ 18
9	♌ 10	♎ 26	♎ 17	♐ 1	♑ 3	♑ 20	♒ 27	♉ 20	♊ 13	♌ 21	♎ 9	♏ 12
11	♍ 6	♏ 14	♏ 4	♐ 25	♒ 28	♒ 17	♓ 25	♊ 18	♋ 10	♍ 17	♏ 3	♐ 6
13	♎ 25	♐ 8	♐ 28	♑ 19	♒ 24	♓ 15	♈ 23	♋ 17	♌ 7	♎ 12	♐ 27	♑ 29
15	♏ 19	♑ 3	♑ 23	♒ 15	♓ 21	♈ 14	♉ 22	♌ 15	♍ 3	♏ 6	♑ 20	♒ 23
17	♐ 13	♒ 28	♒ 20	♓ 12	♈ 20	♉ 13	♊ 22	♍ 12	♎ 28	♐ 0	♒ 14	♓ 18
19	♑ 7	♓ 26	♓ 18	♈ 11	♉ 20	♊ 13	♋ 20	♎ 7	♏ 22	♑ 24	♓ 8	♈ 13
21	♒ 4	♈ 24	♈ 18	♉ 12	♊ 20	♋ 12	♌ 17	♏ 2	♐ 16	♒ 18	♈ 4	♉ 9
23	♓ 1	♉ 24	♉ 18	♊ 12	♋ 19	♌ 9	♍ 12	♐ 26	♑ 9	♓ 12	♈ 0	♊ 8
25	♓ 29	♊ 22	♊ 17	♋ 10	♌ 17	♍ 4	♎ 6	♑ 20	♒ 4	♈ 8	♉ 29	♋ 7
27	♈ 27	♊ 20	♋ 14	♌ 8	♍ 13	♎ 28	♏ 0	♒ 14	♓ 1	♉ 7	♊ 29	♌ 7
29	♉ 25	♋ 20	♌ 11	♍ 3	♎ 7	♏ 22	♐ 24	♓ 9	♓ 28	♊ 6	♋ 0	♍ 6
31			♍ 11		♏ 1		♑ 18	♈ 6		♊ 6		♎ 6

1929	Jan.	Feb.	Mar.	April	May	June	July	Aug.	Sep.	Oct.	Nov.	Dec.
1	♍ 19	♓ 5	♏ 13	♐ 27	♑ 28	♓ 14	♈ 19	♊ 10	♋ 4	♍ 12	♏ 2	♐ 6
3	♎ 15	♏ 29	♐ 7	♑ 20	♒ 23	♈ 10	♉ 17	♋ 10	♍ 3	♎ 10	♏ 28	♑ 0
5	♏ 9	♐ 23	♐ 1	♒ 15	♓ 18	♉ 8	♊ 16	♌ 10	♎ 29	♏ 7	♐ 22	♑ 24
7	♐ 3	♑ 16	♑ 25	♓ 10	♈ 16	♊ 8	♋ 16	♍ 9	♏ 24	♐ 2	♑ 16	♒ 18
9	♐ 26	♒ 11	♒ 19	♈ 7	♉ 14	♋ 8	♍ 16	♎ 7	♐ 18	♐ 26	♒ 10	♓ 12
11	♑ 20	♓ 7	♓ 15	♉ 6	♊ 14	♌ 6	♎ 15	♏ 4	♑ 12	♑ 20	♓ 4	♈ 7
13	♒ 15	♈ 3	♈ 13	♊ 5	♋ 12	♍ 3	♏ 12	♐ 28	♒ 6	♒ 14	♈ 29	♉ 4
15	♓ 10	♉ 0	♉ 10	♋ 4	♌ 10	♎ 28	♐ 7	♑ 22	♓ 0	♓ 9	♉ 26	♊ 2
17	♈ 6	♉ 28	♊ 9	♌ 2	♍ 6	♏ 22	♑ 1	♒ 16	♈ 26	♈ 4	♊ 24	♋ 2
19	♉ 3	♊ 26	♋ 7	♍ 29	♎ 1	♐ 16	♒ 25	♓ 10	♉ 22	♉ 0	♋ 23	♌ 2
21	♊ 1	♋ 25	♌ 5	♍ 26	♏ 25	♑ 10	♓ 19	♈ 4	♊ 19	♊ 29	♌ 23	♍ 2
23	♋ —	♌ 24	♍ 3	♎ 22	♏ 19	♒ 4	♈ 13	♉ 0	♋ 17	♋ 28	♍ 22	♍ 29
25	♋ 0	♍ 21	♎ 26	♏ 17	♐ 13	♓ 28	♉ 7	♉ 26	♌ 15	♌ 27	♎ 19	♎ 26
27	♌ 0	♎ 18	♏ 21	♐ 11	♑ 7	♈ 23	♊ 3	♊ 23	♌ 14	♍ 25	♏ 16	♏ 21
29	♍ 27		♏ 21	♑ 5	♒ 1		♋ 29	♋ 20		♍ 22	♐ 11	♐ 15
31	♍ 23		♐ 15		♓ 7		♌ 26	♋ 19		♎ 19		♑ 9

208

Ephemeris table (moon sign and degree for 1930), read in zodiac-sign progression. Degrees given with each sign glyph.

1930	Jan.	Feb.	Mar.	April	May	June	July	Aug.	Sep.	Oct.	Nov.	Dec.
1	♑ 21	♓ 6	♓ 15	♉ 1	♊ 8	♌ 1	♍ 10	♏ 2	♐ 19	♑ 22	♓ 6	♈ 8
3	♒ 15	♓ 0	♈ 9	♉ 28	♋ 6	♍ 0	♎ 8	♏ 28	♐ 14	♒ 16	♈ 0	♉ 3
5	♓ 8	♈ 25	♉ 5	♊ 25	♌ 4	♍ 28	♏ 5	♐ 23	♑ 8	♓ 10	♈ 25	♉ 29
7	♈ 3	♉ 21	♊ 1	♋ 23	♍ 3	♎ 25	♐ 1	♑ 17	♒ 1	♈ 4	♉ 21	♊ 27
9	♈ 28	♊ 19	♊ 28	♌ 22	♎ 1	♏ 21	♑ 25	♒ 11	♓ 25	♈ 29	♊ 17	♋ 25
11	♉ 26	♋ 18	♋ 27	♍ 21	♏ 28	♐ 16	♒ 20	♓ 4	♓ 20	♉ 24	♋ 15	♌ 24
13	♊ 25	♌ 18	♌ 27	♎ 19	♐ 25	♑ 11	♓ 14	♈ 28	♈ 14	♊ 21	♌ 13	♍ 22
15	♋ 25	♍ 19	♍ 27	♏ 16	♑ 20	♒ 5	♈ 7	♉ 22	♉ 10	♋ 18	♍ 11	♎ 20
17	♌ 26	♎ 17	♎ 25	♐ 12	♒ 15	♒ 29	♈ 1	♊ 18	♊ 8	♌ 16	♎ 10	♏ 17
19	♍ 25	♏ 14	♏ 22	♑ 7	♓ 9	♓ 23	♉ 26	♋ 14	♋ 7	♍ 16	♏ 8	♐ 14
21	♎ 22	♐ 9	♐ 17	♒ 1	♓ 3	♈ 17	♊ 22	♌ 13	♌ 6	♎ 15	♐ 5	♑ 9
23	♏ 18	♑ 3	♑ 11	♒ 25	♈ 27	♉ 13	♋ 19	♍ 13	♍ 6	♏ 13	♑ 5	♒ 4
25	♐ 12	♑ 27	♒ 5	♓ 19	♉ 22	♊ 11	♌ 19	♎ 13	♎ 5	♐ 10	♑ 26	♒ 28
27	♑ 6	♒ 20	♒ 29	♈ 14	♊ 19	♋ 11	♍ 20	♏ 11	♏ 2	♑ 6	♒ 20	♓ 22
29	♒ 0		♓ 23	♉ 10	♋ 17	♌ 11	♎ 20	♐ 7	♐ 28	♒ 1	♓ 14	♈ 16
31	♒ 24		♈ 18		♋ 16		♎ 18			♒ 24		♉ 11

1931	Jan.	Feb.	Mar.	April	May	June	July	Aug.	Sep.	Oct.	Nov.	Dec.
1	24	13	21	14	23	15	20	6	20	22	9	16
3	21	13	21	15	22	12	15	29	13	17	6	14
5	20	13	21	14	20	7	9	23	8	13	3	12
7	19	13	20	12	17	1	3	17	4	10	2	10
9	19	11	17	8	11	25	27	12	1	9	2	10
11	17	7	12	3	5	19	21	9	1	9	2	9
13	14	3	6	27	29	13	17	8	1	9	1	9
15	10	27	0	21	23	9	15	7	1	8	27	5
17	6	21	24	14	18	6	13	7	0	6	23	1
19	0	15	18	7	13	4	11	6	27	2	17	25
21	25	9	12	0	8	2	9	4	23	26	10	18
23	18	3	7	27	5	0	7	0	17	20	4	12
25	12	27	3	25	4	28	3	26	11	14	28	7
27	6	23	0	24	2	26	1	20	5	7	24	3
29	1		29		1	24	29	14	28	2	19	29
31	29						24	8		27		27

210

1932	Jan.	Feb.	Mar.	April	May	June	July	Aug.	Sep.	Oct.	Nov.	Dec.
1	9 ♎	2 ♐	26 ♐	15 ♒	19 ♓	3 ♉	5 ♊	21 ♋	11 ♍	18 ♎	12 ♐	20 ♑
3	7 ♏	29 ♐	22 ♑	10 ♓	12 ♈	27 ♉	0 ♋	18 ♌	9 ♎	18 ♏	11 ♑	18 ♒
5	5 ♐	26 ♑	18 ♒	4 ♈	6 ♉	21 ♊	26 ♋	15 ♍	8 ♏	18 ♐	9 ♒	14 ♓
7	3 ♑	22 ♒	12 ♓	27 ♈	0 ♊	16 ♋	22 ♌	14 ♎	7 ♐	16 ♑	5 ♓	8 ♈
9	0 ♒	16 ♓	7 ♈	21 ♉	24 ♊	12 ♌	19 ♍	12 ♏	5 ♑	12 ♒	29 ♓	2 ♉
11	26 ♒	10 ♈	0 ♉	15 ♊	19 ♋	8 ♍	17 ♎	10 ♐	2 ♒	8 ♓	23 ♈	26 ♉
13	20 ♓	4 ♉	24 ♉	9 ♋	15 ♌	6 ♎	15 ♏	8 ♑	28 ♒	2 ♈	17 ♉	20 ♊
15	14 ♈	28 ♉	18 ♊	5 ♌	12 ♍	5 ♏	14 ♐	6 ♒	23 ♓	26 ♈	11 ♊	14 ♋
17	8 ♉	23 ♊	13 ♋	3 ♍	11 ♎	4 ♐	13 ♑	2 ♓	18 ♈	20 ♉	5 ♋	9 ♌
19	2 ♊	19 ♋	10 ♌	2 ♎	11 ♏	4 ♑	10 ♒	27 ♓	12 ♉	14 ♊	29 ♋	4 ♍
21	28 ♊	17 ♌	9 ♍	2 ♏	11 ♐	2 ♒	7 ♓	22 ♈	5 ♊	8 ♋	24 ♌	1 ♎
23	24 ♋	16 ♍	9 ♎	3 ♐	10 ♑	29 ♒	2 ♈	15 ♉	29 ♊	3 ♌	21 ♍	29 ♎
25	22 ♌	15 ♎	9 ♏	2 ♑	8 ♒	24 ♓	26 ♈	9 ♊	24 ♋	29 ♌	20 ♎	28 ♏
27	21 ♍	14 ♏	8 ♐	29 ♑	3 ♓	18 ♈	19 ♉	4 ♋	21 ♌	27 ♍	20 ♏	28 ♐
29	20 ♎	12 ♐	6 ♑	24 ♒	27 ♓	11 ♉	13 ♊	29 ♋	19 ♍	27 ♎	20 ♐	28 ♑
31	18 ♏		2 ♒		21 ♈		8 ♋	27 ♌		27 ♏		26 ♒

1933	Jan.	Feb.	Mar.	April	May	June	July	Aug.	Sep.	Oct.	Nov.	Dec.
1	♓9	♈25	♉2	♊16	♋18	♍4	♎10	♐2	♐26	♓4	♎23	♉27
3	♈5	♉19	♉26	♋10	♌13	♎0	♏8	♑1	♒24	♈1	♉18	♊21
5	♉29	♊12	♊20	♌5	♍8	♎29	♐7	♒0	♓22	♈27	♊12	♋14
7	♉22	♋7	♋14	♍0	♎6	♏28	♐7	♓27	♈19	♉22	♋6	♌8
9	♊16	♌1	♌9	♎28	♏5	♐29	♑6	♈23	♉14	♊16	♌0	♍2
11	♋11	♍27	♍6	♏27	♐5	♑29	♒2	♉18	♊8	♋10	♍24	♎27
13	♌6	♎24	♎3	♐26	♑5	♒27	♓28	♊12	♋2	♌4	♎19	♏24
15	♍1	♏22	♏2	♑24	♒4	♓24	♈22	♋6	♌26	♍28	♏16	♐23
17	♍28	♐20	♐1	♒21	♓1	♈19	♉16	♌0	♍20	♎24	♐15	♑23
19	♎25	♑19	♐0	♓17	♈27	♉13	♊9	♍25	♎16	♏22	♐15	♒23
21	♏23	♒17	♑27	♈12	♉22	♊7	♋3	♎20	♏13	♐21	♑13	♒23
23	♐23	♓15	♒24	♉7	♊16	♋0	♌28	♏17	♐11	♑20	♒11	♓23
25	♑22	♈12	♓20	♊1	♋10	♌24	♍24	♐15	♑10	♒19	♓7	♈21
27	♒20	♉8	♈16	♋25	♌3	♍18	♎20	♐13	♒8	♓17	♈2	♉17
29	♓17		♉10	♋25	♌27	♍14	♏20	♐13	♒6	♓14	♉2	♈6
31	♈12		♊4		♌22		♏18	♐11		♓10		♊29

1934	Jan.	Feb.	Mar.	April	May	June	July	Aug.	Sep.	Oct.	Nov.	Dec.
1	11	26	5	22	29	23	0	23	10	12	26	28
3	5	21	0	20	28	22	26	19	4	6	20	23
5	29	16	26	18	27	20	26	13	28	0	15	20
7	24	13	23	16	25	16	22	6	21	24	11	18
9	19	10	21	14	23	12	10	1	15	19	9	17
11	17	9	19	12	19	7	4	25	10	16	7	16
13	16	9	18	10	15	1	27	19	6	13	5	14
15	16	7	17	7	11	25	21	13	2	10	4	12
17	16	4	15	2	5	19	16	9	0	9	1	9
19	15	29	12	27	29	13	12	6	28	7	29	5
21	13	23	7	21	22	7	10	4	27	6	26	0
23	8	17	1	14	16	4	10	4	27	4	21	24
25	3	10	25	9	12	2	10	3	25	1	16	18
27	26		18	4	9	2	9	1	23	26	10	12
29	20		13	1	8	2		27	18	20	4	6
31	14		9		8					14		1

213

1935	Jan.	Feb.	Mar.	April	May	June	July	Aug.	Sep.	Oct.	Nov.	Dec.
1	♏ 14	♐ 4	♑ 12	♓ 5	♈ 14	♊ 6	♋ 10	♌ 25	♎ 10	♏ 13	♐ 1	♒ 8
3	♏ 11	♐ 4	♑ 12	♓ 5	♉ 13	♊ 2	♌ 5	♍ 19	♏ 4	♐ 8	♑ 27	♓ 6
5	♐ 11	♒ 4	♒ 12	♉ 5	♊ 10	♋ 27	♌ 29	♎ 13	♏ 29	♐ 4	♒ 25	♈ 4
7	♑ 11	♓ 4	♓ 11	♊ 2	♋ 6	♌ 21	♍ 23	♎ 7	♐ 24	♑ 1	♓ 24	♉ 3
9	♒ 10	♈ 2	♈ 8	♊ 29	♋ 1	♍ 15	♎ 17	♏ 2	♑ 22	♒ 0	♓ 24	♊ 1
11	♓ 9	♉ 29	♉ 3	♋ 23	♌ 25	♎ 9	♏ 11	♏ 29	♒ 21	♓ 0	♈ 23	♊ 29
13	♈ 6	♊ 24	♊ 27	♌ 17	♍ 19	♏ 3	♏ 8	♐ 28	♓ 21	♈ 0	♉ 21	♋ 25
15	♉ 2	♋ 18	♋ 20	♍ 10	♎ 13	♏ 29	♐ 5	♑ 28	♈ 21	♉ 29	♊ 17	♌ 20
17	♋ 27	♌ 12	♌ 14	♎ 5	♏ 8	♐ 27	♑ 4	♒ 28	♉ 22	♊ 27	♋ 12	♍ 14
19	♌ 21	♍ 5	♍ 8	♏ 29	♏ 4	♑ 25	♒ 3	♓ 25	♊ 19	♋ 22	♌ 6	♎ 8
21	♍ 15	♎ 29	♎ 3	♐ 25	♐ 2	♒ 24	♓ 2	♈ 21	♋ 18	♋ 16	♍ 0	♏ 2
23	♎ 8	♏ 23	♏ 28	♑ 21	♑ 29	♓ 23	♈ 29	♉ 16	♋ 13	♌ 10	♎ 24	♐ 27
25	♏ 2	♏ 18	♏ 24	♒ 19	♒ 28	♈ 21	♉ 24	♊ 10	♍ 8	♍ 4	♏ 19	♑ 23
27	♐ 26	♐ 15	♐ 22	♓ 17	♓ 26	♉ 18	♊ 19	♋ 4	♍ 1	♎ 28	♐ 14	♒ 20
29	♑ 22		♑ 21	♈ 15	♈ 24	♊ 15	♋ 14	♎ 28	♎ 25	♏ 23	♐ 11	♓ 18
31	♒ 19				♉ 22			♍ 28		♐ 18		♈ 17

214

1936	Jan.	Feb.	Mar.	April	May	June	July	Aug.	Sep.	Oct.	Nov.	Dec.
1	1 ♈	24 ♉	18 ♊	6 ♌	9 ♍	23 ♎	25 ♏	11 ♑	1 ♓	9 ♈	3 ♊	10 ♋
3	29 ♈	21 ♊	14 ♋	0 ♍	3 ♎	17 ♏	20 ♐	8 ♒	1 ♈	10 ♉	2 ♋	8 ♌
5	27 ♉	17 ♋	9 ♌	24 ♍	26 ♎	12 ♐	16 ♑	7 ♓	1 ♉	9 ♊	0 ♌	4 ♍
7	24 ♊	12 ♌	3 ♍	18 ♎	20 ♏	7 ♑	13 ♒	6 ♈	29 ♉	7 ♋	25 ♌	29 ♍
9	20 ♋	6 ♍	27 ♍	11 ♏	15 ♐	3 ♒	11 ♓	5 ♉	27 ♊	3 ♌	20 ♍	22 ♎
11	16 ♌	0 ♎	21 ♎	6 ♐	10 ♑	0 ♓	9 ♈	3 ♊	23 ♋	28 ♌	14 ♎	16 ♏
13	10 ♍	24 ♎	14 ♏	0 ♑	6 ♒	28 ♓	8 ♉	0 ♋	19 ♌	23 ♍	7 ♏	10 ♐
15	4 ♎	18 ♏	9 ♐	26 ♑	4 ♓	27 ♈	6 ♊	27 ♋	14 ♍	17 ♎	1 ♐	4 ♑
17	28 ♎	13 ♐	4 ♑	24 ♒	2 ♈	26 ♉	4 ♋	22 ♌	8 ♎	10 ♏	25 ♐	0 ♒
19	22 ♏	9 ♑	1 ♒	23 ♓	2 ♉	25 ♊	1 ♌	17 ♍	2 ♏	4 ♐	20 ♑	26 ♒
21	18 ♐	7 ♒	29 ♒	23 ♈	2 ♊	22 ♋	26 ♌	11 ♎	25 ♏	28 ♐	16 ♒	23 ♓
23	15 ♑	6 ♓	0 ♈	23 ♉	0 ♋	18 ♌	21 ♍	5 ♏	19 ♐	23 ♑	13 ♓	21 ♈
25	13 ♒	7 ♈	0 ♉	22 ♊	27 ♋	13 ♍	15 ♎	29 ♏	14 ♑	19 ♒	11 ♈	20 ♉
27	13 ♓	6 ♉	0 ♊	19 ♋	23 ♌	7 ♊	9 ♏	23 ♐	11 ♒	18 ♓	11 ♉	19 ♊
29	12 ♈	4 ♊	27 ♊	15 ♌	17 ♍	1 ♏	3 ♐	19 ♑	9 ♓	18 ♈	11 ♊	18 ♋
31	10 ♉		23 ♋		11 ♎		28 ♐	17 ♒		18 ♉		16 ♌

1937	Jan.	Feb.	Mar.	April	May	June	July	Aug.	Sep.	Oct.	Nov.	Dec.
1	♌ 29	♎ 14	♎ 22	♐ 6	♈ 9	♒ 25	♓ 2	♉ 24	♋ 18	♌ 25	♎ 14	♏ 17
3	♍ 24	♏ 8	♏ 16	♑ 0	♒ 3	♓ 22	♈ 0	♊ 23	♌ 15	♍ 22	♏ 8	♐ 11
5	♎ 19	♐ 2	♐ 10	♑ 24	♒ 29	♈ 20	♉ 29	♋ 22	♍ 13	♎ 17	♐ 2	♑ 4
7	♏ 12	♐ 26	♑ 4	♒ 20	♓ 27	♉ 19	♊ 28	♌ 20	♎ 9	♏ 12	♐ 26	♑ 28
9	♐ 6	♑ 21	♒ 29	♓ 18	♈ 26	♉ 20	♋ 28	♍ 17	♏ 4	♐ 6	♑ 19	♒ 23
11	♐ —	♒ 18	♓ 26	♈ 18	♉ 26	♊ 19	♌ 26	♎ 13	♐ 28	♑ 29	♒ 14	♓ 18
13	♑ 26	♓ 16	♈ 25	♉ 18	♉ 26	♋ 18	♍ 23	♏ 8	♐ 21	♒ 23	♓ 9	♈ 13
15	♒ 22	♈ 14	♉ 24	♊ 17	♊ 25	♌ 14	♎ 18	♐ —	♑ 15	♓ 18	♈ 6	♉ 13
17	♓ 20	♉ 13	♊ 23	♋ 16	♋ 22	♍ 9	♏ 12	♐ 25	♒ 10	♈ 15	♉ 5	♊ 14
19	♈ 18	♊ 11	♋ 22	♌ 13	♌ 18	♎ 3	♐ 5	♑ 20	♓ 7	♉ 13	♊ 6	♋ 14
21	♉ 16	♋ 9	♌ 19	♍ 8	♍ 12	♏ 27	♑ 29	♒ 15	♈ 4	♊ 12	♋ 6	♌ 11
23	♊ 14	♌ 6	♍ 16	♎ 3	♎ 6	♐ 21	♒ 24	♓ 12	♉ 3	♋ 12	♌ 5	♍ 7
25	♋ 13	♍ 2	♎ 11	♏ 27	♏ 0	♑ 15	♓ 19	♈ 9	♊ 2	♌ 11	♍ 2	♎ 2
27	♌ 10	♍ 28	♏ 6	♏ 21	♐ 24	♒ 5	♈ 15	♉ 7	♋ 0	♍ 9	♎ 28	♏ 26
29	♍ 7		♏ 1	♐ 15	♐ 18		♉ 12	♊ 5	♌ 28	♎ 5	♎ 23	♐ 20
31	♎ 2		♏ 24		♑ 12		♉ 10	♋ 3		♏ 1		

1938	Jan.	Feb.	Mar.	April	May	June	July	Aug.	Sep.	Oct.	Nov.	Dec.
1	♐ 1	♒ 16	♒ 25	♈ 13	♉ 20	♋ 14	♌ 23	♎ 13	♐ 0	♑ 2	♒ 15	♓ 17
3	♑ 25	♓ 12	♓ 21	♉ 11	♊ 20	♌ 13	♍ 21	♏ 9	♐ 24	♑ 26	♓ 10	♈ 13
5	♒ 20	♈ 8	♈ 18	♊ 10	♋ 19	♍ 14	♎ 17	♐ 3	♑ 18	♒ 20	♈ 5	♉ 10
7	♓ 15	♉ 5	♉ 15	♋ 8	♌ 17	♎ 8	♏ 12	♐ 27	♒ 11	♓ 14	♉ 2	♊ 8
9	♈ 11	♊ 2	♊ 13	♌ 6	♍ 15	♏ 3	♐ 7	♑ 21	♓ 6	♈ 10	♊ 0	♋ 8
11	♉ 8	♋ 1	♋ 11	♍ 4	♎ 11	♐ 28	♑ 0	♒ 15	♈ 1	♉ 7	♋ 29	♌ 8
13	♊ 7	♋ 0	♌ 10	♎ 1	♏ 6	♐ 21	♑ 24	♓ 9	♉ 27	♊ 5	♌ 28	♍ 7
15	♋ 7	♌ 29	♍ 8	♏ 27	♐ 1	♑ 15	♒ 18	♈ 4	♊ 24	♋ 3	♍ 26	♎ 4
17	♌ 6	♍ 27	♎ 6	♏ 22	♐ 25	♒ 9	♓ 12	♉ 0	♋ 22	♌ 29	♎ 24	♏ 0
19	♍ 3	♎ 24	♏ 2	♐ 16	♑ 18	♓ 3	♈ 7	♉ 27	♌ 20	♍ 27	♏ 21	♐ 26
21	♎ 29	♏ 19	♏ 26	♐ 10	♒ 12	♓ 28	♉ 4	♊ 25	♍ 19	♎ 24	♐ 16	♑ 20
23	♏ 23	♐ 13	♐ 20	♑ 4	♓ 7	♈ 24	♊ 1	♋ 25	♎ 18	♏ 21	♑ 11	♒ 14
25	♐ 16	♑ 6	♑ 14	♒ 28	♈ 2	♉ 22	♋ 1	♌ 25	♏ 16	♐ 16	♒ 6	♓ 8
27	♑ 10	♒ 0	♒ 8	♓ 24	♈ 0	♊ 22	♋ 1	♍ 24	♐ 12	♑ 10	♓ 0	♈ 2
29	♒ 4		♓ 3	♈ 22	♉ 29	♋ 23	♌ 1	♎ 21	♑ 8	♒ 3	♈ 23	♉ 26
31	♓ 4		♈ 0		♊ 29		♌ 0	♏ 17		♓ 3		♊ 21

217

Ephemeris table for 1939 (Moon positions — zodiac sign and degree for each date).

1939	Jan.	Feb.	Mar.	April	May	June	July	Aug.	Sep.	Oct.	Nov.	Dec.
1	♉ 4	♊ 24	♋ 3	♌ 27	♎ 6	♏ 26	♐ 1	♒ 16	♈ 0	♉ 4	♊ 22	♌ 0
3	♊ 2	♋ 24	♋ 3	♍ 26	♏ 4	♏ 22	♐ 25	♓ 10	♈ 24	♉ 29	♋ 20	♌ 29
5	♋ 1	♋ 25	♋ 3	♎ 25	♏ 0	♐ 17	♑ 19	♈ 3	♉ 19	♊ 25	♋ 18	♍ 27
7	♋ 2	♌ 25	♌ 1	♏ 22	♐ 26	♑ 11	♒ 13	♉ 28	♊ 15	♋ 23	♌ 16	♎ 25
9	♌ 2	♍ 23	♍ 28	♐ 18	♑ 21	♒ 4	♓ 7	♊ 23	♋ 13	♌ 22	♎ 15	♏ 22
11	♍ 0	♎ 19	♎ 23	♑ 13	♒ 15	♓ 28	♈ 1	♋ 20	♌ 12	♍ 21	♏ 13	♐ 19
13	♍ 27	♏ 14	♏ 17	♒ 7	♓ 8	♈ 23	♉ 28	♌ 19	♍ 13	♎ 19	♐ 11	♑ 15
15	♎ 23	♐ 8	♐ 10	♓ 0	♈ 3	♉ 19	♊ 26	♍ 19	♎ 13	♏ 16	♑ 7	♒ 10
17	♏ 17	♑ 2	♑ 4	♈ 25	♉ 28	♊ 17	♋ 25	♎ 19	♏ 11	♐ 12	♒ 2	♓ 4
19	♐ 11	♒ 26	♒ 29	♉ 20	♊ 25	♋ 16	♌ 26	♏ 16	♐ 8	♑ 6	♓ 26	♈ 28
21	♑ 5	♓ 20	♓ 24	♊ 16	♋ 23	♌ 16	♍ 25	♐ 12	♑ 4	♒ 0	♈ 20	♉ 22
23	♒ 29	♈ 14	♈ 19	♋ 13	♌ 21	♍ 15	♎ 23	♑ 7	♒ 28	♓ 24	♉ 14	♊ 17
25	♓ 23	♉ 9	♉ 16	♌ 11	♍ 20	♎ 13	♏ 20	♒ 1	♓ 22	♈ 18	♊ 9	♋ 13
27	♈ 17	♊ 6	♊ 14	♍ 9	♎ 18	♏ 10	♐ 15	♓ 25	♈ 15	♉ 13	♋ 5	♌ 11
29	♉ 13		♋ 13	♎ 7	♏ 16	♐ 6	♑ 10	♒ 25	♉ 9	♊ 9	♋ 2	♍ 9
31	♊ 10				♐ 13		♒ 4	♓ 18				

1940	Jan.	Feb.	Mar.	April	May	June	July	Aug.	Sep.	Oct.	Nov.	Dec.
1	♍ 24	♏ 16	♐ 9	♐ 26	♒ 29	♈ 13	♉ 15	♋ 1	♋ 22	♎ 0	♏ 24	♈ 1
3	♎ 22	♐ 12	♐ 5	♒ 21	♓ 23	♉ 7	♊ 10	♌ 29	♍ 22	♏ 1	♐ 23	♈ 28
5	♏ 19	♑ 8	♑ 29	♓ 14	♈ 16	♊ 2	♋ 7	♍ 28	♎ 22	♐ 0	♑ 20	♒ 24
7	♐ 15	♒ 2	♒ 23	♈ 8	♉ 11	♋ 28	♌ 5	♎ 28	♏ 21	♐ 28	♒ 16	♓ 18
9	♑ 11	♒ 27	♓ 17	♉ 2	♊ 5	♋ 25	♍ 3	♏ 27	♐ 18	♑ 24	♓ 10	♈ 12
11	♒ 6	♓ 20	♈ 11	♊ 26	♋ 28	♌ 23	♎ 0	♐ 25	♑ 15	♒ 19	♓ 4	♉ 6
13	♓ 0	♈ 14	♉ 5	♋ 18	♋ 26	♍ 21	♏ 28	♑ 21	♒ 10	♓ 13	♈ 27	♉ 0
15	♓ 24	♉ 8	♊ 29	♋ 15	♌ 24	♎ 19	♐ 25	♒ 18	♓ 4	♈ 7	♉ 21	♊ 25
17	♈ 17	♊ 3	♋ 25	♌ 14	♍ 23	♏ 17	♑ 21	♓ 13	♈ 28	♉ 1	♊ 16	♋ 21
19	♉ 12	♋ 29	♋ 22	♍ 14	♎ 22	♐ 15	♒ 17	♈ 7	♉ 22	♊ 24	♋ 11	♌ 18
21	♊ 7	♌ 27	♌ 20	♎ 14	♏ 21	♑ 12	♓ 11	♉ 1	♊ 15	♋ 19	♌ 7	♍ 15
23	♋ 5	♍ 27	♍ 21	♏ 12	♐ 17	♒ 8	♈ 5	♊ 25	♋ 10	♌ 14	♍ 4	♎ 13
25	♌ 4	♎ 28	♎ 21	♏ 9	♑ 13	♓ 3	♈ 29	♋ 19	♌ 5	♍ 11	♎ 3	♏ 12
27	♍ 4	♏ 27	♏ 20	♐ 5	♒ 7	♈ 27	♉ 23	♌ 13	♍ 2	♎ 9	♏ 2	♐ 10
29	♎ 4	♐ 26	♐ 18		♓ 1	♉ 21	♊ 18	♎ 10	♎ 0	♏ 8	♐ 2	♑ 9
31	♏ 2		♐ 14					♏ 7		♐ 9		♒ 6

219

1941	Jan.	Feb.	Mar.	April	May	June	July	Aug.	Sep.	Oct.	Nov.	Dec.
1	♒ 19	♈ 4	♈ 12	♉ 26	♊ 29	♋ 16	♍ 24	♏ 16	♐ 10	♒ 17	♈ 4	♉ 7
3	♓ 14	♈ 28	♉ 6	♊ 20	♋ 24	♍ 13	♎ 21	♐ 15	♑ 7	♓ 13	♈ 28	♊ 1
5	♈ 8	♉ 21	♉ 29	♋ 15	♌ 20	♎ 11	♏ 20	♐ 13	♒ 3	♈ 7	♉ 22	♋ 25
7	♉ 2	♊ 16	♊ 24	♌ 11	♍ 17	♏ 10	♐ 19	♑ 11	♓ 29	♉ 2	♊ 16	♌ 19
9	♉ 26	♋ 11	♋ 19	♍ 9	♎ 16	♏ 10	♐ 18	♒ 8	♓ 23	♊ 25	♋ 10	♌ 14
11	♊ 21	♌ 9	♌ 16	♎ 8	♏ 17	♐ 8	♑ 16	♓ 3	♈ 17	♋ 19	♌ 4	♎ 9
13	♋ 17	♍ 7	♍ 15	♏ 9	♐ 16	♑ 4	♒ 13	♈ 27	♉ 11	♌ 13	♍ 0	♏ 6
15	♌ 12	♎ 6	♎ 15	♏ 7	♑ 13	♒ 29	♓ 7	♉ 21	♊ 5	♍ 8	♎ 27	♐ 4
17	♍ 10	♏ 5	♏ 14	♐ 4	♒ 9	♓ 23	♈ 1	♊ 15	♋ 0	♎ 5	♏ 26	♐ 4
19	♎ 8	♐ 3	♐ 11	♑ 29	♓ 3	♈ 17	♉ 25	♋ 10	♌ 27	♏ 3	♐ 27	♑ 5
21	♏ 6	♐ 27	♑ 7	♒ 24	♈ 26	♉ 11	♊ 19	♌ 5	♍ 24	♐ 3	♐ 26	♒ 4
23	♐ 4	♑ 23	♒ 2	♓ 18	♉ 20	♊ 5	♋ 14	♍ 2	♎ 24	♐ 3	♑ 23	♓ 28
25	♑ 1	♒ 18	♓ 27	♈ 11	♊ 14	♋ 1	♌ 10	♎ 0	♏ 23	♑ 1	♒ 19	♈ 22
27	♒ 27		♈ 21	♉ 5	♋ 8	♋ 27	♍ 7	♏ 29	♐ 20	♒ 27	♓ 13	♉ 16
29	♓ 22		♉ 14		♌ 4		♎ 4	♏ 28		♓ 22		♉ 10
31							♏ 2	♐ 26				

1942	Jan.	Feb.	Mar.	April	May	June	July	Aug.	Sep.	Oct.	Nov.	Dec.
1	♊ 22	♌ 7	♌ 15	♎ 4	♏ 11	♐ 5	♒ 13	♈ 3	♉ 20	♊ 22	♌ 5	♍ 7
3	♋ 16	♍ 3	♍ 12	♏ 2	♐ 11	♑ 5	♓ 12	♈ 29	♊ 14	♋ 15	♌ 29	♎ 3
5	♌ 11	♍ 29	♎ 9	♐ 2	♑ 11	♓ 3	♈ 7	♉ 24	♋ 7	♌ 9	♍ 25	♏ 0
7	♍ 6	♎ 27	♏ 7	♐ 1	♒ 9	♓ 29	♉ 3	♊ 17	♌ 1	♍ 4	♎ 22	♏ 29
9	♎ 2	♏ 25	♐ 6	♑ 29	♓ 6	♈ 24	♉ 27	♋ 11	♌ 26	♎ 0	♏ 21	♐ 29
11	♏ 0	♐ 23	♐ 4	♒ 26	♓ 2	♉ 18	♊ 21	♌ 5	♍ 22	♎ 28	♐ 20	♑ 29
13	♏ 28	♐ 22	♑ 2	♓ 22	♈ 27	♊ 12	♋ 14	♍ 0	♎ 18	♏ 26	♐ 18	♒ 28
15	♐ 28	♑ 20	♒ 29	♈ 17	♉ 21	♋ 6	♌ 8	♍ 25	♏ 16	♐ 25	♑ 15	♓ 26
17	♑ 26	♒ 18	♓ 26	♉ 12	♊ 15	♋ 29	♍ 3	♎ 22	♐ 14	♐ 24	♒ 12	♈ 21
19	♒ 23	♓ 13	♈ 21	♊ 6	♋ 8	♌ 24	♍ 28	♏ 19	♐ 13	♑ 21	♓ 7	♉ 16
21	♓ 18	♈ 8	♉ 16	♋ 0	♌ 2	♍ 19	♎ 25	♐ 17	♑ 11	♒ 19	♈ 1	♊ 11
23	♈ 12	♉ 2	♊ 10	♋ 24	♍ 27	♎ 15	♏ 23	♐ 17	♒ 9	♓ 15	♉ 26	♋ 5
25	♉ 6	♊ 26	♊ 4	♌ 18	♎ 23	♏ 13	♐ 22	♑ 16	♓ 6	♈ 11	♊ 20	♌ 28
27	♊ 0	♋ 20	♋ 28	♍ 14	♏ 20	♐ 13	♑ 22	♒ 14	♈ 2	♉ 5	♋ 13	♍ 22
29			♌ 23	♎ 12	♏ 19	♐ 14	♒ 22	♓ 11	♉ 27	♊ 0		♎ 16
31	♊ 24		♍ 20		♐ 20		♓ 20	♈ 7		♋ 23		♏ 11

221

1943	Jan.	Feb.	Mar.	April	May	June	July	Aug.	Sep.	Oct.	Nov.	Dec.
1	♎25	♐16	♐26	♒19	♓27	♉17	♊21	♋6	♍21	♎25	♐14	♑22
3	♏22	♑15	♑25	♓18	♈24	♊12	♋15	♌20	♎15	♏21	♑12	♒21
5	♐22	♒16	♒24	♈15	♉21	♋7	♌9	♍24	♏11	♐17	♒10	♓19
7	♑23	♓15	♓23	♉12	♊16	♌0	♍3	♎18	♐7	♑15	♓8	♈17
9	♒23	♈13	♈21	♊8	♋10	♍24	♎27	♏14	♑5	♒13	♈6	♉14
11	♓21	♉10	♉18	♋26	♌4	♎18	♏22	♐11	♒3	♓12	♉4	♊10
13	♈18	♊4	♊13	♋20	♍28	♏13	♐18	♑10	♓3	♈11	♊1	♋5
15	♉13	♋28	♋7	♌14	♎22	♐8	♑16	♒9	♈2	♉10	♋27	♌0
17	♊8	♌22	♌0	♍7	♏18	♑8	♒17	♓9	♉29	♊7	♋22	♍23
19	♋2	♍16	♍24	♎1	♐15	♒8	♓16	♈7	♊24	♋2	♌16	♎17
21	♌25	♎10	♎19	♏5	♑14	♓8	♈14	♉3	♋18	♋26	♍9	♏11
23	♍19	♏5	♏14	♐3	♒13	♈7	♉11	♊27	♌12	♌20	♎3	♐7
25	♎13	♐1	♐11	♑2	♓12	♉5	♊6	♋21	♍5	♍13	♎29	♑4
27	♏8	♏28	♑8	♒0	♈10	♊1	♋0	♌15	♎0	♎8	♏26	♒2
29	♐4		♒6		♉8	♉27	♋24	♍9		♏4	♐24	♓1
31	♐1		♒5		♉4					♐0		♓1

1944	Jan.	Feb.	Mar.	April	May	June	July	Aug.	Sep.	Oct.	Nov.	Dec.
1	♓ 15	♉ 7	♊ 0	♋ 17	♌ 19	♎ 2	♏ 5	♐ 22	♒ 12	♓ 21	♉ 14	♊ 21
3	♈ 14	♊ 4	♊ 26	♌ 10	♍ 12	♎ 27	♏ 0	♐ 20	♓ 13	♈ 21	♊ 13	♋ 18
5	♉ 11	♊ 29	♋ 20	♍ 4	♎ 6	♏ 22	♐ 27	♑ 19	♓ 13	♉ 21	♋ 10	♌ 14
7	♊ 7	♋ 23	♌ 14	♍ 28	♏ 1	♐ 19	♐ 26	♑ 19	♈ 12	♊ 19	♌ 6	♍ 8
9	♋ 2	♌ 17	♍ 7	♎ 22	♏ 27	♐ 16	♑ 25	♒ 18	♉ 10	♋ 15	♍ 0	♎ 2
11	♋ 26	♍ 10	♎ 1	♏ 17	♐ 23	♑ 13	♒ 24	♓ 17	♉ 6	♌ 10	♎ 24	♎ 26
13	♌ 20	♎ 4	♎ 25	♐ 10	♑ 20	♒ 9	♓ 22	♈ 13	♊ 1	♍ 3	♏ 18	♏ 20
15	♍ 13	♎ 28	♏ 16	♐ 7	♒ 16	♓ 7	♈ 20	♉ 9	♋ 25	♎ 27	♐ 12	♐ 16
17	♎ 7	♏ 23	♏ 13	♑ 6	♒ 15	♓ 3	♉ 16	♋ 3	♋ 18	♏ 21	♑ 7	♑ 12
19	♏ 2	♐ 20	♐ 12	♒ 5	♓ 13	♈ 28	♉ 12	♋ 28	♌ 12	♐ 15	♒ 3	♒ 9
21	♐ 28	♑ 18	♑ 11	♒ 5	♈ 11	♉ 23	♊ 7	♌ 21	♍ 6	♑ 10	♓ 29	♓ 7
23	♐ 26	♒ 18	♒ 11	♓ 3	♈ 8	♉ 16	♋ 1	♍ 15	♎ 10	♒ 6	♈ 26	♈ 5
25	♑ 25	♓ 18	♓ 8	♈ 0	♉ 3	♊ 10	♋ 25	♎ 9	♏ 26	♓ 2	♉ 25	♉ 4
27	♒ 25	♈ 18	♈ 4	♉ 25	♉ 27		♌ 18	♏ 4	♐ 22	♈ 0	♊ 24	♊ 0
29	♓ 25	♉ 17			♊ 20		♍ 13	♐ 0	♑ 21	♓ 29	♋ 23	♋ 0
31	♈ 24						♍ 8	♑ 28		♉ 0		♋ 26

223

1945	Jan.	Feb.	Mar.	April	May	June	July	Aug.	Sep.	Oct.	Nov.	Dec.
1	♌ 9	♍ 24	♎ 2	♏ 16	♐ 20	♒ 8	♓ 16	♉ 9	♋ 2	♌ 8	♍ 25	♎ 28
3	♍ 4	♎ 17	♎ 26	♐ 11	♐ 15	♓ 5	♈ 14	♊ 7	♋ 28	♍ 3	♎ 19	♏ 21
5	♍ 28	♏ 11	♏ 20	♐ 5	♑ 11	♈ 3	♉ 12	♋ 5	♌ 24	♍ 28	♏ 13	♐ 15
7	♎ 21	♐ 6	♐ 14	♑ 1	♒ 9	♉ 2	♊ 11	♌ 3	♍ 19	♎ 22	♐ 6	♑ 9
9	♏ 16	♐ 1	♑ 9	♒ 29	♒ 8	♉ 2	♋ 9	♍ 28	♎ 13	♏ 16	♐ 0	♒ 4
11	♐ 11	♑ 29	♒ 7	♒ 29	♓ 8	♊ 28	♌ 6	♎ 23	♏ 7	♐ 9	♑ 25	♓ 0
13	♑ 7	♒ 28	♓ 6	♓ 0	♈ 8	♋ 24	♍ 2	♏ 17	♐ 1	♑ 3	♒ 20	♈ 28
15	♒ 5	♓ 27	♈ 6	♈ 28	♉ 6	♌ 19	♍ 27	♐ 11	♐ 25	♒ 28	♓ 18	♉ 26
17	♓ 3	♈ 25	♉ 6	♉ 25	♊ 3	♍ 13	♎ 21	♐ 5	♑ 20	♓ 25	♓ 17	♊ 26
19	♈ 2	♉ 22	♊ 5	♊ 20	♋ 28	♎ 7	♏ 15	♑ 29	♒ 17	♈ 24	♈ 18	♋ 25
21	♉ 1	♊ 18	♋ 2	♋ 14	♌ 23	♏ 1	♐ 9	♒ 25	♓ 16	♉ 24	♉ 17	♌ 24
23	♊ 29	♋ 14	♌ 28	♌ 8	♍ 16	♐ 26	♑ 4	♓ 23	♈ 16	♊ 24	♊ 14	♍ 22
25	♋ 26	♌ 8	♍ 23	♎ 2	♎ 10	♑ 21	♒ 0	♈ 22	♉ 16	♋ 22	♋ 9	♎ 18
27	♋ 22		♎ 17	♏ 26	♏ 4	♒ 18	♒ 28	♉ 21	♊ 15	♌ 18	♌ 4	♏ 12
29	♌ 17		♏ 11		♐ 29		♓ 26	♊ 20	♋ 12	♍ 13		♐ 6
31	♍ 12		♏ 5		♑ 25		♈ 25	♊ 18				♑ 0

224

1946	Jan.	Feb.	Mar.	April	May	June	July	Aug.	Sep.	Oct.	Nov.	Dec.
1	12 ♐	27 ♑	5 ♒	24 ♓	2 ♉	26 ♊	4 ♌	23 ♍	9 ♏	11 ♐	25 ♑	28 ♒
3	6 ♑	23 ♒	2 ♓	24 ♈	2 ♊	25 ♋	2 ♍	19 ♎	3 ♐	5 ♑	19 ♒	23 ♓
5	1 ♒	21 ♓	0 ♈	24 ♉	2 ♋	23 ♌	28 ♍	13 ♏	27 ♐	29 ♑	15 ♓	21 ♈
7	27 ♒	19 ♈	29 ♈	23 ♊	1 ♌	20 ♍	23 ♎	7 ♐	21 ♑	24 ♒	13 ♈	20 ♉
9	24 ♓	17 ♉	28 ♉	21 ♋	27 ♌	14 ♎	17 ♏	1 ♑	16 ♒	21 ♓	12 ♉	20 ♊
11	22 ♈	15 ♊	26 ♊	17 ♌	23 ♍	8 ♏	11 ♐	25 ♑	12 ♓	19 ♈	12 ♊	20 ♋
13	21 ♉	13 ♋	24 ♋	13 ♍	17 ♎	2 ♐	4 ♑	20 ♒	10 ♈	18 ♉	11 ♋	19 ♌
15	19 ♊	11 ♌	20 ♌	8 ♎	11 ♏	26 ♐	29 ♑	17 ♓	8 ♉	17 ♊	10 ♌	17 ♍
17	18 ♋	8 ♍	16 ♍	2 ♏	5 ♐	20 ♑	24 ♒	14 ♈	7 ♊	16 ♋	7 ♍	13 ♎
19	16 ♌	3 ♎	12 ♎	26 ♏	29 ♐	14 ♒	20 ♓	12 ♉	5 ♋	13 ♌	3 ♎	7 ♏
21	13 ♍	28 ♎	6 ♏	20 ♐	23 ♑	10 ♓	17 ♈	10 ♊	1 ♌	10 ♍	28 ♎	1 ♐
23	8 ♎	22 ♏	0 ♐	14 ♑	17 ♒	7 ♈	15 ♉	8 ♋	0 ♍	6 ♎	22 ♏	25 ♐
25	2 ♏	15 ♐	23 ♐	8 ♒	13 ♓	5 ♉	14 ♊	7 ♌	27 ♍	1 ♏	16 ♐	18 ♑
27	26 ♏	10 ♑	18 ♑	5 ♓	11 ♈	4 ♊	13 ♋	5 ♍	23 ♎	25 ♏	9 ♑	12 ♒
29	20 ♐		13 ♒	3 ♈	11 ♉	4 ♋	12 ♌	2 ♎	17 ♏	19 ♐	3 ♒	7 ♓
31	14 ♑		10 ♓		11 ♊		10 ♍	27 ♎		13 ♑		2 ♈

1947	Jan.	Feb.	Mar.	April	May	June	July	Aug.	Sep.	Oct.	Nov.	Dec.
1	♈16	♊7	♊18	♋11	♍19	♏8	♐12	♑26	♓11	♈16	♊5	♋14
3	♉13	♋6	♋16	♍9	♎16	♐3	♑5	♒20	♈6	♉12	♋4	♋13
5	♊13	♋6	♋15	♎6	♏11	♐27	♑29	♓9	♉2	♊9	♋2	♍12
7	♋13	♍6	♍14	♏3	♐6	♑20	♒23	♈5	♉29	♋7	♍1	♎9
9	♌13	♎4	♎11	♐28	♑0	♒14	♓17	♉2	♊26	♌6	♍28	♏5
11	♍12	♏0	♏8	♐22	♑24	♓8	♈12	♊1	♋25	♍4	♎26	♐1
13	♎9	♐24	♐2	♑16	♒18	♈3	♉9	♋1	♌24	♎0	♏22	♐25
15	♏4	♐18	♐26	♒10	♓12	♉0	♊7	♌0	♍22	♏26	♐17	♑19
17	♐28	♑12	♑20	♓4	♈8	♊29	♋7	♍27	♎18	♐21	♑11	♒13
19	♐22	♒6	♒14	♈0	♉6	♋28	♌7	♎23	♏13	♑15	♒5	♓7
21	♑15	♓1	♓9	♈28	♊5	♌28	♍5	♏17	♐7	♒9	♓29	♈1
23	♒9	♈26	♈5	♉26	♋4	♍26	♎2	♐11	♑1	♓3	♈23	♉27
25	♓4	♉23	♉3	♊25	♌2	♎22	♏27	♑5	♒25	♈28	♉19	♊24
27	♈29	♉20	♊0	♋24	♎0	♏17	♐21	♑29	♓20	♉24	♊16	♋23
29	♉26		♊29	♋22	♎25		♐14			♉22	♊14	♋23
31	♉23		♋27									♌23

Moon sign and degree table for 1948 (every other day).

1948	Jan.	Feb.	Mar.	April	May	June	July	Aug.	Sep.	Oct.	Nov.	Dec.
1	♍ 7	♎ 29	♏ 20	♐ 6	♐ 8	♑ 22	♓ 24	♉ 12	♋ 3	♌ 12	♎ 5	♏ 11
3	♎ 6	♏ 25	♐ 16	♑ 0	♑ 2	♒ 16	♈ 20	♊ 10	♌ 4	♍ 12	♏ 3	♐ 8
5	♏ 2	♐ 19	♑ 10	♒ 24	♑ 26	♓ 12	♉ 17	♋ 10	♍ 4	♎ 11	♏ 26	♑ 3
7	♏ 28	♑ 13	♒ 4	♓ 18	♒ 21	♈ 9	♊ 16	♌ 10	♎ 3	♏ 9	♐ 20	♑ 28
9	♐ 22	♒ 7	♒ 28	♈ 13	♓ 17	♉ 8	♋ 16	♍ 10	♏ 1	♐ 5	♑ 14	♒ 21
11	♑ 16	♓ 1	♓ 22	♉ 8	♈ 14	♊ 7	♌ 16	♎ 8	♏ 26	♑ 0	♒ 7	♓ 15
13	♒ 10	♓ 25	♈ 16	♊ 4	♉ 12	♋ 6	♍ 14	♏ 4	♐ 21	♑ 24	♓ 2	♈ 10
15	♓ 4	♈ 19	♉ 11	♋ 1	♊ 10	♌ 4	♎ 11	♐ 0	♑ 15	♒ 17	♓ 27	♉ 6
17	♓ 28	♉ 14	♊ 7	♋ 29	♋ 9	♌ 28	♏ 7	♐ 24	♒ 9	♓ 11	♈ 24	♊ 3
19	♈ 22	♊ 11	♋ 5	♌ 27	♌ 7	♍ 23	♐ 2	♑ 18	♓ 2	♈ 6	♉ 21	♋ 1
21	♉ 18	♋ 9	♌ 3	♍ 25	♍ 5	♎ 18	♐ 27	♒ 12	♓ 27	♉ 1	♊ 19	♌ 0
23	♊ 16	♌ 9	♍ 2	♎ 23	♎ 1	♏ 12	♑ 21	♓ 5	♈ 21	♉ 27	♋ 17	♌ 28
25	♋ 16	♍ 9	♎ 1	♏ 19	♎ 27	♐ 6	♒ 15	♓ 29	♉ 17	♊ 24	♌ 16	♍ 26
27	♌ 16	♎ 7	♎ 28	♐ 14	♏ 22	♑ 0	♓ 8	♈ 24	♊ 14	♋ 22	♍ 14	♎ 24
29	♍ 15		♏ 24		♐ 16		♈ 3	♉ 21	♋ 12	♌ 21		♏ 20
31					♑ 10		♈ 28	♊ 19		♍ 21		♐ 16

227

1949	Jan.	Feb.	Mar.	April	May	June	July	Aug.	Sep.	Oct.	Nov.	Dec.
1	♑ 29	♓ 14	♓ 22	♉ 7	♊ 11	♋ 0	♍ 8	♏ 1	♐ 23	♑ 29	♓ 15	♈ 18
3	♒ 23	♈ 7	♈ 16	♊ 1	♋ 6	♌ 27	♎ 6	♏ 29	♑ 20	♒ 24	♈ 9	♉ 11
5	♓ 17	♉ 1	♉ 10	♊ 26	♋ 3	♍ 25	♏ 4	♐ 26	♒ 15	♓ 18	♉ 3	♊ 5
7	♈ 11	♉ 25	♊ 4	♋ 23	♌ 0	♎ 24	♐ 2	♑ 23	♓ 9	♈ 12	♉ 27	♋ 0
9	♉ 5	♊ 21	♊ 0	♋ 21	♍ 29	♏ 23	♑ 0	♒ 18	♈ 3	♉ 6	♊ 21	♋ 26
11	♊ 0	♋ 19	♋ 27	♌ 20	♎ 28	♐ 21	♒ 27	♓ 13	♈ 27	♉ 29	♋ 16	♌ 22
13	♋ 27	♋ 19	♋ 27	♍ 20	♏ 27	♑ 18	♓ 22	♈ 7	♉ 21	♋ 24	♌ 12	♍ 20
15	♋ 26	♌ 19	♌ 27	♎ 19	♐ 23	♒ 14	♈ 17	♉ 0	♊ 15	♌ 19	♍ 9	♎ 18
17	♌ 25	♍ 17	♍ 26	♏ 15	♑ 19	♓ 9	♈ 10	♉ 24	♋ 10	♍ 16	♎ 8	♏ 17
19	♍ 25	♎ 14	♎ 23	♐ 10	♒ 13	♈ 3	♉ 4	♊ 19	♌ 7	♎ 15	♏ 8	♐ 16
21	♎ 23	♏ 10	♏ 19	♐ 4	♓ 6	♈ 26	♉ 28	♋ 15	♍ 6	♏ 15	♐ 7	♑ 15
23	♏ 20	♐ 4	♐ 14	♑ 28	♈ 0	♉ 20	♊ 24	♋ 14	♎ 7	♐ 15	♑ 4	♒ 12
25	♐ 17	♑ 29	♑ 8	♒ 22	♈ 25	♊ 16	♋ 21	♌ 13	♏ 7	♑ 12	♒ 0	♓ 8
27	♑ 13		♒ 1	♓ 16	♉ 20	♋ 10	♌ 19	♍ 13	♐ 6	♒ 9	♓ 4	♈ 2
29	♒ 7		♓ 25	♈ 16	♊ 16	♋ 10	♍ 18	♎ 12	♐ 3	♓ 3	♈ 24	♉ 26
31	♓ 2		♈ 25		♋ 16		♎ 17	♏ 10		♈ 3		♊ 19

228

1950	Jan.	Feb.	Mar.	April	May	June	July	Aug.	Sep.	Oct.	Nov.	Dec.
1	♊ 1	♋ 17	♋ 25	♍ 15	♎ 23	♐ 17	♑ 24	♓ 14	♈ 29	♊ 1	♋ 15	♌ 18
3	♋ 26	♌ 15	♌ 23	♎ 15	♏ 23	♑ 16	♒ 22	♈ 9	♉ 23	♊ 25	♌ 10	♍ 14
5	♋ 22	♍ 13	♍ 21	♏ 15	♐ 23	♒ 14	♓ 18	♉ 3	♊ 16	♋ 19	♍ 5	♎ 11
7	♌ 19	♎ 11	♎ 21	♐ 14	♑ 22	♓ 10	♈ 13	♉ 27	♋ 11	♌ 14	♎ 3	♏ 10
9	♍ 17	♏ 10	♏ 20	♑ 12	♒ 19	♈ 5	♉ 7	♊ 21	♋ 6	♍ 11	♏ 2	♐ 1
11	♎ 14	♐ 8	♐ 16	♒ 9	♓ 14	♉ 28	♉ 0	♋ 15	♌ 3	♎ 9	♏ 3	♑ 1
13	♏ 11	♑ 5	♑ 12	♓ 4	♈ 8	♉ 22	♋ 25	♍ 8	♎ 0	♏ 9	♐ 3	♑ 0
15	♐ 9	♒ 2	♒ 7	♈ 29	♉ 8	♋ 16	♋ 19	♎ 6	♏ 29	♐ 8	♑ 2	♒ 8
17	♐ 7	♓ 28	♓ 2	♉ 23	♉ 25	♋ 10	♌ 15	♏ 4	♐ 27	♑ 5	♒ 29	♓ 3
19	♑ 3	♈ 23	♈ 26	♉ 16	♊ 19	♌ 5	♍ 12	♐ 2	♑ 25	♒ 2	♓ 24	♈ 27
21	♒ 28	♉ 18	♉ 19	♊ 10	♋ 13	♍ 1	♎ 9	♐ 0	♒ 22	♓ 27	♈ 18	♉ 21
23	♓ 22	♊ 11	♊ 13	♋ 4	♋ 8	♍ 28	♏ 7	♑ 28	♓ 18	♈ 21	♉ 12	♊ 15
25	♈ 15	♊ 5	♊ 8	♌ 29	♌ 5	♎ 26	♐ 5	♒ 26	♈ 13	♉ 15	♊ 6	♋ 9
27	♉ 9	♋ 29	♋ 3	♍ 25	♍ 2	♏ 25	♑ 4	♓ 22	♉ 7	♊ 9	♋ 0	♌ 28
29	♊ 4		♌ 1	♎ 23	♎ 1	♐ 25	♒ 3	♈ 17		♋ 3	♋ 24	♍ 24
31					♏ 1		♓ 0					

229

1951	Jan.	Feb.	Mar.	April	May	June	July	Aug.	Sep.	Oct.	Nov.	Dec.
1	7	29	10	3	11	29	2	16	2	6	27	5
3	5	28	9	1	7	23	26	10	27	3	26	5
5	4	28	7	27	2	17	20	5	23	1	25	3
7	4	26	5	23	26	11	13	0	21	0	23	0
9	4	24	1	18	20	4	8	26	19	28	20	26
11	2	19	27	12	14	29	3	24	17	26	16	21
13	29	14	22	5	8	24	0	22	16	24	12	16
15	24	8	16	29	2	20	28	22	15	20	7	10
17	18	2	9	24	28	19	28	20	12	16	1	3
19	12	26	4	20	26	19	28	17	8	11	25	27
21	5	21	29	18	26	20	28	13	3	5	19	21
23	0	17	26	17	26	19	26	7	27	29	13	17
25	25	14	24	17	26	17	22	1	21	23	9	14
27	21	12	22	16	24	13	17	25	15	18	6	13
29	17		21	14	21	8	11	19	10	14	5	14
31	15		20		16		5			12		14

1952	Jan.	Feb.	Mar.	April	May	June	July	Aug.	Sep.	Oct.	Nov.	Dec.
1	♒ 29	♈ 19	♉ 10	♉ 26	♊ 28	♍ 11	♎ 14	♐ 3	♑ 24	♓ 3	♈ 26	♉ 2
3	♓ 27	♉ 15	♊ 6	♊ 20	♋ 22	♎ 6	♏ 10	♑ 1	♒ 24	♈ 3	♉ 24	♊ 28
5	♈ 23	♊ 10	♋ 0	♋ 14	♌ 16	♏ 2	♐ 8	♒ 1	♓ 24	♉ 2	♊ 20	♋ 23
7	♉ 18	♊ 4	♋ 24	♌ 8	♍ 11	♐ 0	♑ 7	♓ 1	♈ 24	♊ 29	♋ 15	♌ 17
9	♊ 13	♋ 27	♌ 18	♍ 3	♎ 7	♑ 29	♒ 8	♓ 1	♉ 21	♋ 25	♌ 9	♍ 11
11	♊ 7	♋ 21	♍ 12	♎ 29	♏ 5	♒ 29	♓ 7	♈ 29	♊ 17	♌ 20	♍ 3	♎ 5
13	♋ 0	♌ 15	♎ 7	♏ 26	♐ 4	♓ 28	♈ 6	♉ 25	♋ 11	♍ 13	♎ 27	♏ 0
15	♌ 24	♍ 10	♎ 3	♐ 24	♑ 3	♈ 26	♉ 3	♊ 20	♌ 5	♎ 7	♏ 22	♐ 26
17	♍ 18	♎ 6	♏ 29	♑ 22	♒ 1	♉ 23	♊ 29	♋ 14	♍ 29	♏ 1	♐ 18	♑ 24
19	♎ 13	♏ 2	♐ 27	♒ 20	♓ 29	♊ 19	♋ 23	♌ 8	♎ 23	♐ 26	♑ 15	♒ 23
21	♏ 9	♐ 1	♑ 25	♓ 18	♈ 26	♋ 14	♌ 17	♍ 2	♏ 17	♑ 22	♒ 13	♓ 22
23	♐ 7	♑ 0	♒ 24	♈ 16	♉ 22	♌ 9	♎ 11	♍ 26	♐ 12	♒ 19	♓ 11	♈ 20
25	♑ 6	♒ 0	♓ 23	♉ 13	♊ 18	♍ 2	♏ 5	♎ 20	♑ 9	♓ 16	♈ 9	♉ 18
27	♒ 7	♓ 29	♈ 21	♊ 9	♋ 12	♎ 26	♐ 29	♏ 15	♒ 6	♈ 14	♉ 7	♊ 15
29	♓ 7	♈ 27	♉ 18	♋ 4	♌ 6	♏ 20	♑ 23	♐ 12	♓ 4	♉ 13	♊ 6	♋ 11
31	♈ 5		♊ 14		♍ 0		♒ 19	♑ 10		♊ 12		♌ 7

231

Astrological ephemeris table for 1953. Each cell gives a zodiac sign and a degree value.

1953	Jan.	Feb.	Mar.	April	May	June	July	Aug.	Sep.	Oct.	Nov.	Dec.
1	♋ 19	♍ 4	♍ 12	♎ 27	♐ 2	♐ 21	♓ 0	♈ 24	♊ 15	♋ 20	♍ 5	♎ 7
3	♌ 13	♍ 27	♎ 6	♏ 22	♐ 28	♒ 19	♓ 29	♉ 21	♊ 11	♌ 15	♍ 29	♎ 1
5	♍ 7	♎ 21	♎ 0	♐ 18	♑ 25	♓ 18	♈ 27	♊ 18	♋ 6	♍ 9	♎ 23	♏ 26
7	♎ 1	♏ 16	♏ 25	♑ 14	♒ 22	♈ 16	♉ 25	♋ 14	♍ 0	♍ 2	♏ 17	♐ 21
9	♎ 25	♏ 12	♐ 21	♒ 12	♓ 21	♉ 14	♊ 21	♌ 9	♍ 23	♎ 26	♏ 12	♑ 17
11	♏ 20	♐ 10	♐ 18	♓ 11	♈ 20	♊ 12	♋ 17	♍ 3	♎ 17	♏ 20	♐ 7	♒ 14
13	♐ 18	♑ 9	♑ 18	♈ 11	♉ 17	♋ 9	♌ 12	♍ 26	♎ 11	♐ 15	♑ 4	♓ 12
15	♑ 16	♒ 10	♒ 18	♉ 9	♊ 13	♌ 4	♍ 6	♎ 20	♏ 5	♑ 10	♒ 0	♈ 10
17	♒ 16	♓ 8	♓ 17	♊ 5	♋ 8	♍ 28	♎ 0	♏ 14	♐ 28	♒ 7	♒ 29	♉ 9
19	♓ 15	♈ 5	♈ 14	♋ 0	♌ 2	♎ 22	♏ 24	♐ 9	♑ 27	♓ 6	♓ 29	♊ 7
21	♈ 12	—	♉ 10	♋ 24	♍ 26	♏ 16	♐ 18	♑ 6	♒ 27	♈ 5	♈ 27	♋ 5
23	♉ 8	♉ 25	♊ 4	♌ 18	♎ 20	♐ 10	♑ 14	♒ 4	♓ 28	♉ 6	♉ 24	♌ 2
25	♊ 4	♊ 19	♋ 28	♍ 12	♏ 15	♑ 6	♒ 12	♓ 4	♈ 27	♊ 5	♊ 20	♍ 27
27	♋ 28	—	♌ 21	♎ 6	♐ 11	♒ 3	♓ 10	♈ 4	♉ 25	♋ 3	—	♍ 21
29	♋ 28	—	♍ 21	—	♑ 8	♓ 1	♈ 9	♉ 2	—	♋ 29	—	♎ 21
31	♌ 22	—	♎ 15	—	♒ 8	—	♉ 9	—	—	♌ 23	—	♏ 9

An ephemeris table for 1954 (zodiac sign ingress/Moon positions). Zodiac glyphs precede each number.

1954	Jan.	Feb.	Mar.	April	May	June	July	Aug.	Sep.	Oct.	Nov.	Dec.
1	♏ 21	♐ 7	♑ 15	♓ 5	♈ 14	♊ 8	♋ 15	♍ 3	♎ 19	♏ 21	♑ 5	♒ 9
3	♐ 17	♑ 5	♐ 13	♈ 5	♉ 14	♋ 7	♌ 12	♍ 28	♏ 12	♐ 14	♑ 0	♓ 5
5	♐ 13	♒ 4	♒ 12	♉ 6	♊ 14	♋ 4	♍ 8	♎ 23	♏ 6	♐ 9	♒ 26	♈ 3
7	♑ 10	♓ 3	♒ 12	♊ 6	♋ 12	♌ 0	♍ 3	♏ 16	♐ 0	♑ 4	♒ 24	♉ 2
9	♒ 8	♈ 2	♓ 10	♋ 4	♋ 9	♍ 24	♎ 27	♐ 10	♑ 26	♑ 1	♓ 23	♊ 2
11	♓ 7	♉ 0	♈ 7	♋ 0	♌ 4	♍ 18	♏ 20	♐ 5	♑ 23	♒ 0	♓ 24	♋ 2
13	♈ 5	♊ 27	♉ 3	♌ 25	♍ 28	♎ 12	♐ 15	♑ 1	♒ 22	♓ 0	♈ 23	♋ 1
15	♉ 3	♋ 23	♊ 28	♍ 19	♎ 22	♏ 6	♐ 10	♑ 29	♒ 21	♈ 1	♉ 19	♌ 28
17	♊ 1	♌ 19	♋ 22	♍ 13	♏ 16	♐ 1	♑ 6	♒ 27	♓ 21	♈ 0	♊ 15	♍ 23
19	♋ 27	♍ 13	♌ 16	♎ 7	♐ 10	♑ 27	♑ 3	♒ 26	♈ 20	♉ 27	♋ 9	♎ 18
21	♌ 23	♎ 7	♍ 10	♏ 1	♐ 4	♑ 23	♒ 1	♓ 23	♉ 17	♋ 23	♌ 3	♏ 1
23	♍ 17	♏ 25	♎ 4	♏ 25	♑ 0	♒ 20	♓ 29	♈ 20	♊ 13	♌ 18	♍ 27	♐ 5
25	♎ 11	♐ 19	♏ 28	♐ 20	♑ 26	♓ 19	♈ 28	♉ 16	♋ 8	♎ 12	♎ 20	♐ 29
27	♏ 5		♐ 24	♑ 16	♒ 24	♓ 17	♉ 26	♊ 12	♌ 3	♏ 6	♏ 20	♑ 24
29	♐ 29		♑ 21	♒ 14	♓ 23	♈ 17	♊ 24	♋ 7	♍ 27	♐ 0	♐ 14	♒ 19
31	♐ 24		♒		♈ 23		♋ 20			♐ 23		♓ 15

1955	Jan.	Feb.	Mar.	April	May	June	July	Aug.	Sep.	Oct.	Nov.	Dec.
1	♓ 29	♉ 22	♈ 3	♋ 25	♌ 2	♎ 19	♏ 22	♐ 6	♒ 22	♓ 27	♉ 18	♊ 26
3	♈ 27	♊ 20	♊ 1	♌ 22	♍ 28	♏ 14	♐ 16	♑ 1	♓ 18	♈ 25	♊ 18	♋ 26
5	♉ 26	♋ 19	♋ 28	♍ 18	♎ 22	♐ 7	♑ 10	♒ 26	♈ 15	♉ 23	♋ 17	♌ 25
7	♊ 25	♌ 17	♋ 25	♎ 13	♏ 16	♑ 1	♒ 4	♓ 22	♉ 13	♊ 22	♌ 15	♍ 22
9	♋ 24	♍ 13	♍ 22	♏ 8	♐ 10	♒ 25	♓ 29	♈ 19	♊ 11	♋ 20	♍ 12	♎ 18
11	♌ 22	♎ 9	♎ 17	♐ 1	♑ 4	♓ 19	♈ 25	♉ 16	♋ 9	♋ 18	♎ 8	♏ 12
13	♍ 19	♏ 4	♏ 12	♐ 25	♒ 28	♈ 15	♉ 22	♊ 15	♋ 8	♌ 15	♏ 3	♐ 6
15	♎ 14	♐ 27	♐ 5	♑ 19	♓ 23	♉ 12	♊ 20	♋ 13	♌ 5	♍ 11	♐ 27	♑ 0
17	♏ 8	♑ 21	♐ 29	♒ 14	♈ 19	♊ 10	♋ 19	♋ 12	♍ 2	♎ 7	♑ 21	♒ 23
19	♐ 1	♒ 16	♑ 23	♓ 10	♉ 17	♋ 10	♋ 19	♌ 10	♎ 28	♏ 1	♒ 15	♓ 17
21	♐ 25	♓ 11	♒ 19	♈ 9	♊ 17	♋ 11	♌ 18	♍ 7	♏ 23	♐ 25	♓ 8	♈ 12
23	♑ 20	♈ 8	♓ 16	♉ 8	♋ 17	♌ 10	♍ 16	♎ 3	♐ 17	♑ 18	♈ 3	♉ 8
25	♒ 16	♉ 6	♈ 15	♊ 8	♌ 15	♍ 8	♎ 12	♏ 27	♑ 10	♒ 12	♓ 29	♊ 5
27	♓ 12	♊ 4	♉ 14	♋ 8	♍ 12	♎ 4	♏ 7	♐ 21	♒ 5	♓ 8	♈ 27	♋ 4
29	♈ 10		♊ 13	♋ 6	♎ 7	♎ 28	♐ 1	♑ 14	♓ 0	♈ 5	♉ 26	♋ 4
31	♉ 8		♋ 12				♐ 24	♒ 9		♉ 3		♌ 5

234

1956	Jan.	Feb.	Mar.	April	May	June	July	Aug.	Sep.	Oct.	Nov.	Dec.
1	♌ 19	♎ 10	♏ 1	♐ 16	♑ 17	♓ 1	♈ 5	♉ 24	♋ 16	♌ 25	♎ 17	♏ 23
3	♍ 18	♏ 5	♏ 26	♑ 10	♒ 11	♓ 26	♉ 1	♊ 22	♌ 15	♍ 24	♏ 14	♐ 18
5	♎ 14	♐ 0	♐ 20	♒ 3	♓ 6	♈ 22	♉ 29	♋ 21	♍ 15	♎ 22	♐ 10	♑ 13
7	♏ 9	♐ 24	♑ 13	♒ 28	♈ 1	♉ 20	♊ 28	♋ 22	♎ 14	♏ 19	♑ 5	♒ 7
9	♐ 3	♑ 17	♒ 7	♓ 23	♉ 28	♊ 20	♋ 28	♌ 22	♏ 11	♐ 15	♒ 29	♓ 1
11	♑ 27	♒ 11	♒ 2	♈ 20	♊ 26	♋ 20	♌ 28	♍ 20	♐ 7	♑ 9	♓ 23	♓ 25
13	♒ 20	♓ 6	♓ 28	♉ 17	♋ 26	♌ 19	♍ 27	♎ 16	♐ 1	♒ 3	♈ 17	♈ 20
15	♓ 14	♈ 1	♈ 24	♊ 16	♌ 25	♍ 18	♎ 24	♏ 11	♑ 25	♓ 27	♉ 12	♉ 16
17	♈ 9	♈ 27	♉ 21	♋ 14	♍ 23	♎ 14	♏ 19	♐ 5	♒ 19	♈ 21	♊ 8	♊ 14
19	♉ 4	♉ 24	♊ 19	♋ 12	♎ 21	♏ 10	♐ 14	♑ 28	♓ 13	♉ 17	♋ 6	♋ 14
21	♊ 0	♊ 22	♋ 17	♌ 10	♏ 17	♐ 5	♑ 8	♒ 22	♈ 8	♊ 13	♌ 5	♌ 14
23	♋ 28	♋ 21	♌ 16	♎ 8	♐ 13	♑ 29	♒ 1	♓ 16	♉ 4	♊ 11	♍ 4	♍ 13
25	♌ 27	♌ 21	♍ 14	♏ 4	♐ 8	♒ 22	♓ 25	♈ 11	♊ 0	♋ 9	♎ 2	♎ 10
27	♍ 27	♍ 20	♎ 12	♏ 29	♑ 2	♓ 16	♈ 19	♉ 7	♋ 28	♌ 7	♏ 0	♏ 7
29	♎ 27	♎ 17	♏ 9	♐ 24	♒ 26	♈ 10	♉ 14	♊ 3	♌ 26	♍ 5	♐ 27	♐ 2
31	♏ 26		♐ 4		♓ 19		♊ 10	♋ 1		♎ 3		♑ 27

Ephemeris table for **1957** (zodiac sign and degree by day and month)

1957	Jan.	Feb.	Mar.	April	May	June	July	Aug.	Sep.	Oct.	Nov.	Dec.
1	9	24	3	18	22	13	22	15	6	11	25	27
3	3	18	27	13	19	12	21	13	2	5	19	21
5	27	12	21	9	17	10	19	9	26	29	13	16
7	21	6	16	6	15	8	16	4	20	23	7	11
9	15	2	12	4	13	6	12	29	14	16	3	8
11	11	0	9	3	12	3	8	23	8	11	29	6
13	8	0	9	2	10	29	2	17	2	6	26	4
15	7	0	9	1	7	24	26	5	26	2	23	3
17	7	29	7	29	3	18	20	0	22	29	22	1
19	7	26	4	25	28	12	14	26	19	27	21	29
21	7	21	0	20	22	6	8	25	18	27	20	26
23	4	15	24	14	16	0	4	25	18	27	17	22
25	0	9	18	8	10	26	2	25	19	26	14	17
27	24		11	2	5	23	1	25	18	23	9	11
29	18		6	27	1	22	1	23	15	19	3	5
31	12				29		1			13		29

236

1958	Jan.	Feb.	Mar.	April	May	June	July	Aug.	Sep.	Oct.	Nov.	Dec.
1	11	27	5	26	5	28	5	24	9	11	26	1
3	6	25	3	26	5	27	2	18	2	5	21	27
5	3	25	3	27	4	24	28	12	26	29	17	24
7	2	25	3	26	3	20	22	6	20	25	15	23
9		24	3	24	29	14	16	0	14	22	14	23
11	29	22	2	21	24	8	10	25	13	21	14	22
13	28	19	29	16	18	2	4	22	13	21	13	21
15	25	14	24	10	12	26	0	20	12	20	20	18
17	22	9	19	3	6	21	27	19	11	18	5	13
19	18	4	13	27	0	18	25	18	8	14	29	8
21	13	28	6	21	25	15	23	17	4	8	23	1
23	7	21	0	15	21	13	22	14	29	2	17	25
25	1	15	24	11	18	11	20	11	23	26	11	19
27	25	9	18	8	16	9	18	7	17	20	5	15
29	19		14	6	14	8	15	2		14		11
31	14		12		14		11	27				8

1959	Jan.	Feb.	Mar.	April	May	June	July	Aug.	Sep.	Oct.	Nov.	Dec.
1	♍ 21	♏ 14	♏ 25	♈ 17	♒ 24	♈ 10	♉ 12	♊ 26	♌ 12	♍ 17	♎ 9	♐ 17
3	♎ 19	♐ 12	♐ 23	♒ 14	♓ 19	♉ 4	♊ 6	♋ 21	♍ 9	♎ 15	♏ 9	♑ 17
5	♏ 17	♑ 10	♑ 20	♓ 9	♈ 13	♉ 27	♋ 0	♌ 17	♎ 6	♏ 15	♐ 9	♒ 16
7	♐ 16	♒ 8	♒ 17	♈ 4	♉ 9	♊ 21	♋ 25	♍ 13	♏ 5	♐ 14	♑ 7	♓ 13
9	♑ 15	♓ 4	♓ 12	♉ 28	♊ 7	♋ 15	♌ 20	♎ 10	♐ 3	♑ 13	♒ 3	♈ 8
11	♒ 13	♈ 29	♈ 7	♊ 21	♋ 0	♌ 9	♍ 16	♏ 8	♑ 2	♒ 10	♓ 29	♉ 3
13	♓ 9	♉ 23	♉ 25	♋ 15	♋ 24	♍ 6	♎ 13	♐ 7	♒ 0	♓ 6	♈ 23	♉ 26
15	♈ 3	♊ 17	♊ 19	♌ 9	♌ 18	♎ 3	♏ 12	♑ 5	♒ 27	♈ 2	♉ 17	♊ 20
17	♉ 27	♋ 11	♋ 13	♍ 4	♍ 13	♏ 1	♐ 11	♒ 4	♓ 23	♉ 27	♊ 11	♋ 14
19	♊ 21	♌ 5	♌ 9	♎ 29	♎ 10	♐ 1	♑ 10	♓ 1	♈ 18	♊ 21	♋ 5	♌ 8
21	♋ 15		♍ 7	♏ 29	♏ 8	♑ 1	♒ 9	♈ 27	♉ 12	♋ 15	♌ 29	♍ 3
23	♌ 10	♍ 29	♎ 6	♐ 29	♐ 7	♒ 28	♓ 6	♉ 22	♊ 6	♌ 8	♍ 24	♍ 29
25	♍ 7	♎ 27	♏ 6	♑ 29	♑ 8	♓ 24	♈ 2	♊ 17	♋ 0	♍ 3	♎ 19	♎ 26
27	♎ 4	♏ 26	♐ 5	♒ 27	♒ 6	♈ 19	♉ 27	♋ 10	♌ 24	♎ 28	♏ 17	♏ 25
29	♏ 2		♑ 5		♓ 3		♊ 20	♌ 4	♍ 20	♏ 25	♐ 17	♐ 25
31	♐ 0		♑ 4		♓ 28		♊ 14	♍ 29		♐ 24		♐ 26

238

1960	Jan.	Feb.	Mar.	April	May	June	July	Aug.	Sep.	Oct.	Nov.	Dec.
1	10 ♒	0 ♈	20 ♈	5 ♊	7 ♋	22 ♌	25 ♍	15 ♏	8 ♑	17 ♒	8 ♈	14 ♉
3	8 ♓	25 ♈	15 ♉	29 ♊	1 ♌	16 ♍	21 ♎	13 ♐	7 ♒	15 ♓	5 ♉	9 ♊
5	5 ♈	20 ♉	9 ♊	23 ♋	25 ♌	12 ♎	19 ♏	13 ♑	6 ♓	13 ♈	0 ♊	3 ♋
7	29 ♈	13 ♊	3 ♋	17 ♌	21 ♍	11 ♏	19 ♐	13 ♒	4 ♈	9 ♉	25 ♊	27 ♋
9	23 ♉	7 ♋	27 ♋	13 ♍	18 ♎	10 ♐	19 ♒	12 ♓	1 ♉	5 ♊	19 ♋	20 ♌
11	17 ♊	1 ♌	22 ♌	10 ♎	17 ♏	11 ♑	19 ♓	10 ♈	27 ♉	29 ♊	12 ♌	14 ♍
13	11 ♋	27 ♌	18 ♍	8 ♏	17 ♐	11 ♒	18 ♈	6 ♉	21 ♊	23 ♋	6 ♍	9 ♎
15	5 ♌	22 ♍	15 ♎	8 ♐	17 ♑	9 ♓	15 ♈	1 ♊	15 ♋	16 ♌	2 ♎	6 ♏
17	0 ♍	19 ♎	13 ♏	7 ♑	15 ♒	6 ♈	10 ♉	25 ♊	9 ♌	11 ♍	28 ♎	5 ♐
19	26 ♍	16 ♏	11 ♐	5 ♒	13 ♓	1 ♉	4 ♊	18 ♋	3 ♎	7 ♎	27 ♏	5 ♑
21	22 ♎	15 ♐	10 ♑	2 ♓	9 ♈	25 ♉	28 ♊	12 ♌	28 ♍	4 ♏	26 ♐	5 ♒
23	20 ♏	13 ♑	8 ♒	29 ♓	4 ♉	19 ♊	22 ♋	7 ♍	25 ♎	2 ♐	26 ♑	4 ♓
25	19 ♐	12 ♒	6 ♓	24 ♋	28 ♉	13 ♋	16 ♌	2 ♎	22 ♏	1 ♑	24 ♒	2 ♈
27	19 ♑	10 ♓	2 ♈	19 ♉	22 ♊	7 ♌	10 ♍	28 ♎	20 ♐	29 ♑	22 ♓	28 ♈
29	18 ♒	7 ♈	28 ♈	13 ♊	16 ♋	1 ♍	5 ♎	25 ♏	18 ♑	27 ♒	18 ♈	23 ♉
31	16 ♓		23 ♉		10 ♌		1 ♏	23 ♐		25 ♓		18 ♊

1961	Jan.	Feb.	Mar.	April	May	June	July	Aug.	Sep.	Oct.	Nov.	Dec.
1	30	14	23	8	13	5	3	7	27	1	15	16
3	24	8	17	4	13	4	3	4	22	25	9	10
5	—	2	—	28	9	2	—	1	17	19	3	6
7	—	27	12	26	7	0	8	25	10	12	27	2
9	5	24	7	25	6	27	3	20	4	6	23	30
11	—	22	2	23	3	24	28	7	8	27	20	28
13	28	21	1	22	—	9	23	—	22	23	8	26
15	28	21	30	19	27	14	6	25	17	21	6	25
17	28	21	29	5	23	8	0	20	3	9	4	23
19	27	20	27	0	8	0	4	7	1	8	2	20
21	25	6	24	4	5	25	28	5	9	7	0	17
23	20	—	2	7	29	20	24	6	9	6	8	12
25	5	6	7	27	25	6	22	9	9	3	4	7
27	9	—	—	2	22	4	22	5	8	9	29	24
29	2	9	7	7	20	4	22	3	5	9	23	24
31		29	26							3		18

1962	Jan.	Feb.	Mar.	April	May	June	July	Aug.	Sep.	Oct.	Nov.	Dec.
1	1	18	26	17	26	20	26	14	28	1	17	22
3	26	16	24	17	26	17	22	8	22	25	12	19
5	24	15	23	17	25	14	18	2	16	20	8	16
7	23	16	24	15	23	10	12	25	6	15	6	15
9	22	15	23	1	19	4	29	20	4	12	5	14
11	21	13	20	9	8	27	24	15	3	12	5	13
13	20	10	15	29	26	21	20	10	4	12	4	11
15	17	5	9	23	20	16	17	0	30	9	0	8
17	13	30	3	17	16	12	16	0	25	4	25	3
19	8	24	26	7	13	9	15	9	20	29	19	27
21	3	17	20	7	10	6	14	6	14	22	13	21
23	27	10	14	2	8	5	12	28	7	16	7	15
25	21	5	10	29	9	3	10	23		10		10
27	14	0	6	27	5	29	9	17		4	26	5
29	9		6				1					2
31	4		3									29

241

This is a rotated astronomical ephemeris table (moon sign/degree positions) for the year 1963.

1963	Jan.	Feb.	Mar.	April	May	June	July	Aug.	Sep.	Oct.	Nov.	Dec.
1	♓ 13	♉ 6	♉ 17	♋ 9	♌ 14	♍ 30	♍ 2	♐ 16	♒ 2	♓ 7	♈ 29	♊ 8
3	♈ 1	♊ 5	♊ 15	♌ 5	♍ 9	♎ 24	♍ 26	♑ 11	♓ 29	♈ 6	♉ 0	♋ 8
5	♉ 0	♋ 2	♋ 12	♌ 30	♎ 3	♏ 17	♐ 20	♒ 7	♈ 28	♉ 6	♊ 30	♌ 7
7	♊ 8	♋ 28	♌ 8	♍ 24	♎ 27	♐ 12	♑ 15	♓ 4	♉ 27	♊ 6	♋ 28	♍ 3
9	♋ 9	♌ 24	♍ 3	♎ 18	♏ 21	♑ 6	♒ 1	♈ 2	♊ 26	♋ 5	♌ 24	♎ 29
11	♌ 3	♍ 19	♎ 27	♏ 12	♐ 15	♒ 1	♓ 8	♉ 1	♋ 24	♌ 2	♍ 20	♏ 23
13	♍ 28	♎ 13	♏ 21	♐ 6	♑ 9	♒ 27	♈ 9	♊ 9	♌ 21	♍ 27	♎ 14	♐ 17
15	♎ 23	♏ 7	♐ 15	♑ 0	♒ 4	♓ 25	♉ 4	♋ 6	♍ 18	♎ 22	♏ 8	♑ 0
17	♏ 17	♐ 1	♑ 9	♒ 25	♓ 29	♈ 23	♊ 3	♌ 27	♎ 13	♏ 17	♐ 2	♒ 4
19	♐ 1	♑ 25	♒ 3	♓ 20	♈ 28	♉ 22	♋ 1	♍ 25	♏ 8	♐ 1	♑ 25	♓ 29
21	♑ 5	♒ 21	♒ 29	♒ 0	♉ 9	♊ 21	♋ 29	♎ 21	♐ 2	♑ 5	♒ 19	♈ 24
23	♒ 27	♒ 19	♓ 27	♈ 0	♉ 6	♋ 18	♌ 26	♏ 17	♑ 26	♒ 28	♓ 14	♉ 20
25	♓ 25	♓ 18	♈ 26	♉ 0	♉ 28	♌ 14	♎ 22	♐ 12	♒ 20	♓ 22	♈ 10	♊ 17
27	23	8	27	0	27	8	16	6	14	18	8	9
29	22		27	8	23	14	0	30	0	15	8	9
31			25	1	18	8	4	24 / 19	0	14		6

Ephemeris table — Moon positions (sign and degree) for 1964.

1964	Jan.	Feb.	Mar.	April	May	June	July	Aug.	Sep.	Oct.	Nov.	Dec.
1	♌ 28	♏ 19	♎ 10	♎ 25	♐ 27	♒ 12	♓ 16	♉ 7	♊ 30	♌ 9	♍ 30	♍ 5
3	♌ 24	♏ 15	♏ 5	♏ 19	♑ 21	♓ 7	♈ 13	♊ 5	♋ 28	♍ 6	♎ 25	♏ 29
5	♍ 19	♐ 9	♏ 29	♐ 12	♒ 15	♈ 3	♉ 10	♋ 4	♋ 27	♎ 3	♏ 20	♐ 23
7	♎ 13	♐ 3	♐ 23	♑ 7	♒ 9	♉ 1	♊ 0	♌ 3	♌ 25	♎ 29	♏ 15	♑ 17
9	♏ 7	♑ 27	♑ 17	♒ 3	♓ 8	♊ 1	♊ 0	♍ 2	♍ 21	♏ 24	♐ 8	♒ 10
11	♐ 1	♑ 21	♒ 12	♓ 30	♈ 8	♋ 1	♋ 0	♎ 0	♎ 16	♐ 18	♑ 2	♓ 4
13	♑ 25	♒ 17	♓ 8	♈ 29	♉ 7	♋ 29	♌ 8	♏ 26	♏ 10	♑ 12	♒ 26	♈ 30
15	♒ 21	♓ 13	♈ 6	♉ 28	♉ 4	♌ 26	♍ 5	♐ 21	♐ 4	♒ 6	♓ 21	♉ 27
17	♓ 17	♈ 11	♉ 5	♊ 27	♋ 29	♎ 21	♎ 1	♑ 14	♑ 28	♓ 1	♈ 19	♊ 25
19	♈ 14	♉ 9	♊ 4	♋ 24	♌ 24	♏ 16	♏ 24	♒ 8	♒ 23	♈ 27	♉ 18	♋ 25
21	♉ 12	♊ 7	♋ 2	♌ 20	♍ 18	♐ 9	♐ 18	♓ 2	♓ 19	♉ 25	♊ 17	♌ 26
23	♊ 10	♋ 5	♌ 30	♍ 15	♎ 12	♑ 3	♑ 12	♈ 27	♈ 16	♊ 24	♋ 17	♍ 25
25	♋ 8	♌ 3	♎ 27	♎ 10	♏ 6	♑ 27	♒ 6	♉ 23	♉ 14	♋ 23	♌ 16	♎ 23
27	♌ 6	♍ 27	♏ 23	♏ 4	♐ 30	♒ 21	♓ 1	♊ 20	♊ 12	♌ 22	♍ 13	♏ 19
29			♐ 18		♑ 26		♈ 26	♋ 18	♋ 11	♍ 19	♎ 10	♐ 14
31			♑ 13		♒ 30		♉ 23	♌ 16		♎ 16		♑ 8

243

CHAPTER XII

The Degrees of the Moon Analyzed

There are 360 degrees in the circle of the zodiac. The position of the moon in an individual chart can be found in any one of these degrees. Each degree responds to a different rate of vibration from the luminary. The 360 degrees are divided into twelve houses, each of 30 degrees.

In this guideline to the degrees of the moon, a final analysis of a chart must also rest on the position of the moon in the house. According to the strength of the house position, some degrees will be modified or exaggerated. This is why a competent astrologer becomes more efficient when he uses the skills of his science, but augments them with both extrasensory perception and common sense. Each horoscope is a unique map of the life of an individual. Looking only at the individual's sun sign is another way of "type casting." This cannot happen when the moon's position is given the respectful analysis that it deserves.

DEGREES OF THE MOON
IN ARIES

1. A shy person.
2. Powers of concentration not good.
3. A degree of recklessness, unable to discriminate in choice of companions.
4. Excessive vanity.
5. Very sensitive, weak eyesight.
6. Weak eyesight but compensated by good hearing.
7. Very imaginative and, if not carefully channeled, will choose to lie.
8. Indecisive.
9. Anxious to be liked but does not find it easy to exert himself with others.
10. Inner fears about being inferior.
11. Irresponsible.
12. Can generally find an easy way to get through life.
13. A slow starter in youth; benefits come after the twenty-sixth year.
14. Inclined to put self first; has good instincts for survival.
15. Basically a lover of peace, but searching for it brings discontent.
16. If he can live in the country, he will thrive better than in urban life.
17. A keen observer of everyone but himself.
18. Cannot face his own faults and overestimates his virtues.
19. The first touch of reality; the person begins to see himself as he really is.
20. Ambitious.
21. Hard-working but never quite successful.
22. Has creative ideas but cannot put them into action.
23. Can be moderately successful in creative work.
24. A contented disposition but not without ambition.

25. Can achieve financial wealth but generally through inheritance.
26. Good money-maker.
27. Money comes through shrewdness.
28. Better in an occupation where he can be close to nature.
29. Possessive.
30. Love of land and an interest in ecology.

DEGREES OF THE MOON
IN TAURUS

1. Strong-willed.
2. Prefers his own company and is generally lonely in old age.
3. Very impressionable and interested in occult matters.
4. Prefers the company of his own sex. Not good for marriage.
5. Very speculative, reckless in early youth.
6. A true romantic who will seek love for its own sake.
7. The lower passions dominate; great interest in the opposite sex.
8. Peace at any price, but makes mistakes through being fearful to take advantage of opportunities which could lead to advancement.
9. Obstinate and moody.
10. An ingenious mind, more flexible than one would expect in this sign but must have encouragement when young.
11. The mind is very restricted. Develops certain views when young and retains them. Will rarely respond to the logic of others. Once his mind is made up, nothing changes it.
12. Unambitious but capable of working hard, resists changes.
13. Antisocial.

14. Needs encouragement in youth to mix with others; feels inadequate.
15. Generally attracted to work in which research is involved.
16. Finds it difficult to be popular, but works hard to be liked.
17. Often involved in religious pursuits; the religion he is brought up in as a child seems to remain with him all his life.
18. A very complex degree. The mind is shrewd to a point of cunning and unless he is guided well in his formative years, he will use his mind in criminal activities—but not very successfully.
19. Given the right environment and education, he can attain genius status.
20. Always seeking to better himself, he is capable of attaining great heights.
21. Very critical, but not always in a constructive manner.
22. Many fine surgeons have the moon in this degree but in creative types it indicates ability to be a good painter.
23. Warmhearted.
24. When he gets set on a good cause, he will devote himself to it with passionate dedication.
25. Not very ambitious but always looking for some scheme to help him, yet he cannot define his own goals.
26. A person to have confidence in; very strong-minded, however.
27. Fascinated by the darker side of occult matters.
28. Good for an uneventful but long life.
29. Rather more happy-go-lucky than one normally associates with Taurus. Can live on happy memories of childhood, and these sustain him in adulthood.
30. Philanthropic and can become a self-made man, financially successful.

DEGREES OF THE MOON
IN GEMINI

1. Many negative attitudes.
2. Negative attitudes but ability to deal with them.
3. A determined will to succeed.
4. Keen powers of observation and awareness of the psyche, sharpened intuition.
5. Good degree for an educator.
6. Indulgent attitude toward young people.
7. Fickle in romantic relationships.
8. Instincts for a successful business life through quick-witted mind.
9. Sharp mentality; important to learn to use it.
10. Whimsical, humorous nature.
11. Dual personality which may develop into schizophrenia.
12. Innovative ideas.
13. Inquisitive about moral codes.
14. Incredible memory for trivia.
15. Self-centered, rather shallow nature.
16. Likely to be impressed by other people devoted to "good causes," but a follower, not a leader.
17. Plenty of extrasensory perception.
18. Very versatile, a Jack or Jill of all trades.
19. Versatile again but more of the "rolling stone gathering no moss" type.
20. Agile mind, capable of absorbing facts and using them.
21. An opportunist.
22. The promise of a good mind, capable of getting good grades at school; does not always fulfill the promise of prosperity in adulthood.
23. Lazy attitude to most things.
24. Dilettante lover of art but not a producer; always lost in admiring the work of others.

25. Will have many jobs and be moderately successful in each one, but is easily bored.
26. Artistic temperament.
27. Will seek and thrive in sophisticated areas of life in any age.
28. Unpretentious, a likable type of academic ability without the dullness associated with this.
29. Capable of deliberately inflicting hurt on himself as well as others. Destructive.
30. Careless. Likely to have some speech difficulties.

DEGREES OF THE MOON
IN CANCER

1. More than ordinary interest in music without being a performer.
2. Lovable nature without too many artifices; natural charm and emphasis on natural amenities.
3. In youth a dreamer, in adult life the dreams can be converted to reality, since there is ambition in this degree.
4. Sensual inclinations not necessarily related to sexuality, more the love of beautiful things. Sense of touch important.
5. Very trusting nature lacking in discrimination, so constantly being hurt emotionally.
6. Unable to cope with money—either the lack of it or too much of it—money just comes and flows away, usually on trivia.
7. This degree is often seen in possessive mothers or aggressive businessmen. They know what they want and have all the instincts to retain it.
8. Self-indulgence becomes a way of life difficult to get away from.
9. Varying degrees of contentment. A person with this degree will seek peace at any price, or be unwilling to

accept challenges, preferring to walk away from them.

10. Capable of leading a hard-working life but must have a touch of success early in life to supply the momentum to carry on.

11. A Pollyanna type of optimism not justified by facts, which are generally ignored.

12. Possibility of self-destruction—not just the act of suicide, but a life-style in which the person finds it hard to do anything constructive for himself.

13. Sustained constantly by hope, it is a vital force in contributing to the success or failure in whatever he does. It is augmented by a constant desire to seek knowledge.

14. Generally found in a person born with a silver spoon in his mouth. He is capable of taking advantage of all his birth and ancestors have contributed. This can lead to spectacular success.

15. Although given to laziness, this person will thrive and get a great deal of pleasure out of life because there is a lot of astuteness in his mentality.

16. Divide-and-conquer attitude, a subtle type of power which succeeds.

17. Nervous energy which, if unchanneled, brings ill health, but when deliberately channeled to creativity or executive action, can bring personal success.

18. There is a capability to make the best of things. May not have the money to be a millionaire, but will always give the appearance of being in better financial circumstances than he actually is.

19. A complex degree. In a person with weak aspects, the character may be pleasing but not productive. With good aspects, the mind is more stable and capable of putting ideas into action.

20. With a desire to be of service to others, this can deteriorate into a martyred existence.

21. Discontented mind and unstable habits.

22. Indolent, never quite able to put things together through lack of willpower. Given good opportunities, he can foul them up by missing appointments and bad timing.

23. Success in the latter part of life; uses personality as a tool when young, but needs experience to reap the benefits of a good mind.
24. Very resourceful and can rise above circumstances which would devastate others.
25. Can be extreme introvert, but more generally this shows in self-reliance. What the world thinks does not matter because he is sure he knows what is good for him.
26. Meteoric rise to fame which can then plunge him into near oblivion only to rise again. Very ephemeral, but how he makes a comeback after the downward plunge depends on his ambitions.
27. Quiet, reserved person who can easily be exploited.
28. In extreme cases, the spiritual nature can take this person into a religious retreat, but generally he is capable of seeking an harmonious existence in other ways.
29. Very much a tool of others, rather content to be exploited. Always needs someone to look after him.
30. Quick mind and conscious of intuitive qualities which he can use well.

DEGREES OF THE MOON
IN LEO

1. Ambitions dominate the life-style.
2. The mind wants acclamation, but is not geared to direct action to obtain it so he invents fantasy situations in which he is the greatest.
3. Lacking in moral fiber.
4. A loyal friend with high ideals and expects friends to appreciate and live up to them.
5. A subtle mind which, when circumstances dictate, can be very cunning and conniving.
6. Pride in achievements and capable of doing great things according to ambitions.

7. Born to greatness and will maintain it at all costs.
8. The passionate lover.
9. Vain and often given to self-praise which his mind rationalizes as his right.
10. Good-natured and versatile, but can become his own worst enemy if he relies too much on the goodwill of others. Needs to choose close companions with great discrimination.
11. Sensuous and self-indulgent.
12. Very much an opportunist, quick to grasp advantages offered by others and sometimes ruthless in walking over the emotions of friends.
13. The early formative years are important because whatever is instilled in him during youth remains with him all his life. Can lead to an inflexible mind.
14. Drifts aimlessly through life.
15. The degree in which fame and general success are possible. Early in life he decides where his superior talents lie and goes all out to supplement them with education or otherwise learning specific skills.
16. Impulsive and restless, yet his spontaneous attitudes can lead to success. Not easy to understand because motivations are rarely clear.
17. Circumstances will take him away from his native land.
18. The degree of brilliance, excellent mentality, and sparkling personality.
19. Although he has flashes of very original thought, he is not good at executing them and often too proud to accept help in doing so.
20. Fame achieved in international affairs. More likely to be successful in a country other than the one he was born in.
21. Remarkable memory.
22. The spirit of adventure is high in this degree. No thought for personal safety when opportunity opens the door to adventure, but can be the degree of a hero as well.
23. A hard-working person who, having achieved fame and fortune, may decide he is not so interested in the results as he was in the act of achievement.

25. Danger through water. Not a strong character, easily influenced.
26. A patient nature, not very ambitious because peace of mind is more important than looking for challenges.
27. Restless mind, always ready for the next challenge. Can be good in an executive position.
28. Very constructive, good for a person taking up architecture as a career. Popular among acquaintances.
29. A good partner either in marriage or business. He will accept responsibilities with equanimity.
30. Very self-centered. Not the best degree to live with since it breeds discontent. Even if the subject appears to be blessed with many good things of life, he does not get the ultimate enjoyment from them.

DEGREES OF THE MOON
IN VIRGO

1. A sociable nature, enjoys friendships to the full without seeking personal popularity.
2. Lacking in direction and motivation, so rarely gets much financial gain during life.
3. The try, try, and try again degree—ultimately he succeeds.
4. Very productive mind which then reflects in his life-style which will not be lacking in the acceptably good things; he is capable of enjoying them with humility.
5. Whatever he chooses to do he will do efficiently and take pride in his achievements.
6. Good looks and a pleasing nature make him a good companion in romance or business. He does not mind using his physical attributes to take him into areas of success.
7. Marital troubles seem to be inevitable, but he rarely complains and will find something good to say about people who have hurt him. Not vengeful.

8. Good for a life of contemplation. Very self-sufficient.
9. If he is born into good circumstances and given plenty of opportunities for advancement, he is likely to waste them through his inability to contribute anything.
10. Attracts friends to him like bees to honey and enjoys this status to the full.
11. Very flexible mind which can lead to inventive qualities.
12. A calm life with not too many highlights but leads to a contented attitude.
13. He will follow any leader he respects without seeking personal acclaim.
14. Better in work of a sedentary nature.
15. Rarely gets the credit he deserves, but is not resentful about it.
16. A good liaison person; enjoys company and bringing people together for a mutual good cause.
17. Not likely to have any gambling instincts either in games, romance, or business. Very prudent and thoughtful.
18. The degree of prosperity which is not only linked to finances but also to friendship and trust.
19. Robust constitution.
20. Aggressive—he believes that attack is the best form of defense.
21. Financially ambitious and will go to great means to achieve this type of security.
22. Sensuous nature rather than sexual.
23. Likely to thrive in working conditions away from his native land.
24. Not likely to marry.
25. Very aggressive and sometimes seen in the horoscopes of soldiers of fortune.
26. Sociable and needs a happy home life to thrive.
27. A sharp tongue which he sees as bluntness but is often construed as lacking in diplomacy.
28. A full quiver of children, and interested in sexual activities.
29. Interested in work of a religious nature.

30. A night person; can develop moods of depression after middle age. This gives way to despondency, and it is not easy to get him to renew active interest in life.

DEGREES OF THE MOON IN LIBRA

1. Quarrelsome and not easy in partnerships of any type. Able to pick a quarrel about literally anything and everything.
2. Overly enthusiastic toward religion, generally those of fundamental persuasion. In extreme cases, this is the degree of religious mania.
3. Self-centered, conscious that he needs help from others but can never bring himself to take advice, so he is constantly searching for needles in haystacks.
4. Given fair abilities, he never gets the best out of life.
5. Impulsive and quick tongue. Given to gossiping without realizing that this can be hurtful to others. He can always improvise on any rumor.
6. Always forced to work hard, he develops a patient attitude toward it. Although he has little motivation to extend himself, he cannot be content, so frustrations develop.
7. Easily led, especially where the opposite sex is concerned.
8. Very sensitive and suffers from family bereavements at an early age.
9. Aggressive nature; the subject enjoys a good fight.
10. At some time of life, he will undergo a period of enforced seclusion. It may be of his own choice as, for instance, in a religious institution, or it may be a hospital or imprisonment.
11. Often found in the horoscope of adopted children when the father is not known, or in those of divorced parents

where the father goes away and does not influence the life of the child.

12. Frivolous and lighthearted nature.

13. The first marriage is rarely successful. If it does not end in divorce, there can be long separations and loneliness, making the person nervous to try romance or marriage again.

14. Insincerity dominates the life-style.

15. Enjoys flattery by the opposite sex. Very indecisive.

16. Will thrive in a northern country.

17. Very critical, but this can be channeled into work of an analytical nature. If this is not done, then the person criticizes everything and enjoys it.

18. Lives a social life and can be a good hostess or host; enjoys work where he meets the public.

19. Proud nature, desires esteem and can live up to it.

20. Important to anyone considering a life in religion. He will take to it with little or no effort but it also produces great singers with a flair for drama. It is an emotional degree.

21. Impractical, looks for opportunities but generally they fall apart. He picks up the pieces and starts all over again.

22. Careless of possessions; dreamy and very content to live in the past, rather than cope with the reality of the future.

23. Good for anyone interested in research work, especially medicine.

24. Suffers at the hands of friends and is unable to discriminate between companions good for him and those who are not. Does not deliberately try to make enemies, but ends up with friends betraying him.

25. Personal charm and attractiveness help him toward a good social life.

26. A passionate defender of what he considers the right. This degree is often found in dedicated people in the legal profession.

27. A kindly nature anxious to help others with less

selfishness than one would expect to find. Lover of ecology and peaceful lifestyle.

28. Hard-working but always knows his limitations which he can offset by choosing the right partner in romance and business.
29. No real ambitions and given to moods of deep depression.
30. Indifferent to the sensitivity of others.

DEGREES OF THE MOON
IN SCORPIO

1. Makes numerous enemies because of agressive nature.
2. Very confident and can tackle a mammoth amount of work.
3. Loves anything mysterious. A good degree for anyone interested in detective work.
4. Fine for an actor or musician, as he will have a natural tendency toward these professions.
5. Plenty of energy, but always misdirected so the person feels that life is a constant battlefield.
6. A probing mind which can encompass details as well as on a large scale. Good for detective work or analysis.
7. Successful in business if related to areas in which his sun sign influences work. This position of the moon gives the right mentality to tackle his profession.
8. Very unconventional in romance, business, morals, and religion.
9. Almost always shows up in the horoscope of an orphaned child or one with some unusual parentage which takes the child out of control of the parents at an early age.
10. Sarcastic and critical nature but given to self-deception.
11. Emotionally insecure.
12. Completely resourceful when it comes to self-preservation.

13. Independence and success come through his own good mind and ability to foresee trends. Intuitive, but he has the advantage of being able to use logic as well.

14. Self-indulgent, but in a likeable manner which gives him many friends. He can have an uncanny understanding of others.

15. Inactive mind and lazy disposition. Overindulgence of intoxicating drinks and drugs can produce setbacks in health.

16. Very generous in a grand manner; attracted to volunteer and charitable work, but likes recognition. It is a very self-serving degree.

17. Physical danger, and is incapable of recognizing enemies or chooses to ignore them.

18. Jealous nature which can be destructive and leads to unhappiness in romance and business.

19. Makes as many enemies as friends and survives the attentions of both because he is resourceful enough to sense enemies before they can really hurt him.

20. Restless nature, often found in the horoscope of explorers and in people who spend long periods of life in the Far East.

21. Ultra-independent nature reinforced by capability to look after his own affairs.

22. Rarely follows intuition or logic, so is at the mercy of being swept away in tides of events he chooses to ignore. A form of self-destruction, but he always rallies from one disaster only to get involved in another.

23. If he inherits money he wastes it, but enjoys every minute of spending it. If he has to work for it, he does not provide for the proverbial rainy day.

24. Very adaptable to circumstances. If one life-style fades out, he tackles another and has no regrets.

25. A wolf in sheep's clothing when it comes to attracting the opposite sex.

26. Takes abnormal risks, survives them, gathers momentum, and plunges into another risky situation. Doubtful if he is capable of profiting by experience, but seems to enjoy an adventurous life.

27. Very forceful, likes to make others do whatever he wills them to do, but not necessarily a good employer. It is more a game of the mind. Mesmeric charm and charisma.
28. Can rise to great heights only to be cut down. Seeks security, believes he has it, and then finds it has disappeared. Superior legalistic mind which can verge toward cunning; but the higher he climbs, the greater his fall.
29. Best when devoted to scientific pursuits.
30. Personal magnetic charm which he uses in all areas of life, but especially thrives in partnerships with opposite sex.

DEGREES OF THE MOON
IN SAGITTARIUS

1. Discovers early that life is not a bed of roses, yet manages to survive and ignore the thorns.
2. Aggressive character but with a lot of bravery in it. He has plenty of courage and ignores personal safety, but is not irresponsible where others are concerned.
3. A philosophical degree, very benevolent and humane.
4. Although there is plenty of courage, it is tempered with logic and prudence. He accepts results from his own actions.
5. Although circumstances bring suffering into his life, he does not complain; but equally so, he does not seem capable of doing anything to alleviate the suffering.
6. An inventive mind, very resourceful.
7. Possibilities of enjoying a happy married life but not a very eventful one. He places a high regard on contentment and strives for it.
8. Changes loves and business pursuits with ease.
9. A lot of fiery enthusiasm which can take a person into

the realms of religious zeal. Whatever he does, he creates an atmosphere of enthusiasm.

10. Very adaptable and prepared to tackle all challenges with resourceful energy.

11. Although he is ambitious, he has to cope with people who seem determined to thwart him; but with other aspects backing up this degree of the moon, he can be very successful despite setbacks.

12. Sensuality is the major part of his life-style. Very concerned with material things and the delights of the flesh, so the sensuality is combined with strong sexual drives.

13. Bigoted in opinions.

14. Excellent for literary work of a philosophical nature.

15. Very enterprising and will tackle anything. Cultivates goals early in life and aims directly at them.

16. Financial windfalls come his way and he uses them well, but a good cash flow is essential to his success. Give him a little money and he has aspirations enough to make it into more.

17. Unstable life-style which he rarely tries to improve. It is not always related to finances; he can be born with a good financial background, be able to make money, but somehow his forces become debilitated—often through a bad partnership.

18. Vain and untidy. This may result in an eccentric life-style or merely one in which he expects someone else to be around to pick up the mess he makes.

19. Generally gets locked into an intolerable partnership situation. The type to make an unhappy marriage and be unable to go through a divorce or face separation. In business he will find himself fighting his partners; but he is generally ineffectual, so a lot of energy is wasted.

20. Very sociable and thrives on an entourage of friends.

21. A very good strong mind. This degree indicates an interest in exploring occult forces or any other means of mind improvement, not necessarily through orthodox methods of education.

22. Should try to steer clear of litigation but generally finds himself involved in it. Found in the horoscopes of those who are involved in disputes of wills or property.
23. Emotionally insecure. Rarely finds a stable companion to share his life, so the insecurity deepens. The search for the right partner gathers momentum even after middle age and several marriages.
24. Short-term projects thrive for him, and so do romantic relationships.
25. Highly ambitious, but rarely has the direction to achieve them, so he lives his life always in partial success but with optimism. Next time is always going to be the best thing in his life.
26. Very faithful and loyal even when it might be advantageous to depart from a friendship or marriage.
27. Sexual drive is important but is greatly abused. Often leads to early impotence.
28. Patient and steadfast. He will not set the world on fire, but will gain some acclaim for his durability and loyalty to projects and people.
29. Circumstances get out of control, and many an honest man finds himself entangled in things which he abhors. It is as if others weave a web of deceit around him, and he becomes a fall guy for their devious work.
30. Likes to probe into the unknown and break new ground in discovery. Very good degree for anyone interested in archaeology.

DEGREES OF THE MOON IN CAPRICORN

1. Good for anyone in the diplomatic service or where diplomacy is an asset to work.
2. Procrastinates so misses opportunities.
3. A great deal of subtle wisdom which he uses well and

leads to emotional and financial security.

4. Very intuitive, grasps trends before they are in vogue.

5. Ultra-discreet, and this discretion is applied to his own life-style. He does not make anyone his confidant, but is not aware of being secretive.

6. Duty often takes a higher rating in his life than affection.

7. Jealous nature. Does not choose to apply logic to difficult emotional situations. Very possessive of people in his domestic sphere.

8. Ambitious and is well directed to achieving these because he does not have a system of checks and balances. Happiness is not always the final resort, although he can be happy through securing his ambitions.

9. He has to work hard, make progress by trial and error, but will keep on doing this until he breaks through to success. He profits slowly by experience.

10. High interest in metaphysics and can use it as his life work.

11. If he is trusted he will never betray the trust and will thrive on positions of responsibility.

12. Has a cruel streak which can rise up in unexpected areas.

13. Highly ambitious, hard-working, and will aim high. He always seems to be able to renew his energy and zeal even if he is pushed down a few notches on the ladder to success.

14. Very critical, but applies criticism to himself and finds himself wanting. He goes through life with an inferiority complex although he may boost himself up when in the company of others.

15. Intelligent enough to see that contentment need not reduce his way of life to being a cabbage, but he knows when to stop being ambitious and rest on achievements.

16. He can be a good teacher, especially if he goes to a country away from the land of his birth. He has patience and ability to try to understand another person's life-style and culture.

17. Philosophical and enjoys quiet.
18. He will fight for the right to express his opinion and wisely listens to those of others who may be diametrically opposed to his own principles.
19. Rarely popular, he can command respect through some singular feat of achievement.
20. Very much an egotist with a high regard for his reputation.
21. Good for a business life in which there is some aspect of scientific research.
22. Gains success through sheer, dogged determination.
23. Generally starts out in life with a good mind but through constant obstacles he may take to drink or drugs and never gain the eminence in his profession which was once the promise of his youth.
24. Although he makes enemies because of his bluntness, his friends recognize sincerity. He may not be the most popular person, but he earns respect.
25. Rather shallow in his approach to life, but it serves him to good purpose if he can settle for superficiality in himself and others.
26. A strong inclination to travel which, if he is able to do it, will give him a great deal of happiness. If restricted, his frustrations take the form of excessive bad temper and dark moodiness.
27. He thrives best in a rural life. Uses his hands well. Many excellent gardeners have the moon in this degree.
28. Whatever he decides to do early in life, he has a chance of achieving. He has a good sense of direction.
29. Not very practical in terms of making money, but he can be a good fighter for ecology or anything to do with conservation.
30. Able to define and concentrate on goals and capable of directing those of others. His greatest difficulty in life is maintaining high standards; for once he falls from public grace, he rarely regains it.

DEGREES OF THE MOON
IN AQUARIUS

1. A dreamer with not enough energy to put them into practice because of laziness.
2. A scientific mind.
3. A badly equipped mind which cannot cope with reality. This degree often occurs in a person preaching a pseudoreligion as an escape route from misfortune but actually becomes the vehicle to take him into further misfortunes and destruction.
4. Relates to authority but prefers to be in control of power himself rather than be told what to do.
5. Morally unstable.
6. Attracted to unorthodox religions and sees himself as a teacher.
7. Impulsive nature which leads him into danger he is not equipped to deal with. This is regarded as a vulnerable degree of the moon.
8. Loves freedom but not inclined to use discipline as a means to achieving ultimate freedom.
9. Found in many people who convert from one religion to another. Indicates changes in spiritual awareness.
10. Has to learn the facts of life through trial and error, but is not quick to take advantage of the lessons, so events repeat themselves.
11. Lacking in self-restraint, this degree can produce violent outbursts of temper.
12. Found in members of religious institutions which demand restraint, such as priests who defect from their religious office.
13. Tremendous instincts for self-preservation.
14. The middle of life is a dangerous period when there can be losses so great that he cannot hope to retrieve them

again, although he will adapt very well to such circumstances.

15. The degree of affluence both of the spirit and material things.

16. The degree of the religious fanatic, especially in evangelistic movements. If not directed into religious activities, the same spark ignites others to follow him in whatever cause he sponsors.

17. At its worst, it can indicate sexual aberrations or severe mental illness.

18. This is a degree associated with bitterness which can bring a person to a point of isolation. Circumstances beyond control can lead to mysterious death. The good name of the person is often at stake several times during life, and to some people this in itself is similar to death. New names and identities are often assumed.

19. Constantly needing to be rescued, which adds to his feelings of insecurity.

20. Plodding disposition will never make waves or achieve much in life, although many people end up content.

21. A sense of apathy indicates many inner weaknesses.

22. Excessive passions can run riot to his detriment. It can lead to an act of violence or at least outbursts of irrational behavior and temper.

23. A great enjoyment of work with plenty of energy although he may not achieve any great recognition or remuneration for his labors.

24. He will survive better as a business partner than an employee. If a marriage partnership deters him from working at something that pleases him, he substitutes financial reward for the sense of achievement.

25. Can be paranoid or manic, often turning against those who have tried to help him in times of trouble.

26. Confused thinking dominates his life-style. He falls into pitfalls, extricates himself, and does the same thing again.

27. He enjoys home life and can be the ultimate patriot.

28. This degree of the moon is found in compulsive gamblers.

29. Excellent degree to find in a defense lawyer or someone in business who takes an aggressive attitude toward his competitors.
30. Can succeed to high positions of authority.

DEGREES OF THE MOON
IN PISCES

1. Life is a constant struggle to achieve harmony, but it is not always recognized when it is achieved. Improvements in contentment after middle age.
2. Life makes demands on the person with this degree, and sacrifice for family and friends often interferes with the talent potential of the subject.
3. The personality varies from being generous with time and talent to periods of petulance when everyday matters get out of control.
4. This person will always be a bulwark against the tide in the affairs of others which tries to sweep them to destruction. Will always act as an arbitrator or lend a shoulder to cry on.
5. Very fond of the good life. This degree is often seen in the chart of successful entertainers. Capable of leading a double life and keeping both in control. The two distinct parts of life are kept well apart, and the world will only see what he wants it to see.
6. Need to guard against speculative ventures. No way to get rich quickly by any magical process and much can be achieved by hard work.
7. Secretive nature not always because there are things to hide in the personal life; generally the person gets involved in detective or journalistic work and holds the secrets of others in his head. His success is linked with his discretion.
8. Life is a seesaw—it's either a feast or famine of love and

prosperity, or loneliness and poverty, and he can cope with both.

9. Thrives best in a foreign land or among foreigners.
10. Analytical mind, whether it is as a critic of the arts or in medicine or chemistry.
11. The most important thing in life is freedom and this is often attained by becoming really proficient in the arts, literature, or the law.
12. Very ambitious and will attain success but not sustain it.
13. Cannot be happy alone. Enjoys sharing pleasures and sorrows, and if the other person is happy, then he will be content.
14. Life is a long series of hard work with not many financial rewards.
15. Will find himself living in remote areas or even foreign countries off the beaten track.
16. Great concern over family but without tremendous possessiveness.
17. Establishment of early romantic relationships which should be carefully nurtured to maturity, as companionship is essential for the well-being of this person.
18. One career will flourish, die away, and be almost forgotten, but another career starts up. He can change horses in midstream without mishap if he feels the urge to continue with hard work and perhaps swimming against the tide.
19. Quite aggressive and good for anyone in the legal profession. Can be quite a showman although not in the entertainment business.
20. Fickle and unstable emotionally and mentally, and should seek companions who will supply strength to counteract his weaknesses.
21. Very proud and intense in building and keeping a good reputation.
22. The female influence can be sinister toward both sexes. Is capable of finding weaknesses in others and exploiting them.
23. A complex degree of both strength and weakness,

everything depends on motivation which is best when aimed at lofty ideals rather than settling for second best.

24. Life can be a luxurious experience if it is thought of in terms of material possession and sensuality. A taker, not a giver.

25. Capable of withstanding many assaults on his good nature; gives freely of affection, time, energy and talent.

26. Learns to be self-confident through an intuitive feeling when there is danger. He is not afraid to face his own weaknesses and try to overcome them.

27. If he tries to build his life through castles in the air, he falls to earth and damages himself. His best way to success is to climb steadily, taking time out for meditation and reflection. Taking a second breath or second thoughts prevents disaster.

28. Very unusual mental powers—telepathic and constantly searching the mysteries of life and death through occult studies from which he profits. Self-improvement becomes the key to a successful life-style.

29. Lack of initiative as much as a lack of opportunity makes the person feel as if he is a leaf swept along by the wind. He can rarely stay where he wants to be or do what he would like to do.

30. An inflexible mind, especially if the person is involved in an orthodox religion. He can make allowances for no one else but himself, and this breeds a unique type of egotism.

CHAPTER XIII

The Influence of the Moon
in the Twelve Houses

One of the more difficult things in astrology is the division of the zodiac into houses; they are especially important to a full understanding of the characteristics of the moon. Of all the celestial bodies, the moon has the most psychological significance. Each house, like each sign, has special functions allocated to it. The moon in each house provides an extra understanding to the awareness that it is in a specific sign. For instance, one of the major characteristics of the Moon in Aries is volatility, but when we add to this that the moon in Aries is in the second house, many of the volatile emotions will be geared to the basic characteristics of this second house which is related to finances. The wayard moon in a fire sign (Aries) placed in the house of finances (second) gives a life of fluctuating money worries. This does not necessarily mean poverty, but may indicate extravagant use of money with little or no ability to conserve it.

To know which house your natal moon resides in, you'll have to have your horoscope done by an astrologer.

THE INFLUENCE OF THE MOON
IN THE TWELVE HOUSES

MOON IN THE FIRST HOUSE

Indicates an emotional, sensitive, and sometimes shy character but very changeable. The shyness may be detrimental at work and lead to missed opportunities. If the shyness can be overcome, the moon in the first house can give a gracious character which can be turned to advantage in work involving meeting the public.

MOON IN THE SECOND HOUSE

In this position, the person can expect many changes in his financial status, but will be capable of earning money. His problem is that he cannot keep it or use it to its best advantage. Periods of being out of work can inflict real hardship on him, for there is rarely a nest egg to use on the proverbial rainy day. In a male, he can expect to have financial aid through his mother, wife, or girlfriend.

MOON IN THE THIRD HOUSE

It is easy for this person to establish rapport with younger relations and work well with them or for them. He is quite sentimental, even toward his work, and inclined to relate stories of what happened on the job while embellishing them with drama. He enjoys traveling and is better in a job where he has some freedom of movement.

MOON IN THE FOURTH HOUSE

If this person can work at home, he will do far better than in any job which involves long periods away from his home base; and for many people with the moon in this position, even eight hours is long enough. If he must work away from home, he should try to live within easy reach of his work environment. Generally he can look forward to a comfortable old age with early retirement. The moon in the fourth house often influences children to give up work to look after an aged parent.

MOON IN THE FIFTH HOUSE

If a person with the moon in the fifth house can keep away from speculative jobs, he will be fortunate—but it rarely happens. The grass is always greener somewhere else. When he speculates on the stock exchange, his finances fluctuate, but he gets quite a kick out of it. Only children will tie him down and make him work solidly; then he will go on speculative adventures from the comfort of his chair.

MOON IN THE SIXTH HOUSE

The person with his moon in this position makes a better employer than employee. He is ambitious and capable of learning a trade while being employed; he is then likely to start his own business, well armed with experience gained at someone else's expense. He changes his occupation several times in life but generally manages to better himself. If he fails, his frustrations affect his health.

MOON IN THE SEVENTH HOUSE

This person can be very popular with the public but manages to have one image for the public and another one at home. At work he may be domineering, but at home he is very considerate and willing to please the people he loves. A lot depends on his partner, whether married or purely a business relationship. He likes to feel he is working as much for someone he loves as for himself and likes appreciation for what he does.

MOON IN THE EIGHTH HOUSE

Many people take up the occult sciences when they have the moon in this position, and it seems to work well for them. Even when employed in other jobs, intuition will help them at work.

MOON IN THE NINTH HOUSE

Inclined to be orthodox in religion and attracted to professions where his religious tendencies can manifest themselves. Although he may not become a clergyman, he will enjoy any work connected with his particular religion either on a voluntary or professional basis. He can be idealistic and instills these feelings into his work.

MOON IN THE TENTH HOUSE

Numerous changes in work, but will ultimately find his best success comes from any of the occupations under the direct rulership of the moon. Has a love of working with the public and if he cannot do so professionally, he will be the first to offer his services on a voluntary basis. Men do not mind working for a woman employer if the financial rewards are great enough, while women will enjoy working with their own sex without putting money first.

MOON IN THE ELEVENTH HOUSE

The person with the moon in this position thrives in any occupation where he can establish his work on a friendly basis. It could be through club life, organizing travel for groups of people, or similar things. He will not do well on his own. Give him the chance to make friends with any group of people, and he will work with them and for them.

MOON IN THE TWELFTH HOUSE

Although the person with the moon in the twelfth house can be very shy and ultrasensitive, many of them gravitate toward jobs in institutions, hospitals, prisons, or any place where caring for people matters. Many people earn their living through occult activities and can always be relied upon to offer sympathy but not always good judgment unless it is based on a natural type of intuition.

CHAPTER XIV

The Effect of the Moon on Vocations

In order that people may be happy in their work,
These three things are needed. They must be fit for it.
They must not do too much of it. And they must
have a sense of success in it.

—John Ruskin, *Pre-Raphaelitism*

To many people, work is something that interferes with pleasure. This is especially noticeable in the second half of the twentieth century. Our ancestors linked their instincts for survival with their ability to work. The men hunted for food, and the women converted it into meals. They also hunted to provide skins to keep their bodies warm and later worked to build shelters to shield them from the vagaries of the weather. The means of survival have changed with every age and, despite our more sophisticated life, work is still connected to our basic instincts for survival. The methods, means, and rewards have changed, but the motivation has not. Today we have many things designed to reduce work and allow more time for leisure, but we never really catch up with enjoying the leisure to the full because the old nightmare of survival intervenes. Build a better house, design better standards for living, have all the laborsaving devices you want in the kitchen—and all you have substituted for the hunter's arrows as his means of survival is a piece of green paper called money. That is just about the yardstick today of our survival: hunt it, catch it, and hope to hold on to it for a while represents work, more work, but the end product is survival in a world where all but this instinct has undergone changing values.

If we can have free choice in doing the work we would like to do and when we would like to do it, then we still have time for pleasure and leisure. Work tires us, mainly because we do not like it, and even the thought of an uncongenial chore can produce fatigue. On the other hand, if we are really suited for the work we do, we rarely feel fatigue and can work for long hours, even getting a feeling of pleasure from it. I work long hours at the typewriter mainly because I love all aspects of writing. The thought that I might ever have to be a secretary fills me with aversion, and following the aversions comes a sense of tiredness. I have the skills to be a secretary but not the motivation to enjoy such a job, but if I had to face up to life in terms of basic survival through money, I expect I could brush up my shorthand, practice greater speeds at typing, and even cope with the intricacies of a filing system in an office. I would do this only to have sufficient money to live on, and that is the position so many people find themselves in. Yet there are secretaries who really enjoy their work and do not see it only as a means of earning a living—they enjoy the confidence an employer may have in them and the chance to get away from the house.

The sun stimulates the body and Mars supplies the energy to work, but the moon stimulates the mind. Getting the sun, Mars, and the moon in tune when it comes to work makes any chores much easier to cope with. If a person is working in a job he wholeheartedly dislikes but cannot change the work because of monetary circumstances, then the only thing to do is to change his consciousness and attitude to it. Once the dislike is overcome, it is a curious fact that the work becomes easier although it may not be totally enjoyable. Understanding the position of the moon in your chart often helps you to ease the strain of work and give enough time to have pleasure because the moon softens attitudes toward work. It also indicates through its position in sign and house, the type of work which you are likely to find most naturally congenial. The luminaries of the sun and moon together with each planet have specific rulerships over various types of work. Because you are born under a water sign or have the moon in one, it does not mean that you are cut out to be a sailor; but it will certainly affect your interest in any work which gives a degree of freedom.

In studying the effect of the moon on work or vocations, we find the keynote word is change. The main vocations ruled by the moon are occupations which involve traveling—sailors, nurses, fishermen; dealers in liquids—laundry proprietors and workers; cabbage and cauliflower growers; chicken raisers; cheese manufacturers; health spa attendants and owners; interior decorators with a special interest in bathrooms; bakers; brewery workers and owners; boat owners; dairy farmers; dairy workers; household help; chinaware salespersons; also glassware salespersons, melon growers, midwives, obstetricians, gynecologists—any work connected with plastics, mold makers, restaurant proprietors and workers, innkeepers, waiters and waitresses, night watchmen, antique dealers, collectors, genealogists, heraldic designers, perfume makers and workers, real estate (the sale of homes rather than commercial buildings), hypnotists, clairvoyants, writers of romantic novels, impressionist painters, silversmiths, makers and workers of home appliances.

In considering work and its attendant failure or success, the tenth house is of considerable importance, and any planets in this house have to be considered as well as the position of the moon. Many people, seeing a chart for the first time, get worried if there are houses which do not contain any planets—leaping to the conclusion that the departments of life so governed by these houses must remain blank for him. This is illogical. He should not conclude that if in the seventh house, for instance, he will never get married because of the same rationale of thought, if the fourth and tenth houses are devoid of planets, he would have had no mother or father. Houses containing planets certainly affect life much more than houses without any, but the planet governing the sign on the cusp of any empty house may be so strongly placed by sign, house, and elevation, that it projects its influence onto the vacant house. So, although we must first consider planets in the tenth house as major significators of occupation, if no planets are there it is not always detrimental. According to aspects, it may well mean that the person has difficulties in holding down a job for any length of time, or has an allergy to work because he prefers to slide through life relying on friends to support him.

Adolph Hitler certainly had an impressive career, albeit a diabolical one, but in the tenth house he had Saturn, alone in all its restrictive glory. He also had good aspects in his chart, including a good one from his moon to his tenth house. Under ordinary circumstances, Hitler would never have emerged as a successful writer but, by circumstances connected with his ambitions, *Mein Kampf* became required reading for every Nazi, and so millions of copies were sold. Through this work, he was able to spread his gospel of Nazism and reap the rewards of being the leader of this political cult, so that leadership became his career. At the time of his regime, the personal chart of Hitler was in good aspect to that of his country. This often happens when the charts of heads of state are compared with the national chart of their countries. With his moon in Capricorn in the third house aspecting Saturn in the tenth, there was no way in which Hitler could be freed from the restrictions of Saturn and the desire to be at war with the world. The position of the moon—while aiding his verbosity, hypnotic quality and his luck in publishing—was not strong enough to offset the restrictions of Saturn in the tenth house and in aspect to the moon in Capricorn.

If there is a good unafflicted planet in the tenth house, the next consideration in assessing the working potential is to consider any planet in the second house because this is connected with money. The normal second house ruler is Venus but, according to the position of the planet on the horizon at the time of birth, known as the Ascendant, the house of Taurus, ruled by Venus, will be changed. For financial results from work, it takes a good aspect to the second house to bring the money into your bank account. A point to be considered in work is whether you are going to be employed by someone or be self-employed. If you are in the position when you need an employer, then it is hopeful that you have a good aspect from the sixth house ruling employment to the tenth as well as the second. An ideal astrological layout has to be backed up with some energy and motivation from the subject himself. Mars affects the energy, but the moon affects the mental attitude toward work. No single planet alone affects work, but its sign, house position, and aspects give some clues as to the occupation which the subject will find most congenial.

The moon rules the female but Venus rules young women and girls, so a combination of these two planets may influence the occupation so that we find women as cosmeticians, beauty parlor operators, dressmakers, and dress saleswomen. All these occupations are not, however, exclusive to women but generally, if a male is in this work, he will have a strong affinity to the moon and Venus—at least, enough to make him relate to the more feminine things of life.

The moon rules liquids, of which oil is one type, and Neptune governs occupations connected with oil, so this aspect would be very good for anyone with the inclination to take up a career in the oil business, even if he does not become a tycoon. The moon rules the personality, and who can deny that there are many occupations which rely on this characteristic? If it appears in the second house trining a planet in the tenth house, it is a good indication that the subject will be successful in his work. The most simple rule to follow in assessing work is to consider the planets in the tenth, second, and sixth houses, and then apply a lot of common sense in the interpretation. The more charts an astrologer prepares and studies, the more he is able to apply common sense to his technical skill in analyzing the chart.

Some people succeed through trial and error in finding their right profession, but going through years in the wrong field is not smart, although it may add some needed experience to the karma of the subject. All too many people lead a hard life, always working without any enjoyment in it, and retire with thankfulness only to find that the accumulated tension built up by being a square peg in a round hole forces them into the grave. Exceptionally talented people will somehow find their niche and the type of work which is a joy to them, and others by sheer willpower make good in a difficult vocation.

How much one should accept the wrong working life is not always within the free will of the person concerned. His hatred of his job may be overruled by the need to provide for a family, an aged relation, or a sick child. Then, hopefully, he tries to bear it, with the end product of money being the consolation for personal unhappiness.

If you are considering a working life in partnership with another, then it is better to find someone who has his moon in the same position as the sun is within your own chart. It also helps to have Jupiter, the planet of expansion, in conjunction to the sun, moon, Ascendant or Midheaven of the other. These are basic indications of a successful partnership.

There is a new moon when it reaches the same degree of the sign in which the sun happens to be. Growth takes place at the time of the new moon, and with growth there is activity until the time of the full moon, when there is a lessening of activity. The moon takes roughly twenty-eight days to travel through the twelve signs—that is, from two to three days to go through each sign, or a total of thirteen times around the zodiac each year.

MOON IN ARIES

Mental activity is stimulated and new ideas and projects flourish. It is a good time to start on a new job because there is plenty of optimism and enthusiasm to come to grips with the challenges presented.

MOON IN TAURUS

When the moon is in Taurus, collect all your resources around you and balance the budget. If you run out of ideas at work, just fall back on plain old-fashioned common sense, and it will pay dividends. Any work at home needing patience or extra perseverance will prosper.

MOON IN GEMINI

This is a very stimulating time when the mind is active even if you work with your hands. You can always think of a better way to do something, and the main thing you will notice when the moon is in this sign is that you will always be busy but you have enough energy to cope with it. Watch out for the "blahs" though, as the period ends, for you'll often feel like a deflated balloon.

MOON IN CANCER

Take care at work when the moon is in Cancer because you are liable to run into situations you do not understand and overdramatize them. It is a time when bossiness should be used only when you are really sure you can be authoritative and know your facts. It is comparatively easy to deal with elderly employers and employees as you will relate better to older people than those younger than you. This is the period when an elderly secretary gets tired of working for a new youngster and gives her notice.

MOON IN LEO

This is a time when you can safely mix business with pleasure and neither will be any worse for it. If the boss praises you for your work, though, and you have dreams that he will back this up with a raise in pay, do not rely on it. Sweet words are not always followed by appropriate actions. Take praise and flattery with a grain of salt.

MOON IN VIRGO

If you have a problem at work, this is the time to sit down and weigh the pros and cons with the assurance that you will be nearer to a satisfactory solution than at any other time of the month. If relationships with employees or employer have deteriorated, this is the time to get them back on an even keel without any loss of pride or face.

MOON IN LIBRA

You will work best in any tandem situation and feel quite secure in harness at this time, so it encourages you to express opinions which you have been a bit nervous to discuss previously. The moon in Libra encourages you to want to see life through rose-tinted spectacles. It never does you any harm because no one hates the sordid elements of work more than you. You'll come out of this period much more enthusiastic and optimistic because of renewed self-confidence.

MOON IN SCORPIO

This is not a good time to put any new enterprise into action or go into a new job. However, the moon gives a lot of courage. You may feel like throwing in the towel and going home but remember: the courage may only last as long as the transit of the moon in this sign. So look before you leap into action, walk away from difficulties, and keep calm. Second thoughts help you to catch up with reality.

MOON IN SAGITTARIUS

If a person with the moon in this position can work in travel, sports, or law enforcement, he will be at his best, working hard at his job and deriving satisfaction from it. He likes to be outdoors and feel free even though he knows he has to report back to someone else. Moon people in Sagittarius often lack caution and talk too much, and it is only under exceptional good aspects that this position is good for anyone in the FBI, CIA, or diplomacy.

MOON IN CAPRICORN

People born with the moon in this position do best in a job where there is hope of promotion because the moon enhances ambitions and the desire for the power which comes with high positions. It also brings reserve into play, so that the subject does not make the best of friends who could help him achieve his ambitions. When somehow he succeeds and becomes a self-made man, he will always insist that whatever achievements he has attained he has done without help from anyone else. Generally this is true.

MOON IN AQUARIUS

The moon is in the sign associated with distribution, and this is exactly what a person born with the moon in this position loves to do. He may distribute ideas or goods, but can often go into politics. Before he begins to distribute ideas, he likes to collect facts, and these are his ammunition which can literally fire him up the ladder of success. It is not unusual for a lunar Aquarian to spend many years working behind the scenes and then appear at the top of his profession. Ex-President Nixon had his Moon in Aquarius in his sixth

285

house, associated with work. In this sign, the moon resists any attempts of outsiders to improve the subject in whose horoscope it appears. Once he has attained success in work, he relates it to power and seems to develop immunity from criticism.

MOON IN PISCES

A person with his moon in Pisces always takes his dream world right into his working life. He thrives best in the arts or any form of work where the imagination is an asset. He is also capable of leading a double life or working at two different jobs. He thrives when hugging secrets in his heart. Born with Moon in Pisces, he is able to present a different picture to his employer or employees and then go home to work just as hard on a secret project with a different image. He is no man's fool.

CHAPTER XV

Ring Around the Moon

The heavens themselves, the planets and this center,
Observe degrees, priority, and place,
Insisture, course, proportion, season, form,
Office and custom, in all line of order.

—Shakespeare, *Troilus and Cressida*

The study of astro-meterology, or the influence of the sun, moon and planets on the weather, is of ancient origin. It was originally an important branch of astrology although today there must be a generation of youngsters who are sure the weather is created by svelte young men in television studios. It is certainly not necessary to believe in astrology to know that every member of the solar system exerts an important influence by gravitation upon every other. The main difference between astro-meteorology and the methods employed by ordinary meteorologists is that the astrologer takes a long-term look at weather patterns. Most meteorologists do not profess to foresee weather changes more than one to five days ahead. A combination of astro-meteorology plus the advancements made by modern methods could produce a near-perfect method of weather forecasting.

*　　*　　*

The planets carry their rates of motion in the zodiac according to their relative positions with regard to the earth and the sun. Jupiter, Saturn, Uranus, and Neptune move their fastest through the zodiac as seen from the earth when in conjunction with the sun—that is, when they are on the opposite side of the sun from the earth. As they move away from this position, mainly because of the earth's revolution in its orbit round the sun, they are stationary in the zodiac. This is because the swifter-moving earth overtakes them and seems to leave them behind. Then the planets are called retrograde while they are in opposition to the sun—that is, at the time the earth is passing between them and the sun. They become stationary a second time and finally move direct again. Jupiter, Saturn, Uranus, and Neptune are stationary in the zodiac twice a year, moving direct for more than half the year and retrograde for less than half. Mercury, Venus, and Mars also become stationary and retrograde, but in periods that differ considerably from those of the larger planets.

The symbol "R" in the ephemeris means that a planet is stationary in the zodiac the day before and is now retrograde or appearing to move in the reverse direction. It continues retrograde until the letter "D" appears in the ephemeris, which means that the planet was stationary the day before and is now moving direct again. The positions in the ephemeris are given for noon Greenwich Mean Time except in the case of the moon, which is also given, appropriately enough, at midnight.

Changes in the weather are produced by the sun, moon, and planets under certain specific conditions which, for convenience are classified under two headings: "positions," when each acts alone, and "aspects," when two or more celestial bodies act in combination. The influence of the moon on the weather is paradoxically the easiest and at the same time the most difficult to explain. It is the easiest because its effects are produced more quickly than is the case with other aspects. It is the most difficult because it is capable of forming a multitude of aspects within a very short period. It is therefore not easy to decide which are strong enough to make themselves felt. The nature of the sun is classified as hot and dry and the moon as cool and moist, but in weather forecasting, the two luminaries operate entirely through aspects to the planets. When either luminary is in aspect to a planet, it is the characteristic influence of that planet which is felt, such as cold with Uranus or Saturn, warm with Jupiter or Mars.

The moon moves through the zodiac twelve times faster than the sun and six times faster than Mercury at its swiftest, so lunar aspects to planets are formed rapidly but dissolve equally quickly. The result is that their influence on the weather does not last more than a few hours. Lunar aspects do not produce such decided results as the more slowly formed solar and interplanetary aspects. One effect of the rapid movement of the moon is that it may form two, three, or even more strong aspects to the planets on the same day. This does not result in storms or unsettled weather, as is the case with the solar and interplanetary aspects. True to the erratic character of the moon, however, it can do so if the lunar aspects are supported by other concurrent influences.

If the moon is in square to Jupiter, the natural result would be to anticipate fine weather with a rise in temperature for at least several hours before and after the time when the aspect is exact. If the sun is in trine to Jupiter, the weather will tend to be fine, dry, and warm for a day or two before and after the aspects. If during this period the moon aspects Jupiter and Mars, there will be an increase in sunshine and warmth at the time of the lunar aspect. But when the moon aspects Saturn or Uranus, there is a decrease in temperature, and cloud formations can be expected according to the strength of the aspect. When the moon aspects Venus and Saturn, cold rain can be expected but will clear up when the moon aspects Jupiter and the sun.

At the times when the sun and moon both aspect a planet at the same time, which sometimes happens at the time of the new or full moon, the influence of the particular planet on the weather is strongly felt because the two aspects reinforce each other.

There is a widespread belief that a change of weather is likely to occur at the time of the new moon, but astronomers point out that statistics do not justify this idea. They have often used it as an argument against the influence of the sun and moon on weather, but modern meteorology has produced some good research to prove there is a link with weather conditions through the sun and moon. So we are now back to the old, accepted astrologers' premise that it is the planet the two luminaries aspect which causes the changes. Lunar aspects when the moon is on the equator or in the tropics or in extreme declination gain in strength and importance just as solar aspects do at such times. On the average, there is more rain during the increase of the moon than during its decrease and more during the second quarter than at any other time. A full moon tends to banish clouds and produce a clear sky.

A brief guide to astro forecasting can be seen when the following aspects occur.

MERCURY AND VENUS

Two of the faster-moving planets nearest to the sun produce mild weather, rain, and cloudiness with slight wind.

MERCURY AND MARS

This produces dry, windy weather with an increase in temperature. According to the season, these strong aspects may cooperate with other influences to cause a gale, thunderstorm, or snow.

MERCURY AND JUPITER

An increase in temperature with fine warm weather, but sometimes brings an increase in wind. With exceptionally strong aspects, hail and thunderstorms occur in summer months.

MERCURY AND SATURN

According to the season, rain or snow can be expected. There is a fall in temperature, and in winter months there can be a very cold spell with wind.

MERCURY AND URANUS

Similar to the above, but with much more wind.

MERCURY AND NEPTUNE

Mist, fog, or light rain, temperate to cool.

VENUS AND MARS

Mist, fog, or rain, which can be heavy. Temperate to warm.

VENUS AND JUPITER

Fine weather with an increase in temperature. In cooperation with other influences, showers or thunderstorms.

VENUS AND SATURN OR URANUS

A fall in temperature, cloudy with mist or fog. According to the seasons, there will be rain or snow.

VENUS AND NEPTUNE

Temperate but rain, mist, or fog.

MARS AND JUPITER

An increase in temperature and fine, dry weather. Strong aspects disturb the atmosphere, bringing winds and thunderstorms, after which there is a fall in temperature.

MARS AND SATURN

Disturbs the atmosphere—winds, gales, storms, and heavy rain. It tends to break up and disperse extreme heat in summer and extreme cold in winter.

MARS AND URANUS

Wind squalls.

MARS AND NEPTUNE

Generally fine but light rain, temperate to warm.

JUPITER AND SATURN

The planet of expansion in aspect to the planet of restriction tends to destroy extreme heat in summer and extreme cold in winter. Cloudy, unsettled, mist or fog. These strong aspects are liable to cause wind and storms, also thunderstorms.

JUPITER AND URANUS

Similar to Jupiter and Saturn, but brings in more wind than anything else.

JUPITER AND NEPTUNE

Increase of temperature, but with mist or rain.

SATURN AND URANUS

Fall in temperature with cloudiness, cold winds, rain, or snow.

SATURN AND NEPTUNE

Temperature falls, heavier mists, fog, and rain.

URANUS AND NEPTUNE

Similar to Saturn and Neptune.

All these aspects can be clearly seen by learning how to use an ephemeris. If you are planning an outdoor activity at some future date, it is safer to rely on the ephemeris than to wait for a regular television weather forecast only a day or two before the event. Organizers of public fund-raising events often have to take out high insurance policies to cover the possibility of having all their work destroyed by inclement weather. The investment of a few dollars in an ephemeris plus a few hours devoted to studying it could save quite a lot of money on insurance premiums which, like so many things today, have increased considerably. Basic astro-meteorology is not very difficult to learn. A few trial runs are needed, and it is well to understand the basic influences of each individual planet.

1. The influence of the sun is dependent on the planet with which it is in aspect, although the essential influence of the sun is fine, hot, and dry.

2. The moon seems to act as a collector and also as a discharging rod. She lets loose or discharges the accumulat-

293

ed influence of the planets as and when she aspects them. Her essential influence is fair, cool, and moist.

3. The influence of Neptune is fair, foggy, and misty. In winter it can be stormy or bring an excess of fogginess depending on the aspect to another planet.

4. Saturn's influence is persistent and lasting, mainly concerned with storms, rain, and cold.

5. The influence of Jupiter brings fine, hot, dry, pleasant air with thunder after heat and breezes.

6. The influence of Mars is hot and dry, with thunder after heat.

7. The influence of Venus is gentle, pleasant, mild, leading into light rain.

8. The influence of Mercury is very changeable, often with considerable wind, rain, and storms.

These separate influences will vary according to the seasons of spring, summer, autumn, and winter: that is, when the sun enters the cardinal signs of Aries, Cancer, Libra, and Capricorn.

If I were hoping to find some fine days within any one month, I would first look for a solar aspect with Jupiter followed in a few days with a solar aspect to Mars or Neptune. If I can find this within three or four days intervening, then I would expect a spell of fine weather. If I found a square aspect of Uranus or Mercury intervening, I would expect rough weather with rain as soon as the moon on the day of the aspect became parallel or in aspect to either Uranus or Neptune. If I were going on a short trip when I needed to be sure of fine weather, I would pay special attention to the moon and calculate to the hour the aspects she formed with the planets during the day. If the moon was in conjunction to Jupiter, then the three hours before the conjunction and three hours afterward would be fine.

Folklore tells of various omens that can be read from the state of the moon. If two moons occur in a single calendar month—especially May—there will be floods and calamities. Rings around the moon foretell storms, and the intensity of such storms can be gauged by the number of rings. Heavy rains occur most frequently in the days immediately following the new and full moons, and the richest dew is found on moonlit nights. A full moon at Christmas is a bad omen for the coming harvest, while a full moon on a Sunday is regarded as a harbinger of bad luck. A new moon on a Saturday augurs bad weather.

When you first see the new moon, turn over a piece of silver in your pocket but never look at it through glass, then make a wish. If you live in a place like the British Isles, with its vagaries of weather, the best thing to do is to wish for a fine day. It is primitive weather magic, but somehow all these omens have a place in our lives even today.

CHAPTER XVI

The Moon in Medical Astrology

Kill thy physician and the fee bestow
Upon the foul disease.

—William Shakespeare, *King Lear*

Astrology was once closely linked to religion and medical science, and it is not too many centuries ago since astrology was taught in such great medical universities of the world as Bologna. There is an old saying, "A doctor without astrology is like a lamp without oil," but when medical science became a business, astrological references were thrown out of the door. The formation of various national medical associations throughout the civilized world has made astro-medical studies a subculture, with research limited to astrologers who are unable to put into practice all the things they know. Since most astrologers are mostly quite law-abiding people, they rarely make waves by talking about medical astrology. We are now in an age when the members of medical profession are classified as just one grade below God, and with this has come a terrible reliance on medical men to the exclusion of people trying to help themselves.

The old idea of prevention being better than cure is absent from such a highly sophisticated country as the United States. When herbalists were forbidden to prescribe their simple remedies, we were left as victims to the vast organized big-business concerns of the pharmaceutical companies. True, we can buy medicine off the racks of pharmacies, and the rationale for buying is often generated by the amount of brainwashing advertising the company makes. If a rose is a rose is a rose, then an aspirin is an aspirin is an aspirin—but roses have many names and so do aspirins. The medical profession has stretched itself now to a point where to be sick is a luxury; we pay heavily for the misfortune while doctors seek exotic means for tax shelters in order to keep the vast sums of money they are legally allowed to earn. Take the financial angle out of that dread scourge, cancer, and we should soon find a cure for it.

In 1970 I wrote an article stating that red dyes in foodstuffs were a possible contributory cause to cancer; we were literally being fed the diabolic stuff with the sanction of the Food and Drug Association. Numerous fortunes have been made by food producers who with vast resources of research chemists must surely have known as much as I knew purely from astrological reasoning. Until 1976 nothing was done about the red-dyed foods. Now we have a new ruling that food manufacturers must cease adding red dye to their products, but they have given plenty of time to retailers to get these products off their shelves. Red dye has been extensively used for the past twenty years, and still the product will take anything up to five years to be eliminated from our food. The people who make these laws have the nerve to fight astrologers in practically every community in the United States unless we work under the umbrella of a registered church.

*   *   *

If we examine innumerable combinations in ancient classical tests on the subject of medical astrology, we find there are an amazing series of parallels between the regular motion of the planets in the solar system, of which earth is a part, and the ebb and flow of physical, mental, and emotional phenomena peculiar to life on earth. A few isolated scientific minds now indirectly corroborate the basic concepts of medical astrology which have always been known by astrologers. For instance, it is well known that there is a correspondence between low and high tides of the ocean and the lunar-solar movement. When the sun and moon are 90 degrees apart, low tides occur; when they are 180 degrees apart, we get the high tides. The same geometrical positions of the sun and moon affecting seawater also affects the store of fluids on the surface of the earth contained in the animal and vegetable kingdom and the body fluids of human beings. There is a known astrological reference that the eighth lunar day removes or cures an ailment because on this day the sun and moon, being 90 degrees apart, diminish each other's attraction for fluids. There is a similarity between the salts in the blood and seawater and this is not accidental.

Astrologers know that skin diseases, disturbed mental conditions, and epilepsy increase in virulence at the time of the new moon. At this time, the sun and moon are closer together in the sky pulling at the particles of the gases forming the atmosphere and exerting a pull on human beings. In many illnesses, the fourteenth lunar day is the time when the sun and moon are 160 degrees from each other, and it is at this time that a crisis in illness can occur. Intense emotional disturbance occurs, acting as a trigger to the crisis.

The Swedish scientist Svanté Arrhenius showed through statistical investigation that menstruation in the female occurs at one particular point in the lunar month. His statement is not new. It was remarked upon by Varahamihira, a remarkable astrologer-astronomer who lived in the first century B.C. He said, "The menses in a woman sets in every month when the moon arrives at a particular position from the rising sign in her horoscope, and that is due to the interaction of the moon and Mars."

While half of the world today worries about zero population growth, another half worries about women who are unable to conceive or bear a living child. Modern gynecologists might consider that there are some very clear ideas about the periodic fertility in women which correspond with specific cosmic patterns. The best fertile period for conception are the fourteenth, fifteenth, and sixteenth days from the commencement of menstruation. The pituitary controls the uterus up to the sixteenth day from the rupture of the Graafian follicle. These astrological observations agree with the research done by professors Ogino and Knaus who came up with their own evidence that on the fifteenth night from the last day of menstruation, the ovum is released. By knowing the lunar cycle and relating it to the first menstrual period and the position of the moon in her horoscope, a woman has a surefire chance of being able to control her own fertility. It is certainly less dangerous than the pill, which was a remarkable invention, but we are now beginning to see some adverse results in more and more women. We may well find out that the pill will go the same way as red dye introduced into foodstuffs since it takes about twenty years for human guinea pigs to show a consistent increase of adverse effects.

Every fourteen days at the time of the new or full moon, there is a considerable voltage increase in the electrical potential of all human beings. These electrical changes correspond with noticeable changes in moods, and the forces behind the influence of the moon can aggravate conflicts and maladjustment. In surgery, bleeding crises occur between the first and third quarter of the moon, with a higher incidence of bleeding during the full moon. Medical statistics are available to prove this, mainly due to the experiments carried out by Dr. Edson Andrews of Florida. Dr. Andrews has been an ear, nose, and throat specialist for some thirty years. He is a member of numerous professional organizations and has served as president of two county medical societies. He came to my notice when I read an article in the *Florida Medical Association Journal* in which he described his original research on the effect of lunar cycles on hemorrhages.

Logically, with medical science so advanced, the number of hemorrhage cases should be minute. There can be nothing so frustrating to a surgeon who has skillfully performed an operation than to find himself with a patient whose life's blood is draining away. This happens despite meticulous skill and postsurgical care. Several years ago a nurse at the Tallahassee Memorial Hospital in Florida presented Dr. Andrews with the idea that the particular phase of the moon might be the influencing factor in bleeding. Unknown to the doctor, she had already begun to compile data on such cases, carefully noting the position of the moon at the time when excessive and sudden bleeding occurred. Maximum cases always coincided with the appearance of the full moon. So definite was the grouping that the doctor and nurse decided to collect more case histories and record them in a methodical scientific manner. The result was Dr. Andrew's paper.

In my old home in the New Forest in England, an area where livestock breeding represents a large portion of the wealth of the inhabitant, I never met a farmer who would castrate pigs or geld horses at the time of the full moon. They told me that excessive bleeding would debilitate the animal, hindering the pigs from putting on weight quickly enough to bring to market at the right time for slaughter. The farmers were inclined to ridicule the nouveau riche townsfolk who came to the forest to start horse breeding stables. They were the ones who did not mind having their horses gelded when the moon was full, but I suppose they could not be expected to understand the ancient laws of husbandry and their relationship to the full moon.

Dr. Nicholas Culpeper, the famous seventeenth-century doctor, astrologer, and astronomer, now remembered for his definitive book on herbs, always set up an astrological chart for his patients. He believed—and to date nothing has happened to upset this belief—that when various crises in acute diseases occur, they can be found in the horoscope. Culpeper knew that the crisis periods related to the position of the moon in the chart, and he duly noted the sign in which the moon appeared, also its degrees. In a lunar month, the moon takes approximately twenty-eight days to complete its course. On the seventh day it reaches a square aspect, then an opposition to the sun on the fourteenth day, and a second square on the twenty-first day. Medical practitioners today know that in acute diseases a crisis is reached on the seventh day, and there is a further crisis on the fourteenth day, when the moon is exactly opposing the position it was in when the illness started. (A crisis is a critical point where there can be a change for better or worse in the course of the illness.) If the crisis can be anticipated at the beginning of the illness, then better precautions can be taken to mitigate its full impact.

In cases where surgery is needed, no astrologer would recommend his client undergo surgery on the day when the sick part of the body is governed by the sign actually occupied by the moon. For instance, a person born with his moon in Aries may have a head injury. Surgery should not take place when the moon is in Aries. The chances of recovering more quickly would be best if the surgery took place when the moon was in the opposing sign of Libra. The same basic rule applies for all the signs of the zodiac and the parts of the body ruled by the various planets.

The sun, moon, and wind are necessary for the regular functioning of life on earth, and we are all involved with motion, energy, and gravitation or inertia. As it is above so it is below, and the living cells are arranged to function on the same lines as the cosmos. Human ailments can be linked to the outcome of gravitational pulls exerted by the planets through rotation and revolution: that is, action and reaction, the basic laws of the universe, science, and astrology. In astrological literature, mostly carefully hidden in the archives of famous libraries, there is a thorough classification of all diseases and the planetary patterns which cause them. We can no longer dismiss such writings as nonsense as long as there is our own moon in the sky exerting its influence on us earthlings.

But we certainly need a more scientific approach to astrology, even though science is not always smart enough in itself. It took years of theoretical reasoning and practical experiments for science to accept that energy is a quality of matter, and then Einstein came along with his theory of relativity. Hindu astrology has always accepted that matter is formed by three qualities of inertia (Sleshnia), energy (Pitta), and motion (Vata), but it took a scientist to present it to the world and make the name of Einstein a memorable one. While scientists will not deliberately acknowledge any astrological sources for their discoveries, astrologers must try to keep up with them by delving into ancient knowledge of their own science and dragging it out to present to the world.

A Russian biologist, Professor Tchijevsky, discovered a relationship between the incidences of cardiovascular diseases and outbreaks of solar energy. In astrology, the sun is associated with diseases of the heart. When the sun reaches its highest state of electric activity during an outburst of sunspots, electric particles bombard the earth, electrifying the atmosphere. According to Tchijevsky, it is during this electrification that nations are physiologically and psychologically goaded to the point of massacring one another. At the same time, bacteria of infectious diseases become more deadly. In astrology, the moon rules the mind, the sun the self or soul, and Mercury rules the nervous system. A combination of moon, Mercury, and the nodes of the moon cause exaggerations of disorders rising from psychosis, neurosis, and mental abnormalities. Many people suffering from mental disorders are able to walk the streets, commit crimes, or upset others, and no one will believe there is any mental sickness behind such criminal deeds or unusual behavior.

I would definitely state that a horoscope is more useful in understanding the true mental condition of any person and much more reliable than a Rorschach test. A Rorschach test shows the condition of the patient only at the time the test is taken, but a horoscope reveals the basic psychological conditions. Afflictions to Cancer and the fourth house in a natal horoscope indicate that the subject may become the victim of mental diseases such as lunacy, retardation, dull thinking, and emotional diseases such as fits, epilepsy, phobia, and coma. The moon is always afflicted by a malefic planet or planetary pattern to bring about these diseases. If the nodes of the moon (known as Dragon's Head or Dragon's Tail) either conjoin or aspect the moon, the situation is worsened. If the moon, the watery planet, is conjoined with or aspected by the fiery Mars, the still ocean of the mind can become a whirlpool, bringing instability of the mind into play. The condition will first manifest itself as sudden huge flashes of temper, an abusive tongue, a malicious nature, and very often a treacherous mind which makes him turn against the very people who want to be friends and help him. When Mars is in square aspect to the moon, there is mental agitation and varying degrees of melancholia. When Saturn, the restrictor, afflicts the moon, the subject is obstinate, dull, and rude. In the emotional diseases, the Dragon's Head or Dragon's Tail influence the fourth house ruled by the moon, or even on the moon itself. The mind, emotions, and desires merge to produce phobias and intense fears, all then reflect on the general state of health, but the source of the phobias may not always be detected by normal psychological means.

n cases of suicide, there is always an emotional disturbance acting as a catalyst to the act of self-destruction. In the horoscopes of such people, the moon and the fourth house are afflicted by malefics, especially Mars and the Dragon's Head. The fifth house is generally afflicted as well, causing enough mental derangement to enable the ghastly act to be done. I have always felt that in legal cases suicide is often presumed, but a horoscope would reveal whether the victim did indeed take his own life or whether it was homicide. Insurance companies as well as the law would benefit by checking out charts of victims of suicide, but we are a long way from achieving this. From time to time I have been invited to prepare charts for families disputing wills or insurance claims, but this is generally done in such an aura of secrecy that it seems absurd. The interesting thing is that while the charts may not be accepted in a court of law, every case I have done has provided enough clues to get the law interested in reviewing the case—so I suppose the end product has been worthwhile. I would prefer that credit should be given to astrology, though, rather than have to pretend everything is due to the smartness of the very lawyer who was content to accept a verdict of suicide when the family did not.

Disease is a state of agitation in the body organism indicating a functional disorder which can be physical, mental, emotional, or a combination of them. The state of agitation becomes sensed through symptoms, and this is generally the time a patient goes to the doctor. This would be fine if the modern scientific concept was correct that "man ages to a strict biological clock." I believe that sickness and disease occur when the biological clock fails to be intricately synchronized to the cosmic clock. Each cell in a living organism has its own miniature clockwork and can act independently, giving a biological rhythm regulating numerous processes which give continuity and design to life.

Getting all these millions of tiny clocks ticking together is only half the route to good health. They are also under the influence of a vast unseen synchronizer and it is this process of synchronization that is so little understood. Someone in the near future will come up with a "new" idea that respiratory, glandular, and reproductive systems are started and controlled by extraterrestial powers. All the biological rhythms ebbing and flowing throughout the body have to be in tune with the beating pulsations of the planetary pattern at specific times, and not the least to influence these is the moon.

We know that as the planets move in their orderly procession in the heavens, from time to time they form angles with other planets, and it is through these angles that the astrologer makes his interpretations. As the planetary patterns change, so the tiny clockwork in the cell organisms have to reset themselves. Illness occurs when this does not happen. The clockwork mechanism becomes agitated, and abnormal conditions set in affecting the vital organs and systems. In severe illnesses, there is a chain reaction. Disease becomes the end product of a shift in the pulse beat of the cosmic clock. The remedy lies in resetting the rhythms, biofeedback may be one of the revolutionary methods to achieve this, although it can be achieved by good scientific astrological wisdom. As the planetary patterns affect the environment, so they also set up specific disorders, and there is a secondary group which are initiated by the effect of the planetary patterns on human life. Tension, worry, unnatural living habits, pollution, and bad food of a chemical content trigger off agitation in the human biological clock. Under present-day conditions, with man living at an abnormally fast pace, his metabolism cannot cope with so many changes, and he is constantly out of synchronization with the cosmic clock.

Within old astrological texts there are time-tested guidelines, the best-known one is that of zodiacal man in which his anatomy is superimposed symbolically on the zodiac. Most people know that Aries people have trouble with headaches, Taureans are vulnerable to throat infections, Geminis are accident-prone, Cancers have chest troubles, Leo is vulnerable to heart afflictions, Virgo to trouble in the intestines, Libra can develop kidney trouble, Scorpio has afflictions of the genitalia, Sagittarians have weak thighs, Capricorns are prone to arthritis, while Aquarians have difficulties with circulation, and Pisces are rarely free from foot afflictions. This is absolutely basic astro-medical data, but there is extended literature on the function of more subtle organs. Each planet has rulership over specific diseases and conditions associated with them. Inherent tendencies to diseases can be seen by planetary afflictions in the natal chart, but they may remain dormant for some time; hence the value of the progressed chart as a means of bringing conditions up to date. The timing for the appearance of disease can be found with emphasis on the changing position of the moon and its nodes, and their relationships to planets in the sixth house associated with health.

As the human body becomes more and more prone to diseases not known to our ancestors, there is plenty of room for further research for any astrologer interested in astro-medicine. The best way to do research is to obtain date, place, and time of birth from a doctor connected with some specific disease. The doctor is not infringing on the privacy of his patients since there is no need to have any names included in the data. Currently I am working on research to find the planetary patterns conducive to indicating a tendency to leprosy, one of the oldest diseases known to man. A student of mine is also working on the planetary patterns of hemophilia. Several hundred birthdates are needed in order to start this type of research.

Here are a few combinations taken from various astrological authorities indicating some selected diseases:

307

BLINDNESS OR DISEASES OF THE EYE

1. Blindness can be expected if the moon is in the fifth house, the sun in the eighth, Saturn in the twelfth, and Mars in the second.
2. The moon in the second house indicates potential trouble in the left eye.
3. Venus in the second house of a water sign with a waxing moon produces people with very watery eyes.

TUBERCULOSIS

1. The moon, Jupiter, or Venus in the ninth house conjoined or aspected by malefic planets indicates death by tuberculosis.
2. A weak moon in conjunction with the sun in the sixth or eighth house of a water sign indicates a tendency to the disease.
3. The moon placed between Mars and Saturn with the sun in Capricorn shows a tendency to the disease.
4. The moon and sun in conjunction in Cancer or Leo indicates a tendency to tuberculosis of the bones.

INSANITY, MENTAL DISEASES

1. Malefic planets in the fourth or fifth house not aspected by any benefic planets creates mental trouble.
2. A weak moon with Saturn in the twelfth house indicates poor mental ability which can deteriorate to lunacy.

LEPROSY

1. The moon in Sagittarius or Leo aspected by Mars or Saturn indicates a tendency to the disease.
2. The moon and Saturn in conjunction in Pisces, Cancer or Scorpio aspected by malefics indicates a tendency to the disease.

3. Jupiter and the moon in the sixth house indicates leprosy breaking out in the twelfth and nineteenth years of life.

LEUKEMIA (cancer of the blood)

The moon and Saturn in the sixth house indicates a tendency to leukemia in the fifty-fifth year of life.

LEUCODERMA (white patches of skin)

1. If the sun and moon in the seventh house have malefics in the second and twelfth houses, leucoderma is indicated.
2. When Mars, the moon and Mercury are in conjunction in the sixth house, leucoderma will occur.

EPILEPSY

The moon, Dragon's Head, Jupiter, and Saturn in the eighth house indicates epileptic conditions.

CANCER

There are many varieties of this scourge, but there seems to be one particular planetary pattern which gives indications of the tendency to the disease. There is generally a conjunction of the moon and Venus above the ascendant in Sagittarius. Saturn in Cancer may retrograde to a square aspect with Mars in Taurus or Libra. The body is incapable of throwing off poison, and the system becomes clogged with debris, giving just the right conditions for a cancerous growth in the colon. Drastic dieting can reduce the potential, especially when Mars becomes sextile to the sun. Then there is hope of overcoming the disease. Cancer is also directly concerned with the Dragon's Tail, an afflicted moon, Jupiter or Saturn, and the signs Aries, Taurus, Cancer, Libra, and Capricorn are involved. The sun refers to cancer of the bowels, stomach and head; the moon to the breast and the blood; Mars to the blood marrow, neck, genitals, and uterus;

Mercury to the nose, navel, and mouth; Jupiter to the liver, ears, tongue, and thighs; Venus to the throat and genitalia, and Saturn to the legs and hands.

Tumors, boils, carbuncles, and abscesses involve the water signs, the fourth, eighth, and twelfth houses, the planet Mars, and the Dragon's Head.

DROPSY

1. Saturn in Cancer while the moon is in Capricorn.
2. A weak moon and Saturn in the eighth house.
3. Neptune in Pisces afflicted by a malefic planet with the moon or Venus also afflicted.

GOUT AND RHEUMATISM

1. Both sun and moon afflicted in a water sign.
2. Saturn in Pisces opposing Mars or in conjunction of the sun and the moon.
3. The moon and Saturn in the sixth house indicates a tendency to rheumatism.
4. Weak moon and Saturn in the twelfth house.
5. Mercury with the Dragon's Tail or Dragon's Head in the sixth house.
6. Afflicted moon, Mercury, Venus, and Saturn.

ITCHES AND SKIN DISEASES

1. Mercury in the second house aspected by the moon.
2. Sun, moon, and Mars in the sixth house.
3. Moon and Mars in the second house aspected by Saturn indicates skin diseases which are difficult to cure and which will flare up from time to time.
4. The Dragon's Head in the eighth house joined with or aspected by a malefic planet.
5. The moon in the sixth house aspected by a malefic.
6. The moon in Virgo between malefic planets.

BROKEN BONES

The planetary patterns for these are numerous.
1. The sun and moon, Saturn, and Mars in the fifth, eighth, or ninth house.
2. The Dragon's Head, Saturn, and Mercury in the tenth house.
3. The moon in the first house, Saturn in the fourth, and Mars in the tenth.
4. The moon in Capricorn placed between malefics.
5. The moon with Mars in the sixth house.

The loss of limbs is closely related to some of the above planetary patterns but more definite combinations are:
1. Saturn in the first house, Dragon's Head in the second, a waning moon in the seventh house, and Venus in Virgo indicates possible loss of hand or foot.
2. Saturn in the seventh house while Mars is conjunct with the Dragon's Head.

WOUNDS

1. Moon in the second house, Mars in the fourth, and the sun in the tenth.
2. Mars and the moon in the sixth house.

DIABETES

The planets involved are Venus, Jupiter, and the moon.
A strong malefic planet in the eighth house with Venus and Jupiter or the moon and Jupiter afflicted.

TROUBLES OF THE MOUTH AND FACE

Mercury and the moon afflicting the second house.

COMPLAINTS OF THE HEART

The planetary patterns are numerous, but a safe assessment can be made that heart trouble will afflict a subject when there is an afflicted moon in the fourth house with three malefic planets in one house.

The Dragon's Head and the moon in the seventh house.

There are probably half a million planetary patterns to be considered in relationship to all known diseases, but a rough guide is that the moon influences eye diseases, the stomach and intestines, the mind, phlegm and congested conditions, tuberculosis, asthma, and other respiratory diseases, fever, and vomiting. The Dragon's Tail and Dragon's Head influence diseases due to the intake of poison substances, diseases of the stomach, insanity, some forms of cancer, some heart diseases, epilepsy, and epidemics.

The zodiacal circle consists of 360 degrees. In each sign there are certain degree areas which are specific of certain diseases when these areas are afflicted. In studying a chart, the nature of a disease can be judged by combining the effects of the sign, the planets within, and the planets aspecting the planets within that sign.

Although we are mainly interested in the effect of the moon on the state of health, it is a good idea for any student of astro-medicine to become conversant with the diseases associated with each planet.

SUN DISEASES

Eye diseases, especially
  in the male
Some spinal troubles
Fevers
Blood disorders
Heart conditions
 Spleen

INFLUENCE OF SUN ON
  ORGANIC DISORDERS

Diseases involving
  structural alteration of
  tissues
Heart and circulatory
  troubles
Overstimulation and/or
  devitalization

MOON DISEASES

Abscesses
Catarrh
Colds
Dropsy
Epilepsy
Female disorders
Eye troubles, especially in
  the female
Giddiness
Nausea
Mental illnesses
Mammary and saliva glands
Breasts
Stomach
Uterus
Upper alimentary tract

INFLUENCE OF MOON ON
  FUNCTIONAL DISORDERS

Childhood and inherited
  diseases
Digestive problems
Diseases of the lymphatic
  system
Growths and tumors

DISEASES OF MERCURY

Asthma
Bronchitis
Deafness
Mental disorders
Nervous ailments
Nerves
Lungs
Central nervous system
The thymus gland
Pancreas
Lower alimentary tract

INFLUENCE OF MERCURY ON NERVOUS DISORDERS

Neuritis
Psychosomatic disorders
Respiratory ailments
Speech impediments

DISEASES OF VENUS

Diphtheria
Hair, neck, and throat
 ailments
Skin afflictions
Ulcers
Small of back
Adrenal glands

INFLUENCE OF VENUS ON GLANDULAR DISORDERS

Afflictions of thyroid gland
Metabolic problems
Kidney problems
Ovary problems
Varicose veins

DISEASES OF MARS

Nasal troubles
Piles
Muscular disorders
Colon
Blood

INFLUENCE OF MARS ON ACUTE DISEASES

Accidents
Blood diseases
Cerebral palsy
Excretory problems
Fevers, inflammations,
 irritations, infections
Malfunctions of the male
 reproductive system

DISEASES OF JUPITER

Arterial diseases
Cancer
Diabetes
Body fluids
Lachrymal gland
Lymph glands
Pineal gland
Lower spine
Accidents to buttocks
Accidents to hips

INFLUENCE OF JUPITER ON DISEASES OF EXCESS

Congestion
Faulty coordination
Growths
Liver troubles
Obesity
Lymphatic system

DISEASES OF SATURN

Ague
Atrophy
Bone diseases
Bronchitis
Chronic colds
Deafness
Accidents to knees
Gallbladder

INFLUENCE OF SATURN ON DISEASES OF DEFICIENCY

Arthritis
Bone and skin diseases
Chronic ailments
Dental decay
Hardening of arteries
Malnutrition
Senility

DISEASES OF URANUS

Accidents to ankles
Hiccups
Wounds
Parathyroid gland

INFLUENCE OF URANUS ON SUDDEN DISORDERS

Ruptures, fractures
Cramps, epilepsy
Paralysis, shocks, spasms
Radiation poisoning

DISEASES OF NEPTUNE	INFLUENCE OF NEPTUNE ON PSYCHOGENIC DISORDERS
Delirium	Addictions such as drugs, alcoholism
Accidents to feet	Comas and fainting
Foot disorders	Schizophrenia
Lachrymal glands	Toxic conditions
Lymph glands	Lympahtic disorders
Pineal glands	

DISEASES OF PLUTO	INFLUENCE OF PLUTO ON DEEP-SEATED DISORDERS
Adrenal glands	Mass neurosis
Internal genitalia	Mass paranoia
Pluto also acts in conjunction with other planets	Obsessions
	Somnambulism
	Sexual complexes and compulsions

Planets, like signs, work in pairs or teams. The moon team is composed of Venus, Jupiter, and Neptune. In many diseases, the moon is the trigger which enables the other planets to exert excessive influence. A good example is considering diabetes. The moon governs the early conditioning of a child when candies are often handed out indiscriminately. Venus rules all sugary things, such as candies and rich desserts. Then Jupiter with its expansive nature comes in and creates obesity, which in itself is a trigger to diabetes. In some cases of diabetes, there can be a blackout period when the subject lapses into a coma, and now Neptune joins the team as the blood sugar ruled by Venus becomes too low.

The sun, Mars, Saturn, and Pluto form a secondary team representing a catabolic or tearing-down process, while the first team led by the moon represents the anabolic or body-building process. This leaves Mercury as the neutral planet of the zodiac capable of causing reactions on both beams through its ability to create nervous disorders. Uranus is a higher octave of Mercury and it contributes to the metabolic functions, sometimes distributing its energies constructively, sometimes destructively.

As each planet forms an angle with one or more planets, so the crossplay of good or bad health is woven in the fabric of life. If the force of strong planets afflicts weaker ones, then the pattern becomes distorted and we have sickness. Understanding the natal and progressed horoscope will give indications when the pattern will be firm and correct, and the periods when the planetary influences cross to throw shadows on the basic design.

CHAPTER XVII

The Moon in Aspect

Everyone is a moon and has a dark side
Which he never shows to anybody.

—Sybil Leek

Astrologically, the moon rules the fourth house of Cancer, the house associated with the home and parents, heredity factors, and psychological roots. It influences all that surrounds, protects, and nourishes the self as well as family and racial traditions. From the placement of the moon, it is possible to see what influence the mother has on her children as compared to the influence of the father and all early subconscious training. When placed in its own fourth house, it gives a desire for peace and contentment at any price. When this is denied by the aspects of the moon to other planets, such a peaceful life is often denied and a restless, dissatisfied nature emerges. The Moon in Cancer person, while disliking changes in residence, is often forced to make these changes but has the ability to adapt to his environment through a determined effort. There is always a powerful attraction to maternal influences which can be constructive or very destructive, or underlie a lifelong search for someone to serve as a mother-image. While the moon represents the feminine principle of life, all its influences affect the male as much as the female, sometimes accenting feminine qualities of gentleness and a desire to protect within the framework of a man who may otherwise be very masculine.

There is always a love for the past, which can be reflected in the enjoyment of antiques, old customs and houses, and an interest in genealogy. There is a craving for a sense of continuity; when carried to extremes, this can lead to a disdain for the future.

Among other important factors, the moon placement shows habit patterns, the sum of inherited traits which operate below the threshold of consciousness as instinctive responses. Taken collectively, the sun, moon, and Ascendant show the sense of direction in life. The sun indicates a person's natural way of expressing himself, his innate inclinations and the qualities he deliberately builds into himself. The Ascendant shows where a person is heading; it is a cohesive bond between the sun and moon qualities. When the sun and moon are in conjunction, it is easier for a person to focus his energies and channel them into specific lines of thought and action. He is able to learn from experience as he goes along his chosen path.

When the sun and moon are in opposition, the subject reacts against the past and encounters resistance in achieving his potential and his ambitions. He constantly feels that something has been left unfinished. When the sun and moon are in square aspect, the subject is torn between innate inclinations and cannot always fulfill the hopes and challenges set before him. Most of all, he finds it hard to fulfill family responsibilities and expectancies. If the moon is on the Ascendant, the subject always tries to do something he has done before but aiming always to improve on his performance. In esoteric astrology, it is possible to see what influence past lives have had on the subject; he will act out some incident in the past, trying to make a better job of it. The average person responds more to the influence of the sun and moon than to his Ascendant; this accounts for popularity of sun-sign astrology, as outward characteristics imposed on by the sun are more easily traceable than the more subtle natal qualities of the moon.

When the moon is in Cancer's opposing sign of Capricorn, it is in its detriment. Being in detriment does not weaken the nature of the luminary, but its power works in a manner contrary to that of the sign, becoming subtle, hidden energy. All too often, the Moon in Capricorn subject will have hidden enemies. The moon is exalted in Taurus, which means that it finds itself in a congenial position and brings into play many of the influences associated with Taurus such as the love of beauty, certain materialistic possessive traits, a more than ordinary interest in sex and love, and it adds a bit of toughness to the normally placid influence of the moon in its own bailiwick. Because the laws of polarity follow all through zodiacal references, if we have a planet capable of being in an exalted position, it is also capable of exerting influence in its fall, and the moon is in its fall when situated in Taurus's opposing sign of Scorpio. Here the moon is restricted and cannot fulfill its normal potential. The protective maternal qualities are debilitated; a person with the Moon in Scorpio is not so tender in love, and the sexual appetite is more demandingly robust. When frustrated and with no real outlet for his basic urges, the Moon in Scorpio exaggerates deviousness and there is often a compulsion to do things dramatically out of context with what one would expect of the Sun in Cancer character or even the Moon in Cancer. Psychologically there are always a lot of emotions churning around below the consciousness in Moon in Scorpio people, making the subject very difficult to understand because he does not understand himself as motivations become more complex.

*   *   *

In astrological reference, the moon is always placed second to the sun. This is because the inhabitants of the planet earth see the solar system from this viewpoint. Although neither the sun nor moon are planets, their correct reference being that of luminaries, they are always referred to as planets in astrology. If we draw a line and place the earth in the center of it with four planets on either side, we find the planets oppose one another and again provide polarity, the influences of each opposing pair supplementing each other.

Transposed onto the zodiacal wheel, the planets retain their natural order commencing with the sun. Just as a doctor must study anatomy before he becomes a surgeon, so it is up to the astrologer to study the anatomy of the zodiac before he slices into the human psyche through his interpreation of a chart. In the polarity of the sign of Cancer in opposition to Capricorn, we produce the moon versus Saturn, the ruling planets respectively of Cancer and Capricorn. Carried a step further, it becomes the home versus the state, since Cancer and the moon represent home life and Capricorn and Saturn become the total of a mass of homes which comprise a state or nation. The moon brings the ability to respond while Saturn brings into force many of the responsibilities which Cancer lacks. The influence of the Moon in Cancer is yielding, passive and feminine in contrast to the influence of Saturn, which is masculine and authoritarian. As the moon expands to fullness, so Saturn is inclined to contraction and conservation.

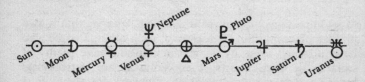

Neptune is a higher octave of Venus and Pluto a higher octave than Mars.

People under the rulership of the moon and Saturn—Cancerians and Capricorns—however, may have similar traits although the Saturnine elements of Capricorn almost always dominate. A person born with his Sun in Cancer and Moon in Capricorn should never be underestimated—despite the seeming soft nature, there is a hard core and a tough spirit which helps him overcome the weaknesses of Cancer. They are very sensitive; the Moon in Capricorn enables them to retain the memory of past hurts to an extent that such a subject can harbor a more intense form of hatred than would the typical Cancerian. The vitally contrasting polarities of the moon and Saturn, of Cancer and Capricorn, are exemplified in the scientific enigma that manifests itself both as continuous waves and discontinuous particles.

When the moon is within 150 degrees from Saturn and Uranus, the aspect is called quincunx, and the signs concerned are Cancer and Aquarius. The meaning of this aspect can be summed up as awareness and replenishment. It brings out humanitarian instincts and a protective attitude toward the general public, although family obligations may debilitate the urge to be philanthropic. This aspect is singularly lacking in the horoscopes of all too many American politicians. The influence of the moon is directed toward providing better living conditions on a national scale, and Saturn and Uranus make a contribution through such things as inventive qualities which help to make this possible. People with this aspect are content to take on long-term projects and if not defected by any speculative aspects in their charts, they manage to succeed. They need plenty of time to plan, force actions, and it is important to them to supervise the operation from beginning to end.

Most horoscopes contain aspects called squares, that is, two planets placed within 90 degrees of each other. People who have attained fame by achievement often have plenty of squares in their charts; these squares are astrological building blocks which make a framework for their life. I have never seen squares as obstacles, but prefer to see them

323

as character-building challenges. There are twelve basic squares possible; they can be likened to the twelve Herculean tasks. A square from the moon to Mars involving Cancer and Aries will bring plenty of activity and challenges into the life of the subject, and he will have enough energy to cope with them although some of them may produce spats of temper. Whatever such people accomplish in their lives, they have paid dearly for it in terms of conflict between the moon's desire for contentment and placidity and Mars's desire to push forward through action. Because of this conflict, the moon squaring Mars brings into play dramatic emotions, with Mars literally goading them forward so that often success and recognition seem to be forced on them. The moon squaring Mars is equivalent to one of the seven ages of man as expressed by William Shakespeare who said that "some have greatness thrust upon them."

In nearly all horoscopes with this moon-Mars square within it, there is a trend toward a break with parents and family traditions or splits in partnerships which would normally be expected to last. Mars ruthlessly forces the moon to use its instincts for the past, relate them to the experiences of the present and get on with future projects, not always with too much thought for the consequences or who gets hurt in the process.

The zodiac is divided into elements—fire, earth, air, and water—and each element is called a triplicity because it includes three signs separated by angles of 120 degrees. These angles are known as trines, and in a chart look like triangles.

The fire signs are Aries, ruled by Mars; Leo, ruled by the sun; and Sagittarius, ruled by Jupiter. The earth signs are Taurus, ruled by Venus; Virgo, ruled by Mercury; and Capricorn, ruled by Saturn. The air signs are Gemini, ruled by Mercury; Libra, ruled by Venus; and Aquarius, ruled by Uranus. In the water triplicity we find Cancer, ruled by the moon; Scorpio, ruled by Mars; and Pluto and Pisces ruled by

Neptune and Jupiter. Trines are known as easy aspects in western astrology, but in all other astrology they are regarded as weak ones. Yet whether easy or weak, they are actually stabilizers of the horoscope; for every period of stress there should be a period of ease; the trines represent areas where life seems spontaneously good. A person can be lulled into a sense of euphoria until he gets wised up to the fact that all good things must come to an end and in his wisdom and through past experiences he begins to see that the easy life will indeed come to an end. If he just rides along with it until the last minute, the jolt of falling from the high cycle to the low can be as drastic as coming off a drug-induced high. No wonder the Hindus call trines the weak aspects!

Even more dramatic is the Grand Trine, which is formed by three ordinary trines and links all the signs of the same element. When people hear of this for the first time, they are intrigued that it represents stability and ease. Living with a Grand Trine is rather tricky, since it has been known to weaken character through lack of incentive; it can produce a parasitical person, someone who would rather be a "hanger on" than do anything so sordid as work. It can be viewed as a "spoiled brat" temperament. A Grand Trine without a planet in square or opposition which acts as a safety valve can become a mind-blowing experience. We get people weeping about their inability to be "fulfilled," and they all have a different idea of what this means. It is not always easy to fill a bottomless pit or a cup with a hole in the base. An astrologer may be able to suggest a means of plugging up the hole, but all too often the subject yawns and walks away. Plugging up the hole might mean he had committed himself to do something for himself and heavens to Betsy—work might be involved. Grand Trine people supply a good income to psychiatrists until the kick of lying on a couch wears off and they go to seek the next time-filling experience.

Cancer trining Scorpio equals the moon trining Mars and Pluto, and what a mess we can find here. It boils down to motherhood and birth versus death and rebirth, prime enemies of a full enjoyable life. Many subjects with this trine go into medical work and still manage to get involved with melodrama. It also produces some very creative writers; if they cannot get into medical work, an outlet may well be to write about hospital life. I have always suspected that the creators of the numerous television soap operas with a medical theme are really frustrated doctors. The trine can be useful in making money—all those fancy doctors looking for tax shelters generally have the moon trining Mars and Pluto. They get away with it, too, leaving enough cash flow to lead an exotic life in contrast to what we understand as the harsh realities of the medical world. If the super doctors in the very top financial bracket have the Grand Trine, it is always helped by having a tough planet in square or opposition to one of the planets in the trine formation. Ever noticed how many fashionable doctors have a god complex? That is because the moon, Mars, and Pluto trine seems to give them power over life and death. One step lower in this trine gives us the doctors who make money by writing books on sex, its joys and problems, and a bit lower down the scale we find the people who harangue about the pros and cons of birth control.

We have another trine of the moon to consider; the Pisces trine Cancer or Jupiter, Neptune trining the moon. It appears in the charts of many psychics and those ultrasensitive to music, art and poetry. Many cannot put the ultimate effort into using their talents and sit back, hoping that destiny will give them a push up the ladder of fame. Sometimes it does, and then those people complain that they are pawns pushed around by literary and entertainment agents, but they thrive and have more than a few moments of pleasure from being successful. Sensibly, as they get into middle age, they view the alternative to success and decide that fate and their friends are not too bad, after all. They are not always able to cope with periods when they slip down a few notches on the ladder of fame and success, but they can generally make noises loud enough to be recognized as a plea for help. So they start all over again...and again...and again. A few politicians have the Jupiter/Neptune/moon trine and through emotional appeals to the public are always able to get back into their chosen milieu.

A sextile aspect is formed by planets sixty degrees apart—that is, it is half a trine. Sextiles are not weak half-trines; they have certain specific qualities uniquely their own. The sextile can bring strength and efficiency into a person's life. In establishing the value and necessary interpretation of sextiles, it is useful to know if the subject of the horoscope is male or female, because sextiles come in two genders—positive ones are masculine and work better if the subject is male. Negative sextiles are feminine and are most effective in the chart of a female. Taurus sextile Cancer—that is, Venus sextile to the moon—is a negative sextile and in the chart of a woman indicates one who is likely to be a good homemaker. In the chart of a male, he is likely to be good at real estate or anything to do with food. Both are concerned with ecology and have the nice qualities of liking children and animals, as well as the attribute of placid patience. Since the Venus-moon sextile is negative, there is a tendency to be engrossed with material things. Energies are directed toward acquiring them, and there is a great determination to progress.

Aspects by any name trace the cause and effect of relationships. All planets and the sun can have planets making angles to them, but those in which the moon has an influence reveal subtle qualities which are not always obvious to friends of the individual in whose chart aspects to the moon appear. They reveal a glimpse of the submerged part of the iceberg.

The various lunar conjunctions are interesting to study. Basically, they represent the blended power of the moon merged with the planet in conjunction. The sun and the moon are like the parents of a family, and both have a certain amount of authority within the family circle. Students of astrology are often perplexed by lunar conjunctions since

327

they are not always clear about which planet is exerting the most influence. Keep in mind that idea of blended power, but then think in terms of a family comprising mother, father, and a few children. The elder children seem by nature capable of exerting influence on the young ones, and so it is with the planets. The lightweight planets—Mercury and Venus—are affected by the heavyweight planets—Mars, Jupiter, Uranus, Saturn, and Pluto—and they have more lasting effects on the life of the subject concerned. Conjunctions occur at 0 degrees, but there is an orb of influence up to 8 degrees.

MOON/MERCURY CONJUNCTION

Mental activities occur when this conjunction is in evidence, and it is an important one to writers, who seem to get inspiration at this time. Thoughts are influenced by both emotions and perception. On the negative side, the conjunction can encourage gossip, the spreading of rumors, and the resultant sensitivity of the nerves and emotions, and some indignation at any form of criticism.

MOON/VENUS CONJUNCTION

If there is going to be a romantic interlude, then this is the time for it, but it generally IS an interlude. There is a tremendous urge to be affectionate and receive affection, but there is not always much discrimination. At its best, the person with this conjunction can feel physically fit with good digestion and circulation, and love can make the adrenaline run quickly. In its negative aspect, there can be periods of moodiness and irritability and malfunctioning of the glandular system.

MOON/MARS CONJUNCTION

Mars produces spurts of intense energy and has a big impact on the emotions, plus a desire to seek excitement at all levels. Because there is so much impulsiveness, mistakes in judgment can be made unless the impulsiveness is channeled. In its negative form, this aspect influences irritability, a feeling that chances have been missed, or that someone has done a dirty trick, and there is a desire for revenge. It is quite a time for quarreling, not always between enemies, but even between lovers.

MOON/JUPITER CONJUNCTION

There is an enormous amount of expansive benevolence in this aspect. You can be the belle of the ball, the favorite son in politics, or the darling of the office—or even just that bit more popular than you normally are or expect to be. This conjunction affects people in religion, giving them the chance to do a Good Samaritan act or even an interest in charity work. It is a great aspect for people working in advertising and public relations, since the fruits of their labors gather momentum and bring in successful results. On the negative side, there can be an excess of sarcasm and a generally cynical attitude to the world. There is very little desire to play fair; carried to extremes, it breeds rebellion and prospers dubious causes and terrorism.

MOON/SATURN CONJUNCTION

Self-control has to be achieved in this aspect, which is a depressing one even at its best. If there is ever a time in your life when you feel lonely, remote, forgotten, then this conjunction brings these emotions right up to the surface. You do not have to like the reality, but you certainly have to endure it. It is a time when happy memories of the past do not raise happiness so much as resentfulness that all the good things seem to be in the past and have no relationship to the present. In its most negative form, there is a feeling of inadequacy, worries which may not be justified but are still here, and nagging doubt that if this is all there is in life, then what's the use of trying to do anything. Separations in love or divorce occurring at this time have an absolute finality about them.

MOON/URANUS CONJUNCTION

Restless and ambitious women get the best out of this conjunction although it can bring the trauma of emotional tension and conflict with it. If you are a female wanting to get away from housework into a professional job, then the moon/Uranus conjunction will catapult you into it but not without some emotion. If you have an objective you have been striving to achieve for some time, then now is the time when you can hit the target and score a bull's eye. It is also the travel or buy-now-and-pay-later conjunction, but the main trend is toward sudden changes. In its negative aspect, this conjunction influences tension, over-taxing strength, and illnesses resulting from overwork, emotional traumas, and nervous strain. Anxiety builds up and makes the subject accident-prone.

MOON/NEPTUNE CONJUNCTION

Great for intuitive powers coming into play and really giving proof that intuition works. A good time to begin studies in psychic awareness or classes in extrasensory perception, or even taking the first dive into a book about psychic experiences. Even your dreams are not exempt from this conjunction, and many predictive ones are likely to occur, rather than nightmares. At its worst, this conjunction can encourage self-deception and a real facility for telling white lies and getting away with them. It is not a time to listen to stories of how to get rich quick because it will be the other person who gets the money while you are likely to be the patsy.

MOON/PLUTO CONJUNCTION

Men come on strong with women seeking sexual experiences more than love, while sons who have not seen a mother or a female relation or old friend for a long time get the urge to contact them. It is a time of extremes, with some deep needs floating up from the turgid contents of the subconscious. Not an easy aspect to handle, since the moon's sensitivity is hard put to cope with the upheaval Pluto demands. In its negative form, the aspect influences violent temper, often generated through jealousy, and frustrated feelings of love and sex. Crimes of passion can occur. Hurt pride and avalanches of emotional shock waves end up with deep-rooted feelings of guilt.

MOON'S NORTH NODE CONJUNCTION

A more exciting name for the north node of the moon is the Dragon's Head, and its opposite number, the south node, is called the Dragon's Tail. If the head is in Cancer, then its tail is in the opposite sign of Capricorn. The nodes are not planets, but a point in the heavens where the moon crosses the ecliptic from the north latitude to the south and vice versa. The north node is considered to be mainly beneficial, but all celestial bodies have good and bad influences. It is simply that the good influences of the north node are more apparent than those of its negatives, while the south node is considered mainly malefic. In predicting weather conditions by astrology, the changing nodes of a planet from north to south or south to north produces definite changes in weather patterns. It takes nineteen years for the nodes to complete the circle of the twelve zodiacal constellations since the nodes move at approximately 3 minutes each day. When studying the natal chart, as the nodes of the moon transit to a conjunction with the various planets in the chart, an astrologer observes that specific conditions and circumstances are brought into play. In this case, we are concerned with the conjunction of the moon and the north node. Since many astrologers ignore the nodes of the moon, a full explanation of their influences, according to the house they appear in, will be found later on in this book.

If you are looking for your soulmate, you are likely to find it when the moon is in conjunction with its own Dragon's Head. It is a time when one is likely to meet someone who is more than the usual type of friend; the chance meeting with a stranger can produce strange emotions as if you have known the person for a long time. In its worst form, this conjunction brings on over-sensitivity, and any form of rejection is a major disaster. The insecure lover may write his poems, gaze on his loved one from a distance, but also experience the agony of not being recognized as the lover.

MOON/ASCENDANT CONJUNCTION

This lunar conjunction is a very personal one. The subject finds it easy to adapt to strange conditions and people; he is always at home, and any stranger is a dear friend. It can be a romantic aspect with strong emotional and physical attraction toward the opposite sex. In its worst aspect, everything is reversed: the subject feels uncomfortable and is likely to quarrel with members of the opposite sex and generally feel a lack of harmony in everything he attempts.

MOON/MID-HEAVEN CONJUNCTION

In astrology, the Mid-heaven—that is, the top of the chart, the tenth house area—is associated with refinements of self. There is a need to get mind, body and spirit in alignment so that they can grow together. It is a good time to try to understand if there has been an imbalance in the past. The deeply religious person may have forgotten that he has a body and a mind. The intellectual professor may have forgotten that spirituality is a necessary part of his being, and that he certainly ought to pay attention to members of his family. In its worst aspect, the subject misses out on opportunities to help this three-part growth of himself and finds himself moody and lonely even in the midst of plenty of activity and people.

KEY WORDS TO MOON ASPECTS

Planets	Conjunctions	Positive	Negative	Refers to
Moon/ Mercury	Awareness Restless Sensitive	Retentive Perceptive Versatile	Forgetful Inconstant Nervous Tension	Responses
Moon/ Venus	Epicurean Poised Attractive	Beautiful Graceful Refined	Hedonistic Sybaritic Uncouth	Sentiments
Moon/ Mars	Passionate Forceful Intense	Enthusiastic Vivacious Zealous	Belligerent Sentimental Quarrelsome	Emotions
Moon/ Jupiter	Expansive Fertile Jovial	Exuberant Happy Generous	Careless Exaggerative Willful	Expansion of Feelings
Moon/ Saturn	Restrictive Depressive Limited	Cohesive Restrained Tenacious	Moody Clannish Miserable	Limitation of Feelings
Moon/ Uranus	Electrifying Impetuous Quixotic	Fascinating Magnetic Unique	Devious Capricious Eccentric	Attraction to the Unusual
Moon/ Neptune	Fanciful Impression- able Receptive	Appreciative Perceptive Sympathetic	Diffuse Fantasizes Lazy	Reception of Spiritual Impulses
Moon/ Pluto	Recessive Receding	Discreet Penetrating	Sarcastic	Hidden Depths

CHAPTER XVIII

Know Your Dragon

We get the dragon we deserve.
—Chinese proverb

Knowing the position of the nodes of the moon can add an extra interest to the natal chart, but it is important mostly when considering any specific year of the horoscope. It then becomes "a progressed chart."

We are all subject to changes, sometimes through educational brainwashing, experiences of an emotional, physical or mental nature in varying degrees of pleasure and pain. It might be important for a person born on February 22, 1923 to know what is likely to be in store for him in 1977. A rough guide to the progressed chart is that the original birthdate is set out and the desired date beneath it:

January 23, 1923

January 23, 1977

The difference between the two dates is 54 years and in order to make calculations, each year is considered as a day and added to the actual birthdate. But when counting the number of days AFTER the birthdate, remember that a child is not a year old until its first birthday. A horoscope is set up as if the person were born on the fifty-fourth day after his original birth, but in the year when the progressed chart is required and its influences will spread over from the 54-55 years of his life. This would give us a new date of March 18, unless February happened to be a leap year, when the new date would be March 17.

A chart is set up for this new date just as a regular natal chart would be prepared, and the astrologer would compare the two, noting the difference now in the placement of the planets from their placement at the time of birth. There is a biblical authority for using the "a day for a year" method, since it is likely that the prophets spoken of in the Bible were astrologers. "A day of prophets' time equals a year." Numbers 14:34; Ezekiel 4:6, "Seven years equal a week of symbolic time." Genesis 29:27.

A good basic guide for studying the influence of the north and south nodes of the moon was written by John Gadbury in 1658, *The Doctrine of Nativities*. The study of ancient documents always provides a fertile field of research for astrologers. In all old books and manuscripts, the nodes of the moon are called by their Latin names: *Caput Draconis* meaning the north node and *Cauda Draconis* meaning the opposite point, the south node. Until recently the Latin names for many of the astrological factors was one means of maintaining the mystique which has been allowed to grow around the subject. By the same token, doctors used to write out their prescriptions in Latin so that the patient did not know he was being given some simple homely herb. In contemporary astrological literature, there is a dearth of writing about the nodes of the moon, and for this reason I am concentrating on them, hopefully to bridge this gap. The position of the nodes can be found in any standard ephemeris, the daily diary of planetary positions compiled each year by naval departments of the governments of most countries which maintain a naval force. The information is in the public domain, but many publishers reprint the information and issue imprints of their own. I believe that today the interpretation of the nodes is becoming increasingly important since we are becoming a nation under strain, and periods of stress and tension are common in most households. The north node position shows any benefits a subject may derive from its specific placement but the south node indicates any possibility of loss and strain. In studying any ephemeris to find the daily position of the nodes, note that they move backward in the zodiac at a rate of 3 minutes a day. This backward movement is called retrograde and is an illusion created by the changing positions of the earth and planets in relation to each other. Retrograde motions are indicated in the ephemeris and transcribed on the chart by the symbol "R." The sun and moon are never retrograde.

NODES OF THE MOON'S FIRST HOUSE

The north node on the ascendant indicates honors, wealth, and respect, generally attainable through religious, educational, or scientific activities. Individuals find they have power in these areas and an ability to wield it through action or words.

The south node on the ascendant indicates losses: financial, emotional, and through scandal. There is also a possibility of an accident affecting the face and eyes. Although other factors must be taken into consideration in anything as dramatic as life and death, there are certain configurations which when linked with the south node on the ascendant that will show the life span will not be long.

NODES OF THE MOON IN THE SECOND HOUSE

The north node in this position indicates unexpected gains noticeable in the area of property, but the gains apply to all material things, including legacies and an excess of gifts There is a gradual expansiveness, so that the increases ma indicate a fortune amassed during the subject's lifetime.

The south node indicates misfortunes in financial affairs constant involvement with debts, and damage to th reputation. The fears generated by financial trouble ultimately affect health.

NODES OF THE MOON IN THE THIRD HOUSE

In this placement, the north node indicates a fine mentality conducive to being always receptive to spiritual and educational matters. Gains come through relations and by knowing helpful friends in the right places. Journeys wil generally be for profit as much as pleasure. This placement of the north node is often found in the horoscope of successful writers and publishers.

The south node shows a tendency to mental anxiety and difficult relationships with relations and friends. Journeys will have elements of danger. There is a lack of ability in the writing skills, which in some cases may reflect on the powers of communication.

NODES OF THE MOON IN THE FOURTH HOUSE

The north node indicates gains through property transactions; real estate can be a profitable business. It is also a very fine placement for anyone interested in treasure hunting, since it denotes success. Many members of ancient families have the moon's north node in this position, and often they inherit family treasures. It is the indicator of longevity and trustworthiness about the care of possessions.

The south node in this position will bring about confusion about land and property, also difficulties in establishing probate of wills through unharmonious family relationships, and in many cases a deterioration in status and reputation.

338

NODES OF THE MOON IN THE FIFTH HOUSE

A person with this placement can always be relied upon to put distance between himself and physical danger or any traumatic emotional calamities. It aids steady employment, especially if the subject holds a public office.

When the south node is in the fifth house, there is a chance that he will not have children of his own. His temper is erratic and his employment is as variable as his temper and moods.

NODES OF THE MOON IN THE SIXTH HOUSE

Here the north node favors good health and a strong body. The influence of a father figure will loom in his life; if not his actual father then someone he respects and admires. He will go through life as an employer rather than an employee or be self-employed, and his working life will be successful. In time he is capable of establishing himself as a father figure to others and, in the case of a woman, she can take on the aspects usually associated with masculinity.

When the south node is in this house, the subject suffers from physical afflictions and may even be born with some physical malformation. He is also susceptible to bites from small animals or reptiles and has a built-in fear of them.

NODES OF THE MOON IN THE SEVENTH HOUSE

The subject goes through life making friends and profits from contact with others who increase his ability to make money. Males delight and profit from association with women and are likely to marry a woman in a good financial situation. Women also have a chance to achieve status and wealth through marriage.

When the south node is in the seventh house, the subject finds himself inadequate in dealing with others, cannot stand competition or challenges which demand responsible action from him, and has a knack of making enemies.

NODES OF THE MOON IN THE EIGHTH HOUSE

Health and a long life are indicated here, and through outliving relations, legacies are possible. Old age does not have too many financial problems; there is always someone around to give help.

The south node shows that the subject will often be deceived by people he trusts and be an easy prey for con artists who relieve him of his money. When certain other planetary configurations are taken into consideration, this placement can indicate a sudden or violent death.

NODES OF THE MOON IN THE NINTH HOUSE

The mental qualities are always wanting to be improved through study, research, or even the everyday experiences of living. The subject can be successful in the legal profession or in teaching, and has an interest in religious instruction. It is very favorable for psychics since it seems to bring with it the ability to prophesy. The subject is likely to spend a good portion of his life traveling.

When the south node is in this position, we can expect to find an atheist or agnostic, someone insecure about his spiritual life and given to highly romanticized premonitions. Travel is often unsatisfactory, and there is danger of imprisonment in foreign lands.

NODES OF THE MOON IN THE TENTH HOUSE

High honors, personal credit, and executive positions in industry can be seen. The subject gets on well through his own determination to succeed in his chosen work, and fortunately his hard labors are appreciated and rewarded.

In the position of the south node, there can be losses through adverse criticism or a reversal of public opinion, also the loss of position through treachery. A large percentage of the politicians associated with the Watergate scandal have the south node in the tenth house.

NODES OF THE MOON IN THE ELEVENTH HOUSE

Friendships blossom to become some of the most meaningful experiences of life, and even acquaintances are capable of making a contribution to the well-being of the subject. He also has a knack of discriminating among his friends, intuitively knowing who is likely to be helpful at the appropriate time.

Conversely, the south node in this position brings undesirable associations into life. There are losses of opportunities and hopes are frustrated; practically everything he attempts seems to be nipped in the bud before it can mature. He is at the mercy of his friends, is easily led into bad habits, and rejects good advice.

NODES OF THE MOON IN THE TWELFTH HOUSE

People with this placement are successful in occult studies and deliberatley seek out unorthodox religions. They do not mind becoming recluses, not that they reject the world, but simply because they have so many inner resources to draw on that they rarely miss the company of others except for a few close friends or colleagues.

When the south node is in the twelfth house, the person will be harassed by enemies, and at some period of his life will know restraint such as being in prison or in an institution. It may be that the restraint is for his own good and for a limited period, but it is almost always unfavorable to health. When certain other planetary patterns are linked to it, this placement of the south node indicates suicidal tendencies, or may indicate that the act will indeed take place.

* * *

In all interpretations, the nodes of the moon are rarely considered in isolation from everything else in the horoscope. They supplement existing factors, either highlighting them or casting them in low profile. They are the dots to the *i* and the cross to the *t* in graphology. Understanding the position of the nodes of the moon gives a little more polish to the interpretation of the chart.

CHAPTER XIX

The Real Moon-Children

You cannot teach a crab to walk straight.

—Aristophanes

Among the countless number of celestial bodies, earth enjoys a special relationship to its satellite, the moon. It is our nearest neighbor (although occasionally a comet approaches the earth more closely than the moon). All other celestial bodies are very much farther away from us than the moon. Every one of the many thousands of stars that can be seen with the naked eye is much larger than our satellite, but we are more conscious of the moon than any of them. It is only 240,000 miles away, a mere bagatelle when compared with the distance between the stars and this planet.

As the sun is the giver of light in the solar system, the moon is the giver of life to our planet earth, a real moon-child, in fact. It is quite possible that life originally began on the moon and then failed, perhaps because of a feud, and the process of evolution came to a standstill. Until the advent of the space program culminating in earthmen walking on the moon, science spoke as if life started on this planet as it was formed. If the results of the space program prove that the moon is much older than the earth, then it may not be so farfetched to believe that there was once life upon it and that life was transferred to earth. All those stories of ancient astronauts may be feasible, after all. When life ended on the moon, it was left as a cold, decaying body. If we really want to understand how life came to the earth, the history of the moon and its failure have to be taken into consideration. Different types of humanity appeared at different times in the evolutionary scale, and not all forms survived. In the photographs brought back by modern astronauts, there is nothing to show that there is any life on the moon. It is indeed a dead, decaying body, but the question still remains to be answered: was it always so?

Madame Helena Blavatsky considered the moon's qualities in *The Secret Doctrine:*

> The Moon is now the cold residual quantity, the shadow dragged after the new body, into which her living powers are transfused. She is now doomed for longer ages to be ever pursuing the Earth, to be attracted by and to attract her progeny. Constantly vampirized by her child, she revenges herself on it, soaking it through and through with the nefarious, invisible and poisonous influence which emanates from the occult side of her nature. For she is a dead, yet a living body. The particles of her decaying corpse are full of active and destructive life, although the body which they had formed is soulless and lifeless.

The Moon is the source of sexual misery experienced on this planet. As a matter of fact, more crimes and erratic actions take place during a full moon than at any other time of the month. In another passage, Madame Blavatsky explains more fully:

The Moon is dead, only as far as regards her inner principles, i.e., physically and spiritually, however absurd the statement may seem. Physically, she is only as a semi-paralysed body may be. She is aptly referred to in Occultism as the "insane mother," the great sidereal lunatic. Isn't it strange that lovers swear their love by the inconstant Moon and that is the way their love is, changeable and inconstant. Why is it nobody swears their love by the Sun? Is it a law of nature that is unconsciously adhered to or is it a quirk of mind passed down by romanticists?

*　　*　　*

All planets and luminaries have bodies and as such have a process of birth, growth, and death. The solar system is a body within the constellation and the planet, the moon, is another body within the body of the solar system. The whole universe becomes one living organism. Energy and motion are the basis for all this. Planet earth is a body and within it are human bodies, mere cells in contrast to the greater whole. As blood and energy circulate through the human body, so energy circulates through the universe, enabling it to perform its function. Since planets have energy and motion, they can transmit this to other planets and so influence them. In this way the moon influences the earth and ultimately the cells—that is, human beings—who inhabit the earth, as the light of the silvery moon strikes us, we pick up some aspects of its cosmic energy. People who scorn astrology often say it is impossible for celestial bodies so many miles away to exert any influence on the earth, but the same thing was said about cosmic rays years ago. Today we know that cosmic rays do indeed affect life on earth.

If the moon were suddenly struck out of existence, a great wail of anguish would go up from the earth. The rise and fall of the tides would cease; this is one of the most important works which our satellite, the moon, performs. The body fluids of each human being would change drastically. Ancient Chinese philosophy links the ebb and flow of life-energy to the waxing and waning of the moon, and the entire theory of Yin and Yang are linked to this, since energy and motion are needed to maintain the correct balance between the Yin and Yang. Both Chinese and Hindu astrology, with their ancient roots, place great importance on the increasing or decreasing light of the moon. In studying numerous horoscopes, it becomes impossible not to see that people born at the time from the new to the full moon have great strength. Their blood, breath, and muscles are stronger than those born when the moon is waning. Light is yet another source of energy, and people born during the waxing of the moon live longer than those who are born during its decrease. There is a definite link between the length of the moon cycle and the life span.

The influence of the moon on the human body relates to its attitudes toward life. The Indians relate this to three qualities called "gunas." The first is the quality of goodness, the second state is passion, and the third is ignorance, or inertia—all qualities which we can see in the human beings around us. The flow of energy from the moon to the human body can become congested or it can flow freely through the body and mind and be utilized. In the first state, the energy flows through and the person learns to control and use it. In the second state, the energy still flows through, but passion engenders a loss of energy in the end, so that there is not enough for other activities. In the third state, the person appears to be lazy, without ambition and inert, being content to do a minimum amount of work. The flow of energy is blocked in an etheric web, becomes congested, and supplies no energy for action. Our ancestors understood these flows of energy from the moon and the planets, and that knowledge opened the gateway to wisdom. Part of that wisdom became known as the science of astrology in which the various forms and qualities of energy were assessed and observed as to their effect on all living things.

346

*   *   *

One day, when groups of men go back to the moon, we shall
have to start on a new type of astrology by assessing the
influence of our planet earth on those who live on the moon.
Astrology today is earth-centered because it is from this
planet we look out on the solar system; in time it may well
become moon-centered. Today's young astrologers may
become the ancient sages of the new colonies on the moon.
Slowly and painfully man is emerging from his planetary
cocoon and beginning to take a different look at the solar
system. The first transition was made when we launched a
man through space to land on the seemingly dead surface of
the moon. Then, slowly, the perception for some people
changed. I have never met any astronaut who has left earth
who did not say that his attitude toward most things on this
planet changed. Edgar Mitchell, as he went through
difficulties in making his own landing on the moon, says he
felt he had gone through the whole thing before. Was he
reviving some old forgotten motions belonging to another
life when he could have been one of those ancient astronauts
who, having traveled from the moon to explore earth, then
had to make the long journey back to his home base? Anyone
who has heard Edgar Mitchell talk of this experience cannot
help but be moved by his vivid remembrance of the emotions
he felt as he fought his way through the difficult landing to
reach the moon. Some past experience may have enabled
him to land and then return to earth; as in his present
incarnation he must go through the experiences of being an
earthman.

The moon is no longer a remote romantic body in the
heavens. It is there and man can reach it with his physical
body. It is a world outside of man who has for long centuries
considered himself as the center of the universe. Although
his scientific training prepares him for the journey, a man
venturing into space and landing on the moon experiences

something he has not experienced on earth. If there ever comes a time when people are again born on the moon, then we open up a new type of astrology. On earth we have Hindu, Chinese, Arabian, and Western astrology, with some variations occurring by reason of the geographical position. The geographical conditions change again when man is on the moon. He will go beyond the influences he would be subjected to during his sojourn on earth. We have to be prepared to go into lunacentric astrology rather than geocentric, and instead of solar and lunar returns we would have solar and terran returns, the latter referring to the motions of the earth as seen from the moon instead of vice versa.

A man on the moon experiences no lunar aspects, just as there are no earth aspects for a person living on the earth. A person on the moon would experience a conjunction of the earth and sun and during the new moon period, as seen by earthmen, the man on the moon would be experiencing an opposition of the earth and sun. The major influence in setting up a chart for a man on the moon would be to understand that the planetary aspects would all be different. On earth, planetary aspects last for several days at the least, and several months when influenced by the outer planets. But viewed from the moon, earth moves by half a degree per hour more rapidly. The aspects would be brief ones, just as the lunar aspects are on the earth. Other planetary positions would be much the same when viewed form either the earth or moon because of the relatively short distance between them. In setting up new astrological data for men on the moon, we may even begin to know more about planet earth.

In the new astrology, we shall also have to begin to assay what living on the moon will do to man's working life. This is a part of the Aquarian Age which many people have not considered. The moon may rule "laundries and laundry workers" through its influence on earth, but it is doubtful what the reverse process will be. What planetary influences will be needed to produce a type of person who takes care of spacemen's suits? We can be sure that Uranus, the ruling planet of Aquarius now in its own age, will have a major influence because it also influences electronics, electric power, and the energy needed to boost a missile from earth to the moon. The men on the moon will be the product of the age of technology and will become the true moon-children, a term we apply now only to those born with the sun in moon-ruled Cancer.

Shall we take our earthly dreads to the moon? This will be as big a problem as the original one of landing on the moon itself. For a few generations, the new moon-children may refer to earth as their home so breeding a new form of superpatriotism which will supersede nationalism. What aspect will be necessary to show this superpatriotism? On earth, the Leo-Cancer combination seems to produce a person who passionately believes in his country, right or wrong. In the past, many people born with Uranus in Cancer have proved to be notable patriots, including Nurse Edith Cavell, heroine of World War I; Rudyard Kipling, poet; and Mahatma Gandhi.

Linked with past experiments of the influence of Uranus in Cancer, we also find elements of drastic changes creeping in to everyday life. In 1865, during the Uranus in Cancer transition, Gregor Mendel formulated his laws of heredity, shocking a world that insisted on believing that the birth of every child was divinely inspired by the Creator as much as by the physical efforts of the parents. John Lister made a major contribution to medicine when he advocated antiseptic surgery methods. It was the year when the carpet sweeper, the mechanical dishwasher, the first electrically powered washing machine were invented. In the same year, Thaddeus Lowe cast his shadow on the world we live in today. No one remembers him, but we all know his invention. He made the first compression ice machine, paving the way to a method of refrigeration as a means of preserving food, new deep-freeze methods in surgical procedures, and the art of freezing bodies, which was further

349

developed in the same period of technology when we launched missiles into space.

In 1869, with Uranus at 11° in Cancer, women made the first attempt to release themselves from laws which saw them as chattels. In Britain, the passing of the Married Women's Property Act, allowing wives the right to own property, almost caused a riot. Three years later, across the Atlantic Ocean in America, Victoria Woodhull became the first woman to run in a presidential election. She was nominated by the National Woman's Suffrage Association. Almost a century later, in 1948, with Uranus again transiting in Cancer, Queen Juliąna ascended the throne of the Netherlands, a country ruled by the moon. In 1951, Elizabeth became queen of England, and her coronation was televised throughout the world. Two Uranus in Cancer influences combined, bringing a female ruler into focus by the Uranus-inspired invention of television. We can expect to see women on the moon making a great contribution to the colonization of the satellite.

Life on the moon will not be a matriarchal one, by any means, but the future transits of Uranus in Cancer will definitely produce a new type of woman who will be equal to men in understanding technology. Each transit of Uranus in Cancer has gradually released women from bondage. In 1952 the first contraceptive pill was made, but it is too soon yet to realize its full implications. In the first twenty-five years, the pill appears to have contributed to the liberation of women, but, like John Lister's invention of antiseptic methods in surgery, the pill may well develop into a much more perfect form with less danger to the women who take it. The new moon-children may find the female taking a variation of the pill which leads to selective breeding patterns. That is just about as revolutionary an idea as Mendel's laws of heredity were in his time. From our position on earth looking out on the moon, the idea of selective breeding is repulsive, but once on the moon, the moon-children will have brought with them memories of the overpopulated and polluted earth; as the moon is a much smaller body than the earth, problems of overpopulation will be evident from the beginning of the colonization.

As an earth person, perhaps the saddest thing of all is to think that the moon-children will look out from their new homeland and see earth as we once looked at the moon—a decaying body which went through the normal process of being born, growing and dying, a point in the universe to be looked at through the latest telescope. Madame Blavatsky described the moon as "a source of sexual misery." Perhaps our descendants, the moon-children, will see earth as a source of misery created by wars.

CHAPTER XX

A Moon Miscellany

THE MOON IN THE NATAL HOROSCOPE OF FAMOUS PEOPLE

MOON IN ARIES

NAME	OCCUPATION	HOUSE
Mark Twain	Author	Sixth
John Adams	President	Eighth
Leonard Bernstein	Composer	Second
Edgar Allan Poe	Author	Fifth
Albert Schweitzer	Doctor, Philan-thropist	Fifth
Jacqueline Onassis	Former First Lady	Fifth
Jerry Lewis	Comedian, Director	Fourth
Tennessee Williams	Playwright	First
Robert Goulet	Singer	Third
Jean Harlow	Actress	Seventh
Rex Harrison	Actor	Seventh
Henry VIII	King of England	Eighth
Isadora Duncan	Dancer	Twelfth
Marlon Brando	Actor	Tenth

Robert Browning	Poet	Third
Yul Brynner	Actor	Tenth
Al Capone	Gangster	Third
Salvadore Dali	Painter	Ninth
Charles de Gaulle	Soldier, Statesman	Second
Liberace	Entertainer	Fourth

MOON IN TAURUS

NAME	OCCUPATION	HOUSE
Edgar Cayce	Clairvoyant	Ninth
Prince Charles	Heir to the English Throne	Tenth
Bob Dylan	Singer	Twelfth
F. Scott Fitzgerald	Author	Third
Greta Garbo	Actress	Twelfth
Barry Goldwater	Politician	Fourth
Billy Graham	Evangelist	Fifth
Helen Hayes	Actress	Ninth
Marshal Tito	Yugoslav Premier	Tenth
Karl Marx	Revolutionary	Second
Joe Namath	Athlete	Second
Florence Nightingale	Nurse	Ninth
Gregory Peck	Actor	Twelfth
James Pike	Clergyman	Tenth
Ronald Reagan	Actor, Politician	Eleventh
Peter Sellers	Comedian	Ninth
George Bernard Shaw	Playwright	Twelfth
Hans Christian Anderson	Author	Eighth
Fred Astaire	Dancer	Twelfth

MOON IN GEMINI

NAME	OCCUPATION	HOUSE
Joan Baez	Folk singer	Second
Jack Benny	Comedian	Fifth

Mary Pickford	Actress	Third
Pius XII	Pope	Eleventh
Dean Martin	Entertainer	Seventh
Benito Mussolini	Dictator	Seventh
Anthony Armstrong-Jones	Photographer	Seventh
Gloria Swanson	Actress	Eighth
Shirley Temple Black	Actress	Seventh
Spencer Tracy	Actor	Sixth
Victoria	Queen of England	Twelfth
Andy Warhol	Pop Artist	Ninth
Joanne Woodward	Actress	Eighth
Frank Lloyd Wright	Architect	Seventh
Christopher Wren	Architect	Ninth
Sigmund Freud	Psychologist	Eighth
Francisco Franco	Dictator	Ninth
Bette Davis	Actress	Seventh
John D. Rockefeller	Financier	Seventh
Brigitte Bardot	Actress	Twelfth

MOON IN CANCER

NAME	OCCUPATION	HOUSE
Humphrey Bogart	Actor	First
Daniel Boone	Explorer	Fifth
Phyllis Diller	Comedienne	Second
Ralph Waldo Emerson	Author	Tenth
Errol Flynn	Actor	Eleventh
Stephen Foster	Composer	Ninth
Clark Gable	Actor	Tenth
Hussein	King of Jordan	Sixth
Jesse James	Desperado	Second
Tom Jones	Singer	Eleventh
Janis Joplin	Singer	Third
Douglas MacArthur	Soldier	Fourth
Margaret	Princess of England	Fifth

Ethel Merman	Singer	Eighth
Will Rogers	Humorist	First
Eleanor Roosevelt	Former First Lady	Eighth
Franklin D. Roosevelt	President	Tenth
Theodore Roosevelt	President	Second
Babe Ruth	Athlete	First
Christiaan Barnard	Surgeon	First

MOON IN LEO

NAME	OCCUPATION	HOUSE
Pearl Buck	Author	First
Chiang Kai-shek	Statesman	Seventh
Winston Churchill	Statesman	Eleventh
Moshe Dayan	Soldier	Third
John Foster Dulles	Statesman	Ninth
Elizabeth II	Queen of England	Seventh
Mahatma Gandhi	Statesman	Tenth
Oscar Wilde	Author	Eleventh
Barbra Streisand	Singer	Fifth
William Howard Taft	President	Eleventh
Lowell Thomas	Commentator	Tenth
Leon Trotsky	Revolutionary	First
George Wallace	Politician	Second
Herbert Hoover	President	Fourth
James Joyce	Author	Seventh
Gypsy Rose Lee	Entertainer	Eighth
Jack London	Author	Third
Guglielmo Marconi	Inventor	Third
Ralph Nader	Consumer Advocate	Seventh
Prince Philip	Consort to Queen of England	Third
William F. Buckley	Author	First
Mao Tse-tung	Statesman	Seventh

MOON IN VIRGO

NAME	OCCUPATION	HOUSE
William Randolph Hearst	Publisher	Fifth
Katherine Hepburn	Actress	Tenth
Andrew Jackson	President	Sixth
Lyndon B. Johnson	President	Second
Edward Kennedy	Politician	Eighth
Deborah Kerr	Actress	First
John V. Lindsay	Politician	Eighth
Shirley MacLaine	Actress	First
John Pierpont Morgan	Financier	Third
Tyrone Power	Actor	Eleventh
Anne	Princess of England	Eleventh
Ingrid Bergman	Actress	Eleventh
Richard Burton	Actor	Second
Joseph P. Kennedy	Financier	Second
Marlene Dietrich	Entertainer	Twelfth

MOON IN LIBRA

NAME	OCCUPATION	HOUSE
Maria Callas	Singer	Eleventh
Elizabeth Barrett Browning	Poet	First
Frederic Chopin	Composer	Second
Amelia Earhart	Aviatrix	Fifth
El Cordobes	Bullfighter	Sixth
Henry Fonda	Actor	Fifth
Zsa Zsa Gabor	Actress	Second
Duchess of Windsor	Socialite	Fourth
Lana Turner	Actress	First
Alfred Hitchcock	Movie Director	Eighth
Joan of Arc	Heroine	Twelfth
Rose Kennedy	Matriarch	Twelfth

Rudolph Nureyev	Dancer	Third
William Shakespeare	Playwright	Fourth
Barbara Stanwyck	Actress	Seventh
Louis Armstrong	Musician	Sixth
Johann S. Bach	Composer	Third
Helena Blavatsky	Occultist	Fourth
Walt Disney	Moviemaker	First
Rudolph Valentino	Actor	Seventh

MOON IN SCORPIO

NAME	OCCUPATION	HOUSE
Truman Capote	Author	Fourth
Carol Channing	Comedienne	Sixth
Charles Chaplin	Comedian	First
James Dean	Actor	Second
Claude Debussy	Composer	Seventh
Dwight Eisenhower	President	Seventh
John Hancock	Statesman	Seventh
Shelley Winters	Actress	Fifth
Joan Sutherland	Singer	Second
Elizabeth Taylor	Actress	Second
Leo Tolstoi	Author	Fourth
Arturo Toscanini	Musician	Tenth
Harry S. Truman	President	First
Jules Verne	Author	Sixth
John Wayne	Actor	Fourth
John F. Kennedy	President	Eleventh
James Madison	President	Twelfth
Henry Miller	Author	Seventh
Laurence Olivier	Actor	Fifth
Aristotle Onassis	Financier	Second
Paul VI	Pope	Twelfth
Nelson Rockefeller	Politician	First
Willie Shoemaker	Jockey	Second
Joseph Stalin	Statesman	Ninth
Julie Andrews	Singer	Second
Warren Beatty	Actor	Second

Alexander Graham Bell	Inventor	Sixth
Roddy McDowell	Actor	Third
Steve McQueen	Actor	Tenth
Melina Mercouri	Actress	Eleventh

MOON IN SAGITTARIUS

NAME	OCCUPATION	HOUSE
Joannes Brahms	Composer	Ninth
Maurice Chevalier	Entertainer	First
Montgomery Clift	Actor	Fourth
Gary Cooper	Actor	Sixth
Charles Dickens	Author	Second
Albert Einstein	Physicist	Sixth
Douglas Fairbanks, Sr.	Actor	Fifth
Judy Garland	Entertainer	Sixth
Kahlil Gilbran	Poet	Third
Jackie Gleason	Entertainer	Eighth
Cary Grant	Actor	Second
Mae West	Actress	Fourth
Gerald Ford	President	undetermined
Robert Taylor	Actor	Third
Martin Van Buren	President	Twelfth
Charlton Heston	Actor	Third
Bob Hope	Comedian	Fifth
Harry Houdini	Magician	Tenth
Howard Hughes	Financier	Fourth
Thomas Jefferson	President	Tenth
Charles Lindbergh	Aviator	First
T.E. Lawrence	Author	Sixth
Franz Liszt	Composer	Fifth
Wolfgang Mozart	Composer	Fourth
Pablo Picasso	Artist	Fourth
Neil Armstrong	Astronaut	Seventh
Bing Crosby	Entertainer	Third
Rock Hudson	Actor	First

MOON IN CAPRICORN

NAME	OCCUPATION	HOUSE
Johnny Carson	Entertainer	Third
Dick Cavett	Entertainer	Fifth
Thomas Edison	Inventor	Second
Adolph Eichmann	Mass Murderer	Tenth
John Glenn	Astronaut	Second
Mia Farrow	Actress	Ninth
Ernest Hemingway	Author	Fifth
Woodrow Wilson	President	Third
Loretta Young	Actress	Seventh
James Stewart	Actor	Twelfth
George Washington	President	Ninth
Robert F. Kennedy	Politician	Tenth
Christine Jorgensen	Transsexual	Fourth
John XXIII	Pope	First
Burt Lancaster	Actor	First
Gina Lollobrigida	Actress	Sixth
Abraham Lincoln	President	Second
Mary Stuart	Queen of Scots	Ninth
Napoleon Bonaparte	Emperor of France	Fourth
George Patton	Soldier	Eighth
Gregori Rasputin	Demagogue	Tenth
Robert Redford	Actor	Sixth
John Quincy Adams	President	Fourth
Lucille Ball	Comedienne	Sixth
Tallulah Bankhead	Actress	Third
Ludwig Beethoven	Composer	Eighth

MOON IN AQUARIUS

NAME	OCCUPATION	HOUSE
Fidel Castro	Dictator	Fourth
Muhammad Ali	Pugilist	Fifth
Joan Crawford	Actress	Third

Arthur Conan Doyle	Author	Ninth
Mary Baker Eddy	Founder of Christian Science	Second
Henry Ford	Manufacturer	Third
George Gershwin	Composer	Third
Richard Wagner	Composer	Tenth
Orson Welles	Actor	Eleventh
Grace Kelly	Princess of Monaco	First
Nikita Khrushchev	Statesman	Sixth
Nikolai Lenin	Communist Leader	Second
John Lennon	Composer, Entertainer	Eleventh
Sophia Loren	Actress	Sixth
Charles Manson	Hippie-Cultist	Tenth
Marilyn Monroe	Actress	Seventh
Gamal Nasser	Former President of Egypt	Tenth
Richard M. Nixon	President	Sixth
Rosalind Russell	Actress	Fourth
Red Skelton	Comedian	Third
Harry Belafonte	Entertainer	Ninth

MOON IN PISCES

NAME	OCCUPATION	HOUSE
Richard Chamberlain	Actor	Tenth
Marie Curie	Scientist	Tenth
Leonardo Da Vinci	Genius	First
Benjamin Franklin	Statesman	Sixth
Ava Gardner	Actress	Eighth
Rita Hayworth	Actress	Sixth
Hugh Hefner	Publisher	Second
Audrey Hepburn	Actress	Tenth
Duke of Windsor	Socialite	First
J. Edgar Hoover	Criminologist	Fourth

361

Martin Luther King	Civil Rights Leader	Eleventh
Michelangelo	Genius	Second
Robert Mitchum	Actor	Eighth
Paul Newman	Actor	Twelfth
Elvis Presley	Singer	Fourth
Frank Sinatra	Singer	Fourth

THE INFLUENCE OF THE MOON AS RULER OF THE FOURTH HOUSE

The fourth sign of the zodiac is Cancer ruled by the moon. It represents the earth; it is from the earth that we emerge; it is part of the inheritance of mankind. We live on the earth, representing the home and parents, and to the earth we return, representing the natural outcome of birth, growth, and the outcome of all things, which we call death.

Agriculture
Birthplace
Breast
Cousins
Digestive organs
Domestic life
End of life
Result or outcome of anything
Environment
Estate
Land, mines and everything underground
Parents
(mother of a man)
Father of a woman, the parent with the least influence
In-law relations
Real estate
Stomach

GUIDE TO AREAS INFLUENCED
BY THE MOON

Alimentary canal
Allergies
Aluminum

Brain
Breasts
Brewing

Cabbage
Change (of all kinds)
Childbearing female organs
Childbirth

Eyes (with sun)

Food and public commodities

Gestation
Glandular system

Home

Laundry
Liquids (with Neptune)
Lymphatic system

Melons

Mother (with Venus)
Mushrooms

Nervous system (with Mercury)
Nursing
Nutrition

Packaging
Period of life 0-4 years
Plant life
Public life
Public (the)

Real Estate (with Saturn)

Saliva
Silver
Stomach
Substance of the body, as
    opposed to vitality

Tradesmen

Water (with Neptune)
Water plants
Wife (with Venus)
Women

CHAPTER XXI

Simple Astrological Definitions

Dictionaries are like watches! the worst is better than none, and the best cannot be expected to go quite true.

—Apothegm from Hawkins' *Life of Johnson*

AFFINITY Having a mutual attraction.

AFFLICTION As aspect of stress in a horoscope such as a square, semisquare, or sesquare.

AGE (ASTROLOGICAL) Also called a Great Month, consisting of 2,150 years or one-twelfth of a Great Year, which consists of 25,800 years. An astrological age represents the time required for the vernal equinox to retrograde through the thirty-degree arc of one constellation. While the signs of the zodiac progress from Aries to Pisces, an astrological age is reckoned from Pisces to Aries. We are now moving from the Age of Pisces to the Age of Aquarius.

AIR SIGNS Gemini, Libra, Aquarius are regarded as the mental signs.

APPARENT MOTION We refer to "sunrise" when actually it is the earth that is moving. Planets seem to rise over the Ascendant but are really traveling in the opposite direction round the sun. "Apparent motion," then, is the motion of a heavenly body as seen from planet earth.

ASCENDANT The zodiacal degree rising over the eastern horizon at the time of birth. Each degree remains on the horizon for approximately four minutes; hence the importance of knowing the time of birth if an exact horoscope is to be charted.

ASPECT The angular relationship between horoscope indicators: the angles involving planets and house cusps. Aspects can be favorable or unfavorable according to the nature of the planets involved and the number of degrees separating them.

ASTROLOGER One who practices astrology.

ASTROLOGIAN An astrological teacher, like a theologian is a teacher of theology.

ASTROLOGIST A believer in astrology, but not necessarily a practitioner.

ASTROLOGY The science of studying the relationships between the celestial bodies and interpreting the influence of these bodies on life.

BENEFIC A fortunate planet. Jupiter is regarded as the greater benefic, and Venus the lesser one.

BIRTHTIME Moment when the first breath is taken.

366

CARDINAL SIGNS Signs which initiate action. These are Aries, Cancer, Libra, and Capricorn.

CHART A horoscope, which is really a map of an individual life.

CONSTELLATION A cluster of stars. Those appearing on the ecliptical belt have the same names but not the same location as the twelve signs.

CUSPS The lines dividing the houses or signs of a natal horoscope.

DEBILITY A detriment: a planet located in a sign opposite the one it rules is said to be in detriment or its influence debilitated.

DECANATE Sometimes called a decan. Each sign has three parts to it, consisting of a 10 degree arc for each part.

DEGREE The zodiacal circle consists of 360 degrees, each having its own specific meaning.

EARTH SIGNS The practical, conserving signs: Taurus, Virgo, and Capricorn.

ECLIPSE May refer to either the sun or moon. In a solar eclipse, the moon passes between the sun and earth so the light of the sun is obliterated. In a lunar eclipse, the earth passes between the sun and moon, casting its shadow on the moon.

ECLIPTIC Apparent track of the sun in the heavens. The plane of the earth's orbit extended to meet the celestial sphere.

ELEMENTS Fire, earth, air, and water. Each element operates through three related signs called a triplicity.

Earth triplicity is Taurus, Virgo, and Capricorn; fire triplicity is Aries, Leo, and Sagittarius; air triplicity is Gemini, Libra, and Aquarius; and water triplicity is Cancer, Scorpio, and Pisces.

EPHEMERIS A calendar listing the positions of the sun, moon and planets day by day.

EQUINOX The beginning of spring and the beginning of autumn. In astrology, the equinoxes are the times when the sun moves into the first degree of Aries, known as the vernal equinox, and when the sun moves into the first degree of Libra, known as the autumnal equinox.

EVOLUTION The ascent of the spirit out of matter.

EXALTATION The sign in which a planet is most congenially placed.

FALL A planet in the opposing sign to its exaltation.

FIRE SIGNS The inspirational or activating sign of Aries, Leo, and Sagittarius.

FIXED SIGNS Taurus, Leo, Scorpio, and Aquarius, known as stabilizing signs.

GEOCENTRIC Astrologers study the celestial bodies from the earth. Astronomers study the solar system from a heliocentric—sun centered—point of view.

GREAT MONTH One-twelfth of a Great Year.

GREAT YEAR The time it takes for the poles of the earth's axis to complete an entire circle round the pole of the ecliptic—25,800 years.

HORARY ASTROLOGY The practice of setting up a chart

for the time when a question is asked and using the horoscope to find the answer.

HOROSCOPE A map of planetary positions with reference to a particular time and place on earth—the birthdate and place of birth.

HOUSES The twelve divisions of a daily cycle of apparent motion resulting from the earth's daily rotation on its axis.

MUM COELI Noted on a chart as I.C. meaning the undersky, the meridian point opposite the Medium Coeli, noted as M.C. meaning Mid-heaven.

INGRESS The entrance of a planet into a sign.

INTUITION The pure form of reason. In astrology, it is the ability to synthesize a multitude of data.

INVOLUTION The descent of spirit into matter.

KARMA The law of cause and effect. The horoscope shows a person's karmic assets and liabilities and indicates how he may fulfill his potential during a given lifetime.

LUMINARIES The sun and moon, although often referred to as planets in astrology, are really lights—or luminaries—of the heavens.

LUNAR RETURN Chart set up for the time the moon returns to the exact degree, minute, and second it occupied at the time of birth.

LUNATION A period of 29 days, 12 hours, 44 minutes, and 3 seconds, during which the moon passes from one conjunction with the sun to the next.

LUNATION CHART A horoscope set up for a time of the

new moon, reputed to give a clue to the significance of the next twenty-nine days.

MALEFIC Planets which exert a strong influence. Saturn is known as the greater malefic, while Mars is the lesser one.

MEDICAL ASTROLOGY The application of astrology to questions of health, used chiefly as a diagnostic aid.

MEDIUM COELI The Mid-heaven, or M.C. The interesting line at the top of the chart equivalent to twelve noon on a clock.

METEOROLOGICAL ASTROLOGY Astrology used for forecasting weather conditions, earthquakes. Sometimes called natural astrology, or astro-meteorology.

MUTABLE SIGNS These are the adaptive signs of Gemini, Virgo, Sagittarius, and Pisces.

MUTUAL RECEPTION Two planets located in each other's signs are in mutual reception. If Mars were in Taurus and Venus in Aries, they would be in mutual reception and would be judged as though they were in conjunction.

NODES The points at which the orbits of the moon and the planets intersect the ecliptic. The moon's nodes are called the Dragon's Head and Dragon's Tail. The sun and the earth do not have nodes.

ORB A range of influence within which a planet or aspect operates.

OWN SIGN A planet in the sign it rules is in its own bailiwick and exerts greater influence. For instance, the moon in Cancer is the moon in its own sign, since Cancer is ruled by the moon.

PLANET A traveling heavenly body. Any of the nine known heavenly bodies that appear to have a motion of their own among the fixed stars and whose positions are charted in the horoscope.

PROGRESSED HOROSCOPE A horoscope erected for a date that is as many days after a given birthdate as the subject's age in years.

QUADRUPLICITES Division of the zodiac into groups of four signs each at right angles to each other, called Cardinal, Fixed, and Mutable crosses.

RETROGRADE MOTION This is an illusion created by the changing positions of the earth and planets in relation to each other. In the ephemeris, retrograde planets are marked "R." Sun and Moon are never retrograde.

RISING SIGN The sign of the zodiac appearing on the eastern horizon at birth.

RULING PLANET The planetary ruler of the ascending sign.

SIGNS Each sign of the zodiac comprises a 30 degree segment of the yearly revolution of the earth round the sun. The twelve divisions are Aries, Taurus, Gemini, Cancer, Leo, Virgo, Libra, Scorpio, Sagittarius, Capricorn, Aquarius, and Pisces, having the same names as the ecliptical constellations. Signs are measured from the point where the sun crosses the celestial equator on or about March 21. This is known as the vernal equinox.

SOLSTICE At the summer solstice of 0 degrees in Cancer and the winter solstice of 0 degrees in Capricorn, the sun appears to stand still when it reaches its greatest distance north or south of the equator. The solstices mark the beginning of summer and winter.

STATIONARY A planet appears to be stationary when its motion changes from direct to retrograde, or vice versa. The sun and moon are never stationary.

SUN SIGN The sign of the zodiac in which the sun appears, ascertained by knowing the birthdate. The basis of commercial astrology.

SYNASTRY The art of comparing two or more horoscopes for mutual aspects.

SYNTHESIS The art of combining various factors in the horoscope and analysing them to give a balanced judgment of the chart as a whole. An intuitive feeling and common sense is as necessary as knowing how to set up a chart and interpreting the aspects.

TRANSIT The passing of a celestial body over a significant point in the natal horoscope. These passages indicate the nature of changing influences.

WATER SIGNS The emotional and psychic signs of Cancer, Scorpio, and Pisces.

ZODIAC The twelve divisions of the heavens as measured along the band of the ecliptic.

EXPAND YOUR MIND

ASTROLOGY AND LOVE   (03545-X—$1.50)
  by Sybil Leek

HANDBOOK OF PSYCHIC
DISCOVERIES   (03126-8—$1.95)
  by Sheila Ostrander &
    Lynn Schroeder

THE HUMAN AURA   (03566-2—$1.75)
  by Nicholas Regush

MIND-SEARCH   (03544-1—$1.95)
  by Nicholas & June Regush

Send for a *free* list of all our books in print

These books are available at your local bookstore, or send
price indicated plus 30¢ per copy to cover mailing costs to
Berkley Publishing Corporation
390 Murray Hill Parkway
East Rutherford, New Jersey 07073

THE KEY TO HAPPINESS

DREAM POWER (03132-2—$1.95)
  by Ann Faraday

LIBERATED SEX (03407-0—$1.50)
  by Ken & Jeanadele Magner

LOVEMAKING: You Can Be Your
Own Sex Therapist (03383-X—$1.95)
  by Carole Altman

MALE CHAUVINISM (03195-0—$1.95)
  by Michael Korda

PUT-OFFS AND COME-ONS (03382-1—$1.50)
  by A.H. Chapman, M.D.